This Is Why We Can't Have Nice Things

This Is Why We Can't Have Nice Things

Mapping the Relationship between Online Trolling
and Mainstream Culture

Whitney Phillips

The MIT Press
Cambridge, Massachusetts
London, England

First MIT Press paperback edition, 2016

This book was set in ITC Stone Serif by Toppan Best-set Premedia Limited, Hong Kong. Printed and bound in the United States of America.

Library of Congress Cataloging-in-Publication Data

Phillips, Whitney, 1983–
This is why we can't have nice things : mapping the relationship between online trolling and mainstream culture / Whitney Phillips.
    pages cm.—(The information society series)
Includes bibliographical references and index.
ISBN 978-0-262-02894-3 (hardcover : alk. paper)—978-0-262-52987-7 (paperback)
1. Online chat groups—Moral and ethical aspects. 2. Online identities—Moral and ethical aspects. 3. Online etiquette—Social aspects. 4. Internet—Social aspects. 5. Internet—Moral and ethical aspects. 6. Internet users. I. Title.
HM1169.P45 2015
302.23'1—dc23
2014034232

10 9 8 7 6 5 4

To J. S.

Contents

Acknowledgments

Since beginning this research in 2008, I've been surrounded by an incredible group of friends, family members, colleagues, and mentors. I am deeply grateful to everyone who contributed to the project and to all those who encouraged me throughout the process.

I am particularly indebted to my parents Dennis and Carol Phillips (first set) and Sami and Steve Salvatori (second set) for their unconditional love and willingness to listen to me rattle on about trolls, lulz, and that which cannot be unseen on the Internet for the past six years. Also, sorry about that.

Countless thanks to Chris Menning, Greg Leuch, Alex Leavitt, Tim Hwang, Mike Rugnetta, Frank Tobia, Erhardt Graeff, Seth Woodworth, Jamie Sherlock, Christina Xu, Stephen Bruckert, Jamie Wilkinson, Dharmishta Rood, Matt Morain, Don Caldwell, Amanda Brennan, Brad Kim, danah boyd, Alice Marwick, Tricia Wang, Danielle Citron, Kelly Bergstrom, Lee Knuttila, Luke Simcoe, Jiashan Wu, Sam Ford, Molly Sauter, Jessica Beyer, Brent Nash, Erik Markovs, Clint Springer, Austin Song, Josh Suyemoto, Natalie Morris, Hatty, Brian Psiropoulos, Lauren Bratslavsky, John Fenn, Daniel Wojcik, Monica Stephens, Stuart Geiger, and Katie O'Connor for being thoughtful readers, respondents, and cheerleaders at various stages of the research project; Lynnika Butler, Karen Wade, and Kate Miltner for their heroic eleventh-hour edits; Gabriella Coleman's Technological Underworlds class at McGill University for providing excellent and much-appreciated revision suggestions; my dissertation committee, which was composed of Carol Stabile, David Li, Doug Blandy, and Lisa Gilman, for their support and extraordinarily helpful comments; the anonymous reviewers through whose capable hands this manuscript has passed; Amanda Ford for coordinating the piles of letters and logistics I've needed sorting over the years; the various trolls who participated in my research, most notably Paulie Socash, Peter Partyvan, Wilson Mouzone, Soveri

Ruthless, Frank Bagadonuts, and Pro Fessor; everyone in the University of Oregon's Folklore Program; the always helpful English Department office staff, with honorable mention going to the administrative oracle known to mortals as Michael Stamm; Maxwell Schnurer, chair of the Communication Department at Humboldt State University, for providing such amazing support in the run-up to this book's publication; and of course the editorial, design, marketing, and legal wizards at the MIT Press, particularly former Senior Acquisitions Editor Marguerite Avery, former Assistant Acquisitions Editor Katie Persons, manuscript editor Kathleen Caruso, and jacket designer Molly Seamans for their enthusiasm and support, and for helping me noodle through all eight hundred thousand of my questions.

As this book is the culmination of my undergraduate and graduate training, it is appropriate—necessary, even—for me to thank the professors and mentors who have influenced me and my work most strongly: John Powell for challenging and enriching my understanding of academic argument; Jonathan Aaron for encouraging me to embrace a writing style that is wholly mine, and for upending my understanding of the traditional essay; Lisa Gilman for introducing me to ethnographic research methods, and for pushing me to think critically and carefully about the politics of trolling; Henry Jenkins for believing in me, and for providing generous and thoughtful critiques from the project's inception to the very last round of revisions; and Biella Coleman for the camaraderie, spot-on feedback and advice, and of course, for the lulz.

I also offer my sincerest and most effusive thanks to Bryce Peake for the constant inappropriate laughter (bivtron, bunnies, and palm fronds, oh my) and for being my favorite part of graduate school; Shane Billings for the precious PLC memories and brutal line edits; Tony and Mrak Unger for being my family away from home; Chelsea Bullock for the cross-room eyebrow raisings (#spoilers); Katie Nash for her special oats; Maurene Goo for keeping the Boston legacy alive; Patrick Davison for being a frolicsome Internet .gif buddy and solid, kind, supportive friend (also Hi Michelle! Hi Doc!); Kate Miltner for the fireside cyberchats; Karen Wade for the blog parties (you had me at pineapple upside dump cake); Lynnika Butler for the surreptitious texting and beautiful wagon wheel light fixture; Ryan Milner for the various hats he wears, most importantly friend, coauthor, and Scully of merciless proportions; Hilary Maroney for her toughness, generosity, and uncanny ability to say the exact same thing at the exact same time, like we're sisters or something ("puuuublix"); Cullen Maroney for appreciating our family jokes even when they aren't normal ("How do unique up on a rabbit?") and for being an all-around excellent addition to our lives; David Phillips for teaching me everything I know, and for giving the best wedding toast in the history of recorded marriage ("I've only met Whitney once, in 1986, in Miami," he began, despite the fact that he grew up with me, has never been to Miami, and was born in 1989); and Nathan, my young wolf, for helping me explore the forest trails, pushing me always to go further and faster, and at the same time reminding me to slow down and be present.

Finally, to the unsinkable, incomparable, honeybadger of my life, my PhD advisor and hero Carol Stabile: I couldn't have written this book without you, full stop. You have supported, protected, and encouraged me in ways that have changed how I see and engage with the world, and your uncompromising feedback and fierce advocacy have provided me with a model for how I hope to advise my own students. I cannot tell you how lucky I feel to have worked with you, and how grateful I am for your friendship. Plus you made me that weird cake I like. You are amazing. Thank you.

Introduction

Project Origins

I first encountered trolling in the summer of 2007, after my then eighteen-year-old brother recommended I spend some time on 4chan's /b/ board, one of the Internet's most infamous and active trolling hotspots. "You should check it out," he kept insisting. "You'll like it." Eventually I caved (how bad could it be?), and one fateful afternoon decided to see what all of the fuss was about. I parked myself in front of the computer, found my way to 4chan's front page, and as my brother had instructed, clicked on the /b/-Random board. After ten minutes of scrolling through the seemingly infinite stream of nameless, faceless posts—nearly everything I saw was attributed to "Anonymous"—I was ready for a break. A break, a shower, and a nap. There was so much porn and gore, so much offensive, antagonistic humor, and so much general foulness I could hardly process what I was seeing. Nor could I understand why my brother, a smart, thoughtful, and generally easygoing kid, would find this space so amusing. Because what was even happening? What language were these posters speaking? And what, exactly, was a Pedobear?

So one night I asked him, along with several of his friends who also frequented the site, a few basic questions. What kinds of people spent time on /b/? ("Trolls and the trolls who troll them.") What do you mean by "troll?" ("A troll is a person who likes to disrupt stupid conversations on the Internet. They have two basic rules: nothing should be taken seriously, and if it exists, there is porn of it.") Are trolls made, or are they born? ("Yes.") What is the appeal of trolling? ("Lulz.") And . . . what is that? ("Amusement derived from another person's anger. Also the only reason to do anything.") The boys then began recounting their own trolling exploits, which they gleefully peppered with the same sharp, disorienting language I'd encountered online. "Who *are* you people," I remember asking, which only made them laugh harder.

Needless to say, I was intrigued. I was also completely at a loss, and began writing my way into an explanation. One short project turned into another, which turned into another, which evolved into full-blown ethnographic research drawing from dozens of formal interviews and thousands of hours of participant observation. Ultimately, I decided to write an entire PhD dissertation on the subject, which I deposited with the University of Oregon in 2012. This book is an enhanced, expanded, and heavily revised version of that initial study.

Before transitioning to the theoretical fruit of those labors, I would like to take a moment to clarify a few basic points. First, when I talk about trolls and trolling behaviors in this study, I do so with a very specific definition in mind: that of the self-identifying, subcultural troll. Chapter 1 addresses this point in much greater detail, but given the ubiquity of the word on the contemporary Internet, it is worth noting at the very outset that I will not be focusing on online aggression generally, cyberbullying specifically, or antagonistic online commentary—all of which are sometimes described as trolling. There is much to say about these behaviors (and the definitional fuzziness they engender), but that is not my focus here. My focus here is trolls who actively and enthusiastically identify as trolls, and who partake in highly stylized subcultural practices.

The geographic scope of my project is also worth mentioning. Although sizable trolling populations exist in the United Kingdom, Australia, Germany, and Finland (interestingly, organized subcultural trolling is most popular in historically Anglo and Nordic regions), I have—with the exception of my analysis of Facebook memorial page trolling, which as I'll soon explain evolved into a global phenomenon—chosen to restrict my analysis to U.S.-based trolling behaviors. This is not to say that American trolls are the only trolls worth studying; there is much work to be done on and with trolling populations outside the United States, particularly those in non-English-speaking countries. Given that trolling in the subcultural sense is steeped in American popular culture and reached critical mass on U.S.-based forums, however, the United States was an obvious place to start.

A third and final point of orientation—one that will go without saying for anyone familiar with trolling subculture—is that trolling can be nasty, outrageous business. That is, in fact, the entire exercise: to disrupt and upset as many people as possible, using whatever linguistic or behavioral tools are available. As this is a study of trolls and their linguistic and behavioral tools, readers can therefore expect to encounter a fair amount of NSFW (not safe for work) content, including expletives, sexual and scatological references, and accounts of shocking or otherwise threatening behaviors.

This is a fine line to walk. Although a certain amount of offensive content is necessary to the coherence and in fact the accuracy of this study (it would not be possible to write a PG-rated history of trolling), I am simultaneously reluctant to uncritically replicate trolls' racist, sexist, homophobic, and ablest output. Participatory media scholar Ryan Milner echoes similar concerns in his analysis of racism and misogyny in the troll space. "Even if it's done in the service of critical assessment," Milner writes, "reproducing these discourses continues their circulation, and therefore may continue to normalize their antagonisms and marginalizations."[1] In the attempt to minimize this outcome, I have chosen to print examples of problematic language and behavior only when its use provides foundational knowledge about the troll space, or when it helps illustrate a larger point. I recognize that even then, I will be further publicizing what is often quite repugnant content. Ultimately, however, I believe that an unflinching look at trolling subculture will yield better and more robust theoretical insights, not just about trolls, but about the cultural conditions out of which trolling emerges.

Jenkem: The Hot New Drug for America's Teens

Keeping those basic points in mind, I will now turn to some legendary trolling lore, which in addition to introducing readers to the spirit of trolling humor, provides a textbook example of the surprising relationship between online trolling and mainstream culture. This particular story is known simply as Jenkem.

The term "Jenkem" first appeared in 1998, in a *New York Times* article chronicling the struggles of AIDS-ravaged Zambia.[2] According to journalist Suzanne Daley, children in this area are so poor and so desperate that in the pursuit of a cheap high, they've (allegedly) taken to huffing bottles filled with fermented urine and fecal matter, known locally as Jenkem. A year later, the BBC picked up on the "recreational raw sewage" story and cited the *New York Times* article as evidence.[3] Eventually Jenkem dislodged itself from its original context and began appearing on a number of shock forums, online spaces where anonymous or pseudonymous participants post the most offensive content possible, often as a punchline or "grossest of the gross" conversation stopper (or starter, depending on the audience). The story reappeared in 2007, when Pickwick, a user of a forum called

Totse, uploaded a series of images chronicling his attempt to "try" Jenkem, including a picture of a half-full jug of waste labeled with the words "Jenkem," "Pickwick," and "Totse," as well as Pickwick appearing to huff its contents.

The subsequent Totse thread eventually made its way to 4chan's /b/ board, a space already infamous for its aggressive, anonymous user base. From there, Totse's narrative and images quickly began generating multiple iterations, including one copypasta post (text posed numerous times by numerous posters) imploring users to copy and paste the provided letter template, which would then be mailed to the principals of participants' local high school(s). As that copypasta explained:

Step 1: email this to school principal

I am writing you anonymously because I do not want my child to get in any trouble, but I need to alert you to something your students are doing that is potentially very dangerous. Yesterday afternoon I came home early to find my son and his friends getting high on something called "jenkem" which they say they heard about at school. This "jenkem" is the most disgusting thing I've ever heard of. They urinate and defecate in plastic bottles and leave them to ferment in the sun, then inhale the resulting gas. I know it sounds unreal but when I came home I found my son and his friends laying on the grass in the backyard and they were acting very strangely. There was a horrible, putrid smell in the air. I can't believe my son would do something like this. I looked it up on the internet and apparently this was something invented by African children that wound up online and now kids all over the world are doing it. My son says most of his friends at school have tried it.

This seems to be a new thing and I can't find any information about the health effects of jenkem—I think it is the methane and ammonia content that provides the desired high, but I don't really know. Both of those are very harmful chemicals. All sorts of diseases are spread through fecal matter. I imagine it could lead to some very serious health problems at your school. My wife and I are utterly shocked and talking about private school. We have spoken to our son about this and he says he won't do it anymore, but because it is on the internet kids all over the country are trying jenkem and they need to be educated about the health risks. It is only a matter of time before somebody dies from methane poisoning or this leads to a hepatitis outbreak. I don't know exactly what you could do about this as jenkem is legal but I needed to inform you of what some of your students are doing.

Step 2: ???

Step 3: PROFIT[4]

According to the "Jenkem" entry on Encyclopedia Dramatica, the unofficial archive of trolling incidents and images, this particular copypasta appeared on the /b/ board on September 17, 2007.[5] A week later, the Collier County Sheriff Department in Florida circulated a now-infamous internal memo featuring precisely the images and even some of the language that Pickwick posted onto Totse, and which had subsequently been cross-posted onto /b/ and Encyclopedia Dramatica. As soon as Pickwick got wind of these developments, he distanced himself from his actions, deleting the original post and asserting in no uncertain terms that it was just a hoax— his "Jenkem" was a slurry of flour, water, beer, and Nutella. "I never inhaled any poop gas and got high off it," he insisted in a September 24 Fox News article. "I have deleted my pictures, hopefully no weirdo saved them to his computer. I just don't want people to ever recognize me as the kid who huffed poop gas."[6]

Despite Pickwick's confession and the fact that there was absolutely no evidence of pervasive (or any) Jenkem abuse in the United States, the media ran with the story. In November 2007, a local Fox affiliate in Florida (Fox 30) aired a news segment, as did a CBS affiliate out of Fort Meyers (WINK), both of which cited the Collier County Information Bulletin. Although Fox 30 was unable to find anyone who had ever even heard of the drug, Fox reporter Jack Miller implored parents to remain vigilant against the dangers posed by this so-called Human Waste Drug. Or as the kids were calling it, "butt hash."[7] Similarly, the WINK team was unable to confirm any actual cases of Jenkem abuse ("Human feces?" squealed one teenager during an interview. "Okay, I'm sorry, that's . . . gross."). Despite the lack of evidence, WINK reporter Trey Radel concluded that the story was "disgusting," and had sent "shockwaves" through the newsroom.[8]

Fox 30 and WINK weren't the only outlets to take the bait. In the same article describing Pickwick's hoax, the unnamed Fox News writer expressed concern over Jenkem's negative health effects, the availability of raw ingredients, and the legality of possessing said ingredients, which a DEA agent explained couldn't be regulated by the government "because it's feces and urine."[9] KXAN News in Austin, Texas, suggested that parents take note of any "funky smell or odor" coming from their children,[10] and Kelli Cheatham of WSBT in Indiana advocated smelling kids' breath before letting them go to bed.[11] Users of both Totse and 4chan were delighted by these developments, and the great Jenkem scare of 2007 entered the pantheon of successful trolling pranks.

In addition to exemplifying trolls' proclivity for gross-out bodily humor, the Jenkem story also showcases trolls' facility with what they call "media fuckery," essentially the ability to turn the media against itself. Trolls accomplish this goal by either amplifying or outright inventing a news item too sensational for media outlets to pass up. By reporting on the story (or nonstory, as the case may be), media outlets give the trolls what they want, namely, exposure and laughs, and participating media get what they want, namely, a story and eyeballs to commodify through advertisements. In this way, each camp ends up benefiting the other, a point of symbiosis I develop in subsequent chapters.

Regarding the Jenkem story, the trolls' approach was two-pronged. First, in order to lend legitimacy to their account, participating trolls chose a "drug" that was Google search–indexed, thus meeting the criterion of online verifiability. So, even if initially dubious, school administrators and/ or law enforcement could quickly and easily confirm that Jenkem was indeed an African street drug. Or at least, that Jenkem had been reported as being an African street drug, by the *New York Times* and BBC no less. Second, by seeding the story with respectable members of the community, trolls engineered a second layer of plausibility—despite the fact that there was no hard evidence suggesting that Jenkem was indeed the hot new drug for America's teens. Under these conditions, how could the local news say no to butt hash?

Given its silly, scatological undertones, some might be tempted to dismiss the Jenkem story as a meaningless prank, and participating trolls' behaviors as aimless and immature. But this position would overlook the fact that the trolls knew exactly how to manipulate the news cycle, and in the process forwarded an implicit critique of the ways in which media research and report the news. Specifically, many outlets are so eager to present the latest, weirdest, and most sensational story that producers often fail to conduct even the most cursory background research—or worse, they do conduct the appropriate background research, but choose to run misleading segments anyway. Journalists have deadlines to meet, after all, and are working under increasing pressure to maintain their audience in an oversaturated market. Trolls' successful manipulation of the news cycle drives this point home, thereby challenging the assumption that the Jenkem story can or should be dismissed as inconsequential mischief.

The Political Significance of Trolling?

Just as it would be a mistake to dismiss participating trolls' behaviors as politically meaningless, the impulse to posit clear political meaning is similarly misguided, both in relation to the Jenkem story and trolling generally. First of all, there is far too much variation within the behavioral

category of trolling (even within the same raiding party) to affix any singular, unified purpose to constituent trolls' actions. Furthermore, the assertion that a given act of trolling is inherently political, or even politically
motivated, suggests that a specific argument or politics is the trolls'
intended outcome. Given trolls' anonymity, this assumption simply isn't
verifiable. Of course this doesn't mean that specific instances of trolling
can't be political, or that individual trolls can't be politically motivated. It
just means that outside observers can't be sure if and when it happens.

Whether or not trolls deliberately forward political or cultural critiques,
however, political or cultural critiques can be extrapolated from the trolls'
behaviors. Take the Jenkem story. Participating trolls may or may not have
been looking to expose sloppy journalistic standards; regardless, sloppy
journalistic standards were exposed. An argument was made, in other
words, regardless of what participating trolls intended to accomplish. I
build upon this basic argument—that trolls' behaviors provide an implicit,
and sometimes outright explicit, critique of existing media and cultural
systems—in later chapters. For now, it's enough to say that there is much
more to trolling than simple shenanigans, even if the behaviors complicate
(or even outright defy) traditional notions of political action.

In addition to challenging overly simplistic explanations of trolling
behaviors, trolls' ability to generate meaningful discourse provides a preemptive answer to the question "Why study trolls?" First, trolls' various
and sundry transgressions—against specific individuals, organizations,
local, state, and national governments, and civil society generally—call
attention to dominant cultural mores, a process that echoes anthropologist
Mary Douglas's exploration of the related concepts of dirt and taboo.
According to Douglas, dirt is best understood as matter out of place, and
is intelligible only in relation to existing systems of cleanliness: you can't
talk or even think about dirt unless you've already internalized some sense
of what qualifies as clean. Similarly, cultural aberration is only intelligible
in the context of an existing social system. Thus by examining that which
is regarded as transgressive within a particular culture or community, one
is able to reconstruct the values out of which problematic behaviors
emerge.[12] Trolls' behaviors, which are widely condemned as being bad,
obscene, and wildly transgressive, therefore allow one to reconstruct what
the dominant culture regards as good, appropriate, and normal.

Of course, the demarcation between "good" and "bad" (to say nothing
of "normal" and "abnormal") is never so straightforward in practice. Trolls
provide a striking example, and through their more outrageous behaviors
call attention to the various points of overlap between negative and

positive, transgressive and acceptable, even cruel and just behavior. Put simply, the more carefully one examines trolling, the more one struggles to differentiate this ostensibly abnormal, deviant pursuit from pursuits that are (or at least appear to be) so natural, necessary, and downright normal that most people assume things couldn't be otherwise.

This study will explore these moments of slippage, and in the process will challenge the seemingly clear-cut distinction between those who troll and those who do not. My first argumentative plank is that, within the postmillennial digital media landscape of the United States, trolls reveal the thin and at times nonexistent line between trolling and sensationalist corporate media. The primary difference is that, for trolls, exploitation is a leisure activity. For corporate media, it's a business strategy. Because they don't have to take censors or advertisers into account, trolls' behaviors are often more conspicuously offensive, and more conspicuously exploitative. But often not by much. And unlike the media outlets that run sensationalist, racist, and exploitative content, trolling behaviors aren't rewarded with a paycheck.

Trolls also fit very comfortably within the contemporary, hypernetworked digital media landscape. Not only do they put Internet technologies to expert and highly creative use, their behaviors are often in direct (if surprising) alignment with social media marketers and other corporate interests. Furthermore they are quite skilled at navigating and in fact harnessing the energies created when politics, history, and digital media collide. In short, rather than functioning as a counterpoint to "correct" online behavior, trolls are in many ways the grimacing poster children for the socially networked world.

That's not the only overlap between trolling and the mainstream. In addition to parroting digital and terrestrial media tropes, trolls are engaged in a grotesque pantomime of dominant cultural tropes. Not only does the act of trolling replicate gendered notions of dominance and success—most conspicuously expressed through the "adversary method," Western philosophy's dominant rhetorical paradigm[13]—it also exhibits a profound sense of entitlement, one spurred by expansionist and colonialist ideologies. Further, trolling embodies precisely the values that are said to make America the greatest and most powerful nation on earth, with particular emphasis placed on the pursuit of life, liberty, and of course the freedom of expression.

Again, this is not to suggest that trolls deliberately forward such an argument. Nor is it to suggest that trolls would necessarily agree with my conclusions. Rather than hinging on trolls' "true" motivations, or more problematically on their approval, my argument hinges on what trolls' behaviors unearth. And what trolls' behaviors unearth places them in unexpected mythological company.

Trolls as Tricksters

In *Trickster Makes This World: How Disruptive Imagination Creates Culture*, Lewis Hyde examines the trickster archetype, focusing specifically on the stories of Hermes, Coyote, and Krishna.[14] A boundary-crosser, trickster is both culture-hero and culture-villain. He—and trickster is almost always gendered male—invents lies to preserve the truth. He is amoral, driven by appetite, and shameless; he's held captive by desire and is wildly self-indulgent. He is drawn to dirt, both figurative and literal. He fears nothing and no one. He is creative, playful, and mischievous. Trickster also has the uncanny ability to "see into the heart of things," making him somewhat prophetic. But not prophetic in the traditional sense, as trickster spends very little time actively reflecting on his own behavior and almost never editorializes. And yet, trickster *reveals*.[15]

As evidence of trickster's latent (if unwitting) perspicacity, Hyde tells a story about the Indian god Krishna. A particularly mischievous young god, Krishna is quick to develop an interest in the village maidens. One night, he takes a walk into the woods and begins playing a magical flute. All the women who hear Krishna's song are mesmerized and follow its call into the forest, where they begin to dance. Krishna then multiplies himself by sixteen thousand and has sex with each woman. Having had his way with his still-bewitched conquests (the sexually assaultive nature of which is apparently par for the culture-hero course), Krishna disappears with the sunrise.[16]

According to Hyde, this moment captures the "negating strain" inherent in trickster's behavior. He rejects laws of propriety, but doesn't attempt to replace these laws with some other set. As Hyde maintains, "[trickster] is not the declarative speaker of traditional prophecy, but an erasing angel who cancels what humans have so carefully built, then cancels himself."[17] In this way, trickster's behavior demands polysemy—he doesn't tell the audience what to make of his actions. He acts, he leaves, and suddenly there is nothing. Suddenly it's the audience's job to figure things out, to "spin out endlessly their sense of what has happened."[18]

As Gabriella Coleman has noted, there is a great deal of behavioral overlap between trolls and mythological trickster.[19] Of course, this is not to say that trolls *are* tricksters, at least not in the culture-hero, mythological sense. First, and most obviously, trickster is a character created by humans to help explain and order the universe, while trolls are all too real, perhaps obscured by the mask of trolling but people nonetheless. Moreover, however crude or amoral trickster might appear, the trickster tale genre presumes moral order, making trickster a pawn in a very specific cultural ethos. Trolls on the other hand actively embrace amorality, and are, or at least profess to be, pawns in the service of nothing but their own amusement.

These practical differences aside, trolls harness similar means as trickster, resulting in similar ends. Specifically, trolls are agents of *cultural digestion*; they scavenge the landscape for scraps of usable content, make a meal of the most pungent bits, then hurl their waste onto an unsuspecting populace—after which they disappear, their Cheshire cat grins trailing after them like puffs of smoke. They may not know it, they may not intend to, but deliberately or not, these grotesque displays reveal a great deal about the surrounding cultural terrain. What they reveal isn't always pleasant. In fact it is often quite upsetting, sometimes because the trolls' behaviors are upsetting, sometimes because what their behaviors reveal is upsetting, and sometimes both.

The ultimate takeaway point of this analysis is that, while trolling behaviors might fall on the extreme end of the cultural spectrum, the most exceptional thing about trolling is that *it's not very exceptional*. It's built from the same stuff as mainstream behaviors; the difference is that trolling is condemned, while ostensibly "normal" behaviors are accepted as a given, if not actively celebrated.

This idea, that trolling behaviors are similar in form and function to "normal" behaviors, is hardly a popular or immediately obvious position. Much more popular, and infinitely more obvious, is the assertion that trolls are why we can't have nice things online, a nod to a well-known image macro featuring a hissing gray cat. (Image macros, also known simply as "macros," are images captioned with lines of text. Typically, one line of text is placed at the top of the image and another line is placed along the bottom, though the format can vary depending on the image and message conveyed) (figure 0.1).

The analogy between "arguecat," as the macro is called, and trolling is apt. Like a spiteful housecat whose sole interest seems to be property damage, trolls take perverse joy in ruining complete strangers' days. They will do and say absolutely anything to accomplish this objective, and in the service of these nefarious ends deliberately target the most vulnerable— or as the trolls would say, exploitable—targets. Consequently, and understandably, trolls are widely regarded as the primary obstacle to a kinder, gentler, and more equitable Internet.

Figure 0.1
Arguecat. First encountered on 4chan/b/ in July 2008. Re-accessed for download on February 27, 2012. Threads since deleted. Original creator(s) and date(s) of creation unknown.

This book complicates the idea that trolls, and trolls alone, are why we can't have nice things online. Instead, it argues that trolls are born of and embedded within dominant institutions and tropes, which are every bit as damaging as the trolls' most disruptive behaviors. Ultimately, then, *this* is why we can't have nice things, and is the point to which the title gestures: the fact that online trolling is par for the mainstream cultural course.

Chapter Overview

This Is Why We Can't Have Nice Things is divided into three parts and is organized into loose chronological order. The first part, which addresses the subcultural origin period from about 2003 to 2007, provides an overview of the troll space and introduces the reader to the book's major themes and concepts. Chapter 1 presents a historical overview of the term *troll*, and describes the slow and uneven process by which trolling took on subcultural connotations. Chapter 2 provides a working definition of *lulz*, perhaps the most critical concept within the subcultural troll space. Chapter 3 discusses my research methods and various methodological complications.

Part II focuses on the "golden years" of 2008–2011, during which time trolling subculture crystallized, and examines trolls' grotesque pantomime of mainstream behaviors and attitudes. Chapter 4 focuses on 4chan's /b/ board and chronicles the emergence of Anonymous, a nebulous trolling collective that would in later years evolve into a progressive "hactivist" powerhouse. The chapter also considers the ways in which early media representations of and subsequent reactions to trolling on /b/ helped create and sustain an increasingly influential subculture. Chapter 5, an ethnographic study of Facebook memorial page trolls (RIP trolls for short), interrogates the rhetorical and behavioral similarities between trolls' behaviors and sensationalist, mass-mediated disaster coverage. Through a close analysis of the 2008 U.S. presidential election and 2009 Obama as socialist Joker poster controversy, chapter 6 maps the overlap between trolls' unapologetically racist humor and "legitimate" corporate punditry. While conceding that racist trolling behaviors are unquestionably problematic, the chapter argues that corporate-backed racism is just as bad, if not worse. Building upon the previous three chapters, chapter 7 surveys the larger cultural logics out of which trolling emerges and argues that, of all the reactions one could have to the pervasiveness of trolling (dismay, concern, frustration, disgust), surprise should not be one of them.

The third and final part, which covers the subcultural transition period from 2012 to 2015, analyzes the ways in which trolling subculture has changed since first coalescing in the early to mid-2000s. Chapter 8 discusses several interpenetrating political, economic, and cultural factors undergirding recent shifts within the troll space, in the process providing a compelling, real-time example of trolls' cultural digestiveness. Chapter 9 considers the implications of the expanding definition of troll, assesses the (potentially) positive applications of trolling rhetoric, and offers a final reminder of the importance of "spinning endlessly" one's sense of what trolls are and why they matter.

Taken together, these chapters challenge the assumption that a fundamental difference exists between trolling and mainstream culture, an argument that is as much a critique of dominant institutions as it is of the trolls who operate within them. This book is not just about trolls, in other words. It's also about a culture in which trolls thrive.

I   Subcultural Origins, 2003–2007

As I discovered that first night talking to my brother and his friends, the troll space is disorienting both in its size and in the rate at which new content is introduced, adopted, and subsequently repurposed by untold thousands of anonymous participants. The more research I conducted, the bigger and weirder the space seemed to get; initially it felt as if I would never know enough to make a coherent argument, let alone write a book on the subject.

Over time I became increasingly familiar with the contours and customs of the troll space, which despite being a great help to my research had an unexpected and often frustrating consequence—because I finally knew what I was looking at, I often made the mistake of assuming that trolling outsiders would also understand casual references to, say, Pedobear, or Jenkem, or lulz, or even trolling generally. Furthermore, because I was a PhD student in an English department and was pursuing a folklore structured emphasis, many people (very reasonably) assumed I was referring to the under-the-bridge variety of trolls, resulting in countless Monty Python–worthy seminar and academic conference interactions (many of which culminated in the question/punchline "Wait, trolls on the Internet?")

It is therefore important, critical even, to open this study with a careful explication of the history, definition(s), subcultural themes, and political stakes of trolling, including the myriad ways in which trolls embody trickster's amorality, impetuousness, and shameless desire to splash about in the muck. By establishing these basic linguistic and behavioral building blocks, readers will have a chance to familiarize themselves with the idiosyncrasies of the troll space before transitioning into more complicated cultural analyses.

1   Defining Terms: The Origins and Evolution of Subcultural Trolling

The first and most important point of orientation in this study is the term *troll* itself; consequently, this chapter focuses on the history and evolution of trolling in an online context. In addition to describing the process by which the term transitioned from accusation (i.e., what you called someone else) to point of identification (i.e., what you called yourself), it provides a working definition of subcultural trolling as understood by subcultural trolls. The chapter concludes by introducing the fundamental asymmetry of trolling, thereby foreshadowing the host of political and ethical questions trolling inevitably raises.

Trolling History

Depending on whom you ask, the etymology of online trolling can be traced either to Norse mythology or to fishing ("trolling" in that sense involves stringing lines of bait behind a fishing boat). The speaker's attitude toward trolls and trolling behaviors often colors his or her understanding of the term's origins. If he or she sees trolling as mean-spirited and abusive, he or she is more likely to link trolling with the snarling, mythological variety. If he or she is ambivalent or even sympathetic to trolling, his or her account will often make mention of the more value-neutral fishing term.

The "official" record—which, per the *Oxford English Dictionary*, indicates 1992 as the first recorded instance of trolling used in an online context— suggests both mythological and piscatorial origins, citing the former as a possible influence, but quoting a 1995 *Toronto Star* article that defines troll responses as those that "fish for flames," "flames" indicating an incensed response.[1]

To make matters even fuzzier, in both the 1992 and 1995 examples cited by the OED, "troll" is used casually, suggesting an existing linguistic and behavioral frame of reference. Indeed, by 1996, trolls were so common on Usenet—a distributed, worldwide discussion board system first introduced in 1980, and which served as a precursor for modern online forums— that Michele Tepper devoted an entire article to their exploits; as she indicates, an "indignant correction" was the ultimate goal of these so-called trollers.[2]

From its categorical inception, and continuing into conversations about socially networked web culture, trolling has been framed as a major, if not *the* major, impediment to online community formation. Internet and media researcher Judith Donath's foundational 1998 exploration of identity deception on Usenet represents the apex of this framing. Throughout her argument, Donath characterizes trolling as a malicious and deliberately destructive *lie*. As Donath argues, the existence of trolls, even the possibility of the existence of trolls, makes community members far less likely to trust outsiders or to tolerate those who haven't yet mastered the community's norms. In short, trolls incite paranoia, and paranoia sours the communal spirit that yearns to express itself online.[3]

Echoing and elaborating upon Donath's concerns, Internet scholar Lincoln Dahlberg argued in 2001 that the most serious problem associated with trolling is that of impersonation. His is not merely a concern over identity theft, however. Whether a troll is impersonating a living person or has invented a fictional persona, he or she undermines the integrity of the community, thereby making a fool of all involved. Consequently, trolls should be ferreted out and ejected from the group as quickly as possible.[4]

Harkening to the introduction's discussion of matter out of place, trolls on the early web were thus understood as *digital* matter out of place. Not only were these trolls a threat to the utopian dream of early cyberspace, they gestured to the norms against which their behaviors were said to transgress—namely that "true" identities do not deceive, that any form of deception undermines community formation, and even more basically, that pure communication is naturally and necessarily preferable to some inauthentic alternative. For early Internet scholars who were just beginning to ask questions about expressions of and threats to online identity, trolls were a genuine concern—a framing that must be understood in the context of early digital theory.

In a more recent study of the Usenet group rec.equestrian, linguist Claire Hardaker examines nearly nine years' worth of posts, including two thousand containing some iteration of the term troll. Although her definition—that a troll is a person "whose real intention(s) is/are to cause disruption and/or to trigger or exacerbate conflict for the purposes of their own amusement"[5]—takes the trolls' perspective into account, and even critiques the aforementioned studies for not considering trolling on its own terms, Hardacker ultimately aligns herself with Donath and Dahlberg; she concludes that trolling is predicated on its effects, the most significant of which is deception.[6] Gender and media studies scholar Kelly Bergstrom makes a similar point in an article examining community expectations on reddit, a wildly popular content aggregator, and suggests that accusations of trolling are often used as a social deterrent against lying.[7]

The possibility that you might be talking to a troll can therefore be likened to the oft-repeated joke/reassurance/warning that on the Internet, no one knows you're a dog, a deep-seated paranoia borne out by a number of sensationalized accounts of people pretending to be something else entirely, maybe the "wrong" gender, maybe the "wrong" profession, maybe the "wrong" age or the "wrong" religion or whatever other fiction someone's avatar might be attempting to pass off as fact. This concern—that who you're talking to online might not be who he or she claims to be—is at the forefront of the film *Catfish*, in which the main character begins to wonder about his online girlfriend's offline identity,[8] and in California's "e-personation" statute,[9] which imposes seriously punitive measures on those who engage in online impersonation. Although the exact frequency and severity of this type of deception online cannot easily be quantified, the moral could not be more straightforward: *We can't know for sure who we're dealing with online*, making the threat of deception nearly as damaging, if not more so, than specific instances of deceit.

Not all conversations about trolling have focused on deception, however. In the mid- to late 2000s, many accounts of trolling behaviors began to focus less on effects-based definitions (i.e., trolling is the process by which others are deceived) and more on communities that already regarded themselves as trollish. Anthropologist Gabriella Coleman conducted much of this early research, along with Internet researcher Julien Dibbell and a score of other journalists, most notably Urlesque's Chris Menning, Nick Douglas, and Cole Stryker. Unlike early academic accounts, the litmus test for this brand of trolling was that the participants were marked by a set of unifying linguistic and behavioral practices. In short, the emerging research began to treat trolling as a subculture.

A Brief History of Not Quite Trolling

It is difficult to pin down exactly when the term troll began to take on self-selective, subcultural connotations. What is certain is that, by 2004, users of Encyclopedia Dramatica were already debating the definition of trolling *from a troll's perspective*,[10] suggesting that the chicken-and-egg question of what comes first, the subculture or the name of the subculture, was already well under way (I will address objections to the term *subculture* later in this section).

One catalyst for this shift was the ascendency of 4chan, originally conceived in 2003 as a content overflow site for a particularly NSFW Something Awful subforum called "Anime Death Tentacle Rape Whorehouse." Its founder, fifteen-year-old Christopher "moot" Poole, was a regular contributor to Anime Death Tentacle Rape Whorehouse who wanted to archive contributions by other Something Awful users, known on-site as "goons."[11]

Like Japan's hugely popular Futaba Channel (also known as 2chan), upon which 4chan's design, layout, and code was based, 4chan was a simple image board. In its earliest phase, 4chan housed only a handful of boards, including /a/-Anime, /b/-Random, /c/-Cute, and /h/-Hentai. Over time more boards catering to more interests were added, including those devoted to technology, video games, even literature.

Soon after its creation, 4chan began attracting users outside the intended Something Awful subforum, and quickly became a destination unto itself, complete with its own lexicon and behavioral norms. One of these norms was the appropriation of the term troll as a point of self-identification. While not all 4chan users would have identified themselves as trolls—the majority of trollish activity on 4chan was confined to the /b/ board—this particular understanding of the term rooted itself into the ethos of the site. Even if you weren't a troll on 4chan, you were well aware of trolling on 4chan, and well aware of the havoc the trolls on /b/ were all too eager to wreak on- and off-site.

Just as it is critical to note that not all 4chan users were trolls, it is also critical to note that the /b/ board was *not* the birthplace of trolling. Far from it. As evidenced by the academic literature mentioned earlier condemning mid-1990s "trollers" and their disruptive antics, trolling behaviors long preceded the creation of 4chan. In fact every aspect of modern trolling culture has had some basic behavioral precedent. Take, for example, users of the infamous Usenet newsgroup alt.tasteless, who were just as crass and disruptive as trolls on 4chan's /b/ board. In 1993, they even engaged in a months-long raid of rec.pets.cats, an otherwise G-rated pet forum.

The opening salvo of this raid was lobbed by a Canadian PhD student. After alerting alt.tasteless to his plans, he posted a message to rec.pets.cats asking for advice regarding his two fictional cats, Choad (slang for "penis") and Sootikin (slang for "vaginal growth"). Although his message was met with some genuine responses, the majority came from other alt.tasteless users. *Wired* reporter Josh Quittner describes the ensuing chaos: "Hordes of new 'cat lovers' suddenly besieged rec.pets.cats, offering extremely tasteless advice. One correspondent suggested nailing the hapless cats to a breadboard. Another thought firing 'multiple .357 copper-jacketed hollowpoints' longitudinally through Sooti and Choad would solve the problem."[12]

Alt.tasteless was hardly the only hotbed of this sort of activity. Late 1990s American Online (AOL) was also home to a flurry of disruptive behaviors, including the following account taken from a troll collaborator who eventually came to identify as a troll:

Back in about 1997, one of my favorite things to do when going online was to crash Backstreet Boys and 'N Sync fan chatrooms on AOL. I was about 13. Using punters, or "proggies" like PhrostByte, a script-kiddie like me could click a button and instantly flood the chat with garbage-text until the room would crash. These punters had all kinds of cool features, like forcing other users to sign-off using some basic HTML scripting. They also featured some other vanity tricks like automatically converting everything you typed into chat into 1337 to make you sound like an uber cool h4x0r, or flashing rainbow text.[13]

And no account of proto-trolling (for lack of a better term) would be complete without mentioning the various shock images that have long provided fodder for online mischief. The most infamous of these images is the "holy trinity" of Goatse, an image series in which a middle-aged man wearing a wedding ring bends over for the camera and stretches open his anus to the size of a mason jar lid; Tubgirl, a bathtub-bound supine woman whose stream of explosive diarrhea cascades into her own mouth; and Lemon Party, an image of three male octogenarians, two of whom are kissing and one of whom is fellating another. Years before 4chan was but a twinkle in moot's eye, online troublemakers across the globe took great joy in sharing these types of images with like-minded Internet users and, more trollishly, in redirecting unsuspecting targets to images that, as the saying goes, cannot be unseen.

In short, there is a great deal of behavioral precedent for "modern" (i.e., post-4chan) trolling. Ultimately, the primary difference between proto- and modern trolling behaviors is that the former didn't always or as consistently flag itself as such—or necessarily flag itself as anything. Sometimes described by participants as hacking, sometimes as flame baiting, sometimes simply as screwing around or being disgusting or as a means to combat boredom, those who engaged in these types of behaviors had no overarching linguistic or subcultural framework with which to describe their online exploits, a point corroborated by many of my research collaborators. To my—and in fact to their—fascination, few could recall how they described their behaviors before the subcultural definition of trolling took hold. They have since come to use the term retroactively, but at the time did not think of themselves as trolls.

Because these early disruptive behaviors—and people's descriptions of these behaviors—were so variable, and because there was no clear center to the trolling universe, a great deal of overlap existed between proto- and early trolling spaces, particularly on the so-called shock sites of the late 1990s and early 2000s, including Rotten (1996), Hard OCP (Hardware Overclockers Comparison Page) (1997), Totse (1997), Stile Project (1999), Something Awful (1999), Gen May (2002), and finally 4chan (2003). Content traveled from forum to forum, regardless of who described themselves as what (recall the ease with which the Jenkem story traveled between Totse and 4chan). At that point, modern trolling was still in flux, and a coherent definition of the word "troll" had yet to crystallize.

With time, that's exactly what happened. As the popularity of 4chan's /b/ board grew, so too did this particular usage of the word "troll," not just with trolls on 4chan's /b/ board, but among other Internet users who began deferring to this newest subcultural iteration—a process that was further accelerated by the various media interventions (and amplifications) discussed in later chapters. So, while it would be incorrect to state that trolling originated on 4chan, and it is certainly not true that trolling remained sequestered on 4chan, the /b/ board provided a critical incubator for what would emerge from the primordial ooze: a clear, coherent, and immediately recognizable subcultural framing of the term "trolling."

Trolling, Subcultures, and the Mainstream

As is common within the endlessly twisty world of trolling, however, even this contextualized framing of trolling subculture requires additional context. The problem is the word "subculture" itself, which posits a singular, monolithic culture under whose umbrella smaller subsidiary cultures are said to emerge. As sociologists Andy Bennett and Kieth Kahn-Harris note, culture is already fragmented before the imposition of subcultural categories[14]—thus calling into question the basic coherence of the term "subculture" (how can something be "sub-" of that which isn't itself singular?).

Although I readily concede this point, I have chosen to use "subcultural trolling" (as opposed to "trolling culture" or simply "trolling") with caution, for the sake of clarity. First, it is helpful to differentiate self-identifying trolls engaged in highly stylized lulz-based trolling from other forms of antagonistic online behavior, which may or may not also be called trolling. My research is focused on the first category of troll, which subcultural trolling helps me communicate quickly and easily.

Second, given trolls' simultaneously symbiotic and exploitative relationship to mainstream culture, particularly in the context of corporate media, it seems appropriate to frame trolling as fundamentally subsidiary. By "mainstream," here, I am not gesturing toward some singular universal culture, but rather the tropes and ideologies born of capitalism and supported by the entertainment industries. The corporate mainstream, in other words, which asserts itself as natural, necessary, and monolithic despite the diversity and fragmentation of concomitant culture(s). Trolling, as I have described it, easily qualifies as "sub" to this culture, even if the overarching concept of culture is much more complicated.

The Meme Connection

My concern over the "sub" in "subculture" is more than political stakes claiming, however; the embedded relationship between trolling and mainstream culture (particularly the corporate mainstream) undergirds this entire study. And what a relationship it has been. Consider the fact that, from about 2003 to 2011, subcultural trolls on and around 4chan's /b/ board were responsible for creating, or at the very least amplifying, nearly every popular meme on the Internet—an assertion that first requires some definitional clarification.

Coined by Richard Dawkins in 1976 to describe the process by which cultural artifacts (technological innovations, fashion trends, catchphrases, ideas) spread and evolve,[15] the term "meme" has become a ubiquitous feature of the socially networked web. Ubiquitous, but often contentious. Many media and communication studies theorists have emphasized the definitional imprecision of the term, particularly in relation to the related notion of "viral" media.[16] Other theorists, including media scholars Henry Jenkins, Sam Ford, and Joshua Green, dislike the term, particularly when used in a marketing or otherwise corporate context ("using memes" to "go viral"), on the grounds that such a framing implies passive transmission between mindless consumers.[17]

It is therefore worth noting that when I discuss memes in this study, I am deferring to subcultural trolls' understanding of the term. This understanding echoes theories forwarded by digital media scholar Limor Shifman, who describes memes as "(a) a *group of digital items sharing common characteristics* of content, form, and/or stance; (b) that were created *with awareness of each other*; and (c) were circulated, imitated, and transformed *via the Internet by many users*,"[18] as well as participatory media scholar Ryan Milner, who theorizes that memes are a "lingua franca" (i.e., a bridge language) uniting participatory online collectives.[19] This last point in particular captures the trolls' use of the term, as memes within the troll space compose a holistic system of meaning: memes only make sense in relation to other memes, and allow participants to speak clearly and coherently to other members of the collective while baffling those outside the affinity network. Furthermore, trolls' ability to reference, recognize, and remix existing memes helps fortify a basic sense of trolling identity, a point I revisit in chapter 4.

Despite the fact that memes within the early troll space were made by subcultural trolls for other subcultural trolls, an astounding number of troll-made artifacts have been adopted by a much wider pop cultural audience. Prominent examples include LOLcats (images of cats and other animals captioned with cute or otherwise absurdist text), Rickrolling (in which individuals are unwittingly redirected to a clip of Rick Astley's 1987 hit "Never Gonna Give You Up"), and rage face comics (crudely drawn comic templates), each of which were thrust into the mainstream spotlight after being created and/or amplified by trolls. LOLcats, for example, which trolls embraced from 4chan's inception, spawned a multi-million-dollar empire for I Can Has Cheezburger founder Ben Huh, whose "meme team" was eventually featured on a reality show on U.S. cable television channel Bravo;[20] Rickrolling became so widespread online that in 2008, Rick Astley was invited to give a surprise performance of "Never Gonna Give You Up" during Macy's Thanksgiving Day Parade, thus Rickrolling millions of parade spectators;[21] and since 2010, t-shirts featuring rage face comics have graced the shelves of retail outlets across the country.[22]

And these are just a few examples. As I explain in chapter 8, mainstream pop culture—the sort of content you might find scrolling through Facebook, while watching television, or wandering through the mall—is overrun with the brainchildren of subcultural trolls, prompting moot to declare in 2009 that 4chan was an outright "meme factory."[23] Conversely, a significant percentage of content that initially percolated through the filter of mainstream Internet culture was intercepted and reappropriated, or at least further popularized, by subcultural trolls.

In this way, trolling—and in a more indirect way, 4chan/b/—quietly positioned itself as one of the most influential forces within the American pop cultural landscape, and during the major subcultural growth period between 2008 and 2011 managed to go mainstream while still underground—a feat that, ironically, helped usher in the end of the "golden age" of trolling. But that is a story for another chapter; for now, it's enough to note that, upon emerging from the bowels of 4chan's /b/ board in the mid-2000s, lulz-based subcultural trolling quickly asserted itself as a highly gravitational force within the online cultural orbit, which itself was a highly gravitational force within the mainstream pop cultural orbit.

Trolls According to Trolls

Having explicated the process (however nebulous) by which trolling rose to pop cultural prominence, I now turn to my definition of subcultural trolling, which I've based on my trolling collaborators' accounts as well as my personal experiences navigating the troll space.

The first and most important point to make—and upon which trolls of the subcultural ilk consistently insist—is that trolling is a spectrum of behaviors. Some trolling is incredibly aggressive, and meets the legal threshold for harassment. Other forms of trolling—for example, Rickrolling—are comparatively innocuous. Some trolling is persistent, continuing for weeks or even months, and some is ephemeral, occurring once and then never again.

Individual trolls are similarly behaviorally diverse. I've worked with certain trolls who take great pleasure in taunting the friends and family of murdered teenagers, while others quietly respect certain ethical lines, choosing not to troll someone or something they don't think they should. Some trolls are surprisingly sensitive, and at least when they're "off the clock"—that is, not performing for other trolls—can be downright pleasant. Some trolls are extremely difficult to deal with, even when they're not actively trolling. Some are remarkably self-reflective and intelligent, and some are remarkably not.

The same emotional and behavioral spectrum holds for groups of trolls. While researching trolls on Facebook from 2010 to 2012, for example, I encountered a number of troll factions, the most basic being between trolls and anti-trolls (I revisit Facebook trolling in chapter 5). Anti-trolls, also known simply as "antis," publicly denounced other trolls, then proceeded to troll as many trolls as possible. Whether anti or regular, these trolls were either pack trolls or rogue trolls; the rogue trolls (those not associated with a stable group of trolling friends) tended, at least in my experience, to be unpredictable and extremely misanthropic. Pack trolls were much more social, and were often quite eager to help with my research, either by answering questions or putting me in touch with other trolls. Facebook trolls could be further divided into RIP trolls, trolls who trolled memorial pages (among other pages), and trolls who trolled everything but memorial pages. Some RIP trolls actively targeted the friends and families of a particular victim (a much less common breed of troll) and some restricted their focus to "grief tourists," people who comment on the pages of dead strangers in order to mourn alongside other strangers.

Facebook was not the only platform privy to subcultural fracture. During this same period on 4chan's /b/ board, fights simmered between self-described "lulzfags," trolls who claimed to value lulz over all else (a concept to which I return shortly), and "moralfags/causefags," trolls who drew the ire of other trolls by wearing their political affiliations on their sleeves (I will discuss trolls' use of the suffix "-fag" in chapter 4). Perhaps unexpectedly, Facebook trolls reviled 4chan trolls, and between 2010 and 2011 would frequently turn their trollish attentions to the "/b/tards" who dared encroach upon the Facebook trolls' territory. The Facebook trolls I worked with referred to these ongoing skirmishes as the "Troll Wars," and seemed to enjoy trolling other trolls almost as much as they enjoyed trolling non-troll targets.

Despite the dizzying variety of trolls and trolling styles, certain behavioral markers have persisted among all the trolling groups I've worked with. First, and perhaps most basically, trolls of the subcultural variety self-identify as such. Simply flaming, or saying provocative things online, does not necessarily make someone a subcultural troll, nor does griefing, raising similar hell during video gameplay. Engaging in racism or sexism or homophobia, disrupting a forum with stupid questions, or generally being annoying does not automatically make one a subcultural troll. Trolling in the subcultural sense is something a self-identifying troll sets out to do, as an expression of his or her online identity.

In addition to self-identifying as such, trolls are motivated by what they call lulz, a particular kind of unsympathetic, ambiguous laughter. Lulz is similar to Schadenfreude—loosely translated from German as reveling in the misfortune of someone you dislike—but has much sharper teeth. Lulz also indicates a particular comedic and visual aesthetic. The following chapter presents a much more detailed account of lulz, including an analy-sis of the affective reorientation necessitated by their extraction. For now, the critical points are as follows: First, behaviors that fail to generate and/ or celebrate lulz do not qualify as trolling, at least not from the subcultural trolls' perspective. Second, and much more problematically, lulz are (lulz can be singular or plural, depending on the context, a point I will elaborate in the subsequent chapter) regarded by many trolls as secondary, if not inconsequential, to the enjoyment of the resulting fallout. That lulz are achieved is said to be more important than where or from whom they are derived.

The claim—and it is a common claim within the troll space—that lulz is equal opportunity laughter is belied by the fact that a significant percent-age of this laughter is directed at people of color, especially African Ameri-cans, women, and gay, lesbian, bisexual, transgender, and queer (GLBTQ) people. That said, historically dominant groups are also frequent objects of lulz. White Christians and Republicans in particular, along with groups of white people committed to a common cause (most notably environ-mentalists and fan communities), have generated a great deal of trollish taunting.

Disparate as these targets might initially appear, there is a through line in the trolls' targeting practices: the concept of exploitability. Trolls believe that nothing should be taken seriously, and therefore regard public displays of sentimentality, political conviction, and/or ideological rigidity as a call to trolling arms. In this way, lulz functions as a pushback against any and all forms of attachment, a highly ironic stance given how attached trolls are to the pursuit of lulz.

The final marker of trolling is the trolls' insistence on and celebration of anonymity. The ability to obscure one's offline identity has a number of immediate behavioral implications. Most obviously, anonymity allows trolls to engage in behaviors they would never replicate in professional or otherwise public settings, either because the specific behaviors would be considered socially unacceptable, or because the trolls' online persona would clash with their offline circumstances—for example, if the troll in question were a schoolteacher or nurse. Even if the person behind the troll avoided explicitly bigoted speech or behavior, his or her extracurricular interests would likely upset or merely baffle family members and cowork-ers, further reinforcing the importance, perhaps even necessity, of keeping one's real-life identity under wraps.

Conversely, successful trolling is often dependent on the target's lack of anonymity, or at least their willingness to disclose real-life attachments, interests, and vulnerabilities. This, according to the troll, is grounds for immediate trolling, since in the trolls' minds, the Internet is—at least should be—an attachment-free zone. The trolling mantra "Nothing should be taken seriously" suggests as much, and functions both as a rallying cry and post hoc justification for trollish behavior. Trolls believe that, by wearing their hearts (or political affiliations, or sexual preferences, or other aspects of identity) on their sleeves, their targets are *asking* to be taught a lesson. Trolling is thus framed by trolls in explicitly pedagogical terms. Maybe next time, trolls argue, the target won't be so stupid. Maybe next time they won't be such obvious trollbait. In this way, trolls are—at least in their own minds—doing their targets a favor.

Needless to say, the power dynamic between the troll and his or her target is, and can only ever be, fundamentally asymmetrical. Trolls don't mean, or don't *have* to mean, the abusive things they say. They get to choose the extent to which their statements match their personal beliefs; they get to establish that they're just trolling (I complicate this notion of "just" trolling in later chapters). Targets of trolling, on the other hand, are expected to take trolls at their word, and are only trolled harder if they resist. Consequently, trolls exercise what can only be described as pure privilege—they refuse to treat others as they insist on being treated. Instead, they do what they want, when they want, to whomever they want, with almost perfect impunity. To call trolling behaviors ethically and ideologically fraught would be an understatement, and is a point that must be taken into consideration—in fact, must be taken as a given—in all subsequent discussions of trolling.

2 The Only Reason to Do Anything: Lulz, Play, and the Mask of Trolling

This chapter focuses on lulz, arguably the most important concept within the troll space, and an absolutely necessary component in any introduction to trolling. After providing a working definition of the term, the chapter presents several concrete examples of lulz, complete with an insider's perspective on what exactly trolls find so lulzy—that is to say, amusing—about these events and these people. It then discusses the relationship between lulz and the performance of trolling, described as the "mask" of trolling. Finally, it considers the ways in which the mask of trolling favors, and in many cases necessitates, highly transgressive humor.

The Lulz Prayer

In the beginning was the Lulz, and the Lulz was with God, and the Lulz was God. He was with God in the beginning. Through him all trollings were made; without him nothing was trolled that has been trolled. In him was drama, and that drama was the light of all mankind. The light shines in the darkness, and the darkness has not overcome it.

So begins the Encyclopedia Dramatica (ED) entry on "lulz," a cornerstone of trolling humor and culture.[1] A corruption (or as the trolls might argue, perfection) of "Laugh Out Loud," lulz celebrates the anguish of the laughed-at victim. According to the lulz entry writer(s) (as mentioned earlier, ED is an open wiki dictionary, meaning collaboratively editable by users), this anguish is precisely what transforms LOL into lulz, "making it longer, girthier, and more pleasurable"—at least for the troll. Lulz is, as the saying goes, the only reason to do anything; "I did it for the lulz" is the troll's catchall excuse, explanation, and punchline.

This, however, is the limit of any traditional definition. In the trolling world, lulz may mean one basic thing—amusement at other people's distress—but can be deployed in any number of directions, for any number of reasons. Trolls derive lulz from other trolls, from trolls attempting to derive lulz from other trolls, from innocent bystanders, from media figures, from entire news organizations, from anything and everything they can get their hands on.

Within trolling communities, lulz functions both as punishment and as reward, sometimes simultaneously. Lulz operates as a nexus of social cohesion and social constraint. It does not distinguish between friend and foe, and is as much enjoyed by the trolling spectator as by the active trolling agent. This makes lulz an extremely slippery term, one that implies active pursuit (lulz don't amass themselves, they have to be sought out), an object (the person place or thing that has been designated as lulzy), and an aesthetic (that which marks a lulzy action or object as such). Both plural and singular and passive and active and static and dynamic, lulz is (or are, depending on how the term is being used) immediately recognizable to those who speak the trolling vernacular, but often inscrutable, if not unrecognizable, to outsiders.

Lulz in Several Nutshells

Although the concept of lulz is often difficult to define, even for trolls— "you know it when you see it" was the most common definition I heard when conducting interviews—the category is marked by three basic characteristics: fetishism, generativity, and magnetism. The following section analyzes each characteristic, taking care to present lulz from a trolling insider's and nontrolling outsider's perspective.

Lulz Are Fetishistic

In 2006, an American seventh-grader named Mitchell Henderson killed himself with his parents' rifle. In response to his death, Henderson's family and friends posted dozens of condolence messages on his MySpace page, which someone subsequently linked onto MyDeathSpace, an archive of precisely what you would expect. Someone lurking on MyDeathSpace found Henderson's page and noticed a message, written in the form of a meandering free-verse poem, praising his choice. According to the poster, Henderson was "an [sic] hero" for taking the fatal shot, a phrase the poster repeated no less than four times. Apparently amused by this ungrammatical outpouring of grief, the MyDeathSpace lurker posted the page onto 4chan's /b/ board. An untold number of trolls were similarly amused and descended upon the Henderson case, eventually discovering that two days before his death, Henderson had lost his iPod.

Whether or not Henderson's lost iPod did indeed factor into his decision to kill himself, and regardless of Henderson's underlying psychological issues, trolls framed his death as the ultimate example of "first-world problems," specifically as consumerism gone terribly wrong. Augmented by their longstanding disdain for suicides, especially when the victim is young, white, and otherwise (apparently) privileged, "an hero" (as the story came to be known) quickly became a raid for the ages. That Henderson's grieving parents would receive the brunt of this onslaught didn't give participating trolls much pause; in fact, the family became a secondary target. Over the next few days, trolls hacked into Henderson's MySpace page, made public his parents' personal information online, and posted dozens of photoshopped pictures featuring floating iPods and zombies onto /b/. Some anon even uploaded a picture of an iPod resting against Henderson's actual gravestone, an image met with much trollish delight.[2]

Of all the factors contributing to the trolls' engagement with Mitchell Henderson's death, emotional dissociation—an orientation to self and other that psychologist John Suler cites as a core pillar of online disinhibition[3]—is the most prominent. In the trolling world, dissociation manifests as an emotional firewall between he who targets and that which is targeted, and isn't just incidental to the existence of lulz, but in fact is regarded as necessary. No matter the circumstance, and whatever their source, emotions are seen as a trap, something to exploit in others and ignore or switch off in yourself. Abandon all feeling, ye who enter here.

From this solipsistic position, one reinforced by the protections afforded by anonymity, trolls are able to dismiss the emotional context of a given story, as well as the harm their actions cause. All trolls see—all they choose to see—are the absurd, exploitable details. In Henderson's case, trolls were either disinterested in or outright blind to the series of events that lead to the young teen's suicide. They were either disinterested in or outright blind to the grief his death caused his parents. Most significantly, they were either disinterested in or outright blind to the ways in which their mockery exacerbated an already traumatizing experience. All that mattered was the punch line. The vast majority of trolling humor, and all humor categorized as "lulzy," is characterized by similar myopia.

In this way, lulz are a *fetish*. Not in the sexual sense (in which specific objects—for example, shoes—become the point of acute sexual desire), and not in the religious sense (in which specific objects are said to be imbued with mystical powers), but in the Marxist sense—specifically as a play on the concept of commodity fetishism, the process by which material commodities (i.e., the stuff we buy) are "made magic" by capitalism so that the social conditions and relations of power that create and sustain economic disparity are rendered invisible. As a direct consequence of commodity fetishism, all the consumer can see is the product itself, not how the product was made or by whom or to what political or ecological effect.[4]

In similar fashion, trolls' "lulz fetishism" obscures the social conditions and interpersonal strife that animate a particular story, the Henderson story providing a striking and archetypal example. Through the magic of trolling, all that remains are the absurd, exploitable details; trolls do not, and in many cases cannot, connect their object of ridicule—for example, the phrase "an hero"—to the emotional context out of which it arises, resulting in highly dissociative and often rabidly antagonistic laughter.

Lulz Are Generative

In 2010, eleven-year-old Jessi Slaughter (given name Jessica Leonhardt) found herself in the middle of an all-out lulz storm. Slaughter, a self-professed "scene kid" (i.e., a person who embraces any number of underground "scenes," usually musical), was accused of sleeping with the twentysomething lead singer of her favorite electro/crunk/post-hardcore band, Blood on the Dance Floor.[5] In response, Slaughter posted a defiant video addressed to her "fucking haters" to YouTube, in which she threatened to "pop a Glock in your mouth and make a brain slushie."[6] Some anon found the video, deemed it amusing, and posted it onto /b/. Over the next few days, anons flooded Slaughter's various social media profiles with harassing messages. They also got hold of her parents' phone number and address, and began inundating the Leonhardt household with obscene messages and phone calls.

Not expecting the blowback to be so ferocious, Slaughter posted a tearful video to YouTube telling the trolls they'd gone too far. Slaughter's father appeared in the video and over the course of several minutes became increasingly enraged. He told the trolls they "done goofed," that he "backtraced" their threats, and that he'd contacted the cyberpolice. He concluded by bellowing that if anyone tried to harm his daughter, "consequences will never be the same."[7] Trolls were delighted; "you done goofed," "backtracing," "the cyberpolice," and discussions of consequences were promptly inducted into the pantheon of lulz. After all, if there is one thing lulzier to a troll than tears, it's rage. By intervening on his daughter's behalf, Slaughter's father supplied trolls with an embarrassment of the latter, inadvertently attracting increasing numbers of trolls to the story.

In their study of humor within SENDMAIL, a university writing center mailing list, Mike Hubler and Diana Bell provide context for the "world building" (i.e., generative) power of precisely this sort of aggressive laughter. As the community establishes the outline of its own borders, Hubler and Bell argue, a set of shared experiences and expectations emerges; the resulting content feeds into and sustains an interconnected nest of constitutive content, which simultaneously contextualizes and reconfigures the explicit meaning(s) of additional content. Within the community play frame, all reading is writing, and all reception is creation; to recognize an in-joke is to participate in community formation, and to participate in community formation is to ensure community growth.[8]

In the trolling world, this cycle could be summarized as follows: someone posts lulzy content onto /b/ or any other trollish forum. This content could be a particularly amusing macro or turn of phrase or grammatical misfire ("done goofed"). Whatever its form, and however obliquely, the reference— or in the trolls' parlance, the meme—gestures toward and/or taps into a previously shared experience and is subsequently integrated into the collective subcultural fabric. The new bit of content is subsequently (re)created and (re)deployed, simultaneously precipitating further memetic creation and fortifying a sense of community between participants.

The link between community and humor, even ostensibly antisocial trolling humor, is well established. As literary scholar James English explains, humor is always a cultural event, never a discrete statement. Even the simplest joke has a context, not just in terms of content but in terms of whom the joke is for (or as is often the case, against). That there is a joke thus implies, in fact requires, that there is an audience—an "us" who laughs versus a "them" who does not.[9] In the case of trolls, this "us" is marked by the recognition and appreciation of lulz. The resulting laughter simultaneously gestures toward and adds value to a spiderweb of previously shared content, as Ryan Milner notes of antagonistic discursive practices on 4chan and reddit.[10] Put simply, trolls laugh themselves into existence and sustain this existence through further laughter.

Lulz Are Magnetic

One of trolldom's simplest yet longest-lived sources of lulz features *Battletoads*, GameStop stores, and coordinated prank calls. *Battletoads*, an early 1990s video game, follows the misadventures of Rash, Zits, and Pimple as they try to transport a princess from one side of the galaxy to another.[11] For whatever reason, "Is this *Battletoads*?" became the standard response on /v/, 4chan's video game forum, and later on /b/, whenever anyone posted a screenshot from a video game. Starting in 2007, trolls began calling GameStop stores en masse asking to preorder a copy of the sequel (which didn't exist). They also seeded their calls with references to Ebaumsworld, a much-derided rival forum and frequent scapegoat. Due to the high number of *Battletoads* requests, and the frustration of having to field the trolls' constant, often wildly obscene calls, GameStop employees would fly into a rage the second the caller mentioned the game or Ebaumsworld. The lulz were so plentiful that trolls continued posting the telephone numbers of local branches onto /b/ well into 2010.[12]

GameStop employees weren't the only source of lulz. Rhetorical one-upmanship between trolls also generated a great deal of trollish laughter. In order to keep things fresh, trolls would constantly dream up new and more outrageous ways to ask the same question, with the goal of keeping the employee on the phone for as long as possible and then making the employee as angry as possible. The most successful of these calls would be posted onto /b/, ensuring further engagement. Battletoads thus provides an example of what Gabriella Coleman describes as the "magnetism" of lulz. According to Coleman, this magnetism is twofold. First, lulz are *externally* magnetic—they literally attract attention, both from within and from without. More metaphorically, lulz lend cohesion to an otherwise faceless collective. Trolls may not know who their comrades are in real life; in fact, they may never interact with the same group of people again, but through lulz they are united.[13]

In addition to courting spectacle and maintaining community ethos, lulz are fundamentally self-replicating. Once a particular piece of content enters the trolling lexicon ("Is this *Battletoads*?"), its comedic exchange value only increases. This occurs for two interconnected reasons. First, lulz contain, and are celebrated for containing, a trace of their memetic origins. Individuals who did not personally witness or participate in a raid can still experience vicarious amusement, increasing the likelihood that the meme will "live on" in the poster. This in turn encourages the creation of additional variations, many of which subsequently engender their own subnest of memetic content. Lulz are therefore triply magnetic; the existence of some predicts, if not outright necessitates, the emergence of more.

Taken together, the aforementioned characteristics undergird the overarching behavioral and aesthetic category of lulz. All necessary and none solely sufficient, each characteristic—fetishism, generativity, and magnetism—builds upon and complicates the next. Emotional detachment allows trolls to home in on the most exploitable details of a given story, which engenders a nest of new and evolving content, upon which newer and more dynamic content is built, thus wedging an even larger emotional gap between those who laugh and that which is laughed at. This ever-increasing distance generates further memetic variation and further distance, in turn encouraging more active and emotionally unmoored participation. Concurrently, and not unlike a series of campfire ghost stories, lulz provide both entertainment and a basic feeling of connection between participants; the pleasure of lulz inheres as strongly in the retelling as it does in the active pursuit of new targets, guaranteeing that new targets will indeed be found.

The Mask of Trolling

Of these characteristics, the most conspicuous, and conspicuously problematic, is trolls' persistent emotional dissociation. In no way are trolls affected by the havoc they wreak, except to the extent that said havoc is highly amusing—at least to them. As mentioned earlier, "I did it for the lulz" is often the only explanation trolls offer, and is indicative of what I have come to describe as the mask of trolling, a concept that ties into and complicates anthropologist Gregory Bateson's articulation of the play frame.

As Bateson argues, the play frame is established when participants indicate through tone of voice or body language that certain behaviors, which otherwise would mean something very different (an unkind word between friends, for example), are to be taken as playful, not real.[14] Trolling establishes a similar frame, but unlike Bateson's account, which implies good faith and reciprocal engagement, the mask worn by trolls precludes reciprocity; only the troll can wear the mask. The recipient of the trolls' playful behavior, on the other hand, is expected to take things seriously, the more seriously the better. If the target does not, then the troll has failed.

The remainder of this section explores the process by which trolls acquire their masks and provides an alternative account of the relationship between trolls, lulz, and their rotating cast of targets. To do so, I will pull from a series of online interviews conducted on Facebook in 2011.

In order to procure these interviews, I posted an interview request onto the wall of one of my Facebook research groups (I describe my research methods in much greater detail in the following chapter). Several of the respondents were longtime collaborators, and several were trolls whom other trolls knew and had recommended. The majority of the trolls who responded identified primarily as Facebook trolls, though several only occasionally used Facebook to troll and instead considered /b/ their trolling home base. Regardless of their provenance, I gave each troll the option to use a pseudonym or be described simply as "anon"; whichever handle they preferred is reflected in what follows. While these trolls' statements are not and should not be regarded as universally representative of all trolls, the attitudes expressed by each are pervasive among the trolls I've personally encountered on 4chan/b/, Facebook, YouTube, and Skype.

The trolls' first and most basic assumption has to do with the relationship between trolling and the real world. As one /b/ troll explains:

If someone called me a chink or gook online I really wouldn't care at all. In real life though, depending on who says it, if someone called me a chink or gook I would want to beat the hell out of them . . . Reason for this is because online they have no clue what race I am and so they are obviously trying to troll me which I find funny. Real life though they are actually attacking my culture/race which I can't stand, unless it's a friend or something.[15]

The vast majority of trolls I've worked with agree, and insist that their troll selves and their offline ("real") selves are subject to totally different sets of rules. Despite the explicit and biologically necessary connection between the troll and the person behind the troll, and despite the correlation between real-life experiences and online behaviors (even simply in terms of search interest or basic technological access), trolls believe that there exists a fundamental difference between what they do as trolls and who they are as people. This presumed disconnect isn't about which behaviors are *real*, exactly, but which behaviors are attributed to what self; the thoughts expressed by a person's trolling persona do not necessarily reflect the thoughts of the person's public persona. Not only is this twain never to meet, according to the trolls I've interviewed, it isn't *designed* to meet; it's something they work hard to make sure isn't *able* to meet.

Of course, the boundaries between online and offline have become increasingly fuzzy; just as average Internet users engage their "real lives" both remotely and in person, trolling behaviors needn't be confined to online spaces. As one respondent explained:

When I am around other "citizens of the internet" (i.e. trolls and other people who I recognize as internet-people), I go through that [same] fracture between my internet and real life persona. When I am with my friends, I act in a similar fashion as I do on the internet, but when I am not around other internet-people, I revert to my soft-spoken, calm, and somewhat shy personality . . . Since we all are experienced with how language transforms on the internet, we can easily bracket each other's words in this way.[16]

The issue, then, isn't *where* the trolling behavior occurs, but what the behaviors signify. And what the behaviors signify is that an individual has switched into trolling mode. He has, in other words, put on his mask.

Like Goffman's "front," which represents the emotional or spatial distance between a performer and that which is performed,[17] the mask of trolling decodes incoming and outgoing signals, framing all subsequent input and output as a particular kind of detached, lulzy play. Other trolls have little trouble recognizing and deciphering these signals, explaining why trolls are so adept at recognizing their own kind; the message that *this is play* could not be clearer to other trolls. Outsiders, on the other hand, who have no decoding mechanism, often don't realize that there are signals to be decoded—making them the perfect target.

The mask of trolling thus establishes a clear insider/outsider distinction. More importantly, it necessitates an affective reorientation to content. By establishing a firewall between person and troll, the mask of trolling simultaneously establishes a second and much more robust firewall between the troll and the object of his attention. This in turn allows, if not outright demands, a lulzy response to content. Unsurprisingly so; echoing philosopher Henri Bergson, humor is predicated on mental dexterity and emotional distance.[18] The mask of trolling is fueled by both, thus positing a gaping affective gap—one perfectly calibrated to the attraction to and extraction of lulz.

Interestingly, trolls' talent for emotional firewalling is matched only by their ability to recognize and exploit their target's attachments. As Peter Partyvan (whom we encounter again in chapter 5) explains:

Being obscene for shock value can only go so far. You have to interact with the people you are trolling. Twist their words, respond to their comments, etc. They get even angrier when you point out the flaws in their argument. And you can make them absolutely rage when you start getting inside their heads. Either by selecting a line of attack based on their previous responses (suicides go to hell for religious types) or trying to guess aspects of their lives based on their profiles. The things that hurt the most are the comments grounded in truth. Ones that echo the thoughts of whoever you are trolling, bringing up the doubts that haunt them every day.[19]

As Peter Partyvan's statement shows, trolls are keenly aware of how their behaviors impact others, and know exactly which issues will get the greatest rise from their chosen targets. From race to class to everything in between, trolls have their fingers on all kinds of powder kegs—all the better to troll you with. As Facebook troll Wilson Mouzone (another troll I revisit in chapter 5) explains, "[Great trolls] fully understand the implications of everything they say and do, and that's what makes them great trolls. They have empathy and can work out the best way to wind people up, but that also means they are fully aware of the harm they cause."[20]

What makes a troll successful, in other words, is his or her ability to empathize. I would argue, however, that even this awareness—which, as Peter Partyvan suggested, can be extraordinarily discerning—is predicated on abstraction. Certain trolls may wage personal vendettas, thus necessitating at least a degree of emotional investment. And occasionally trolls are themselves triggered, in which case the lulz either evaporate, thus suspending the game, or are turned against the offending troll, thus refocusing the game's target. But the vast majority of trolling is explicitly dissociative, as discussed in the previous section on lulz fetishism. Indeed, regardless of what offline experiences a troll might bring to a given interaction, the mask of trolling safeguards trolls' personal attachments, thereby allowing the troll to focus solely on the extraction of lulz. Anon2 emphasized this point in a Facebook interview. "We don't have the intent to demean people," he said. "The intent is to piss them off."[21] To a person who deliberately severs emotion from behavior, for whom the ends always already justify the means, the demarcation between "real" disrespect and trollish taunting is perfectly sensible.

Even if one buys the explanation that trolls are only doing it for the lulz and don't mean any *real* harm (a difficult position for outsiders to accept, but one that is common within the ranks of subcultural trolls), one cannot deny that the pursuit of lulz is, at the most basic level, objectifying. The trolls' targets aren't ends unto themselves, they're fetishized pawns in the trolls' game. Chapter 7 revisits the subject of lulz and considers the cultural logics out of which this impulse emerges. For now, the takeaway point is that lulz are predicated on asymmetry—making their extraction an inherently loaded endeavor.

3 Toward a Method/ology

This is a qualitative, mixed methods study. It engages with digital media studies, folklore studies, cultural studies, subcultural studies, and critical race and feminist theories. The study also draws from extensive ethnographic research. In addition to conducting and transcribing dozens of online interviews with twenty-five trolls spanning several platforms, exchanging endless email and private messages with my trolling collaborators, and introducing myself and being introduced to a snowballing sample of research recruits, I've spent thousands of hours engaging in participant observation on 4chan's /b/ board, Encyclopedia Dramatica, Facebook, Skype, YouTube, and various other online spaces (commercial websites, personal blogs, specific comment threads) recommended by my collaborators.

From its very outset, the project was plagued by a number of methodological complications, including the deceptively simple question of how and where to restrict my research focus, the ever-shifting dynamic between community and platform, trolls' insistence on anonymity, constant subcultural change, and most vexingly, my own research myopia. Rather than undermining my argument, each roadblock yielded new—if unexpected—insight into the project, which I chronicle here.

Establishing Borders

The first and most basic hurdle I faced was determining the scope of my inquiry. In early 2008, when I first began writing about the subject of trolling, this was no obvious task. With the exception of intermittent media interventions that, as I discuss in the subsequent chapter, helped ensure the ascendency of the subcultural understanding of the term troll, the only group of people talking extensively about lulz-based trolling were lulz-based trolls. As time passed, an increasing number of academics and journalists began joining this conversation. But initially, there were very few sources to pull from.

Consequently, and particularly during those first few months of research, the only way to fully understand exactly what qualified as trolling and who qualified as a troll was to go where the self-identifying trolls were and start observing. Because they were spaces frequented by people who described themselves as trolls, I started with 4chan's /b/ board and Encyclopedia Dramatica.

Initially I understood nothing; it felt as if I were trying to read a website written in an entirely different language. I could tell that people were making jokes, but didn't see what was so funny. Still, there was something about the space that intrigued me, so I continued reading and cross-referencing and eventually the indecipherable chaos gave way to what I could recognize as a surprisingly coherent behavioral and linguistic system. More importantly, I was starting to understand the trolls' jokes.

This was a critical moment. As humor folklorist Gershon Legman argues, jokes illuminate the cultural system (and systems of power) out of which the jokes emerge.[1] Tell me what kinds of jokes you make, in other words, and I'll tell you what kind of world you live in. This insight was especially helpful when first encountering trolling humor, particularly given its outrageous and often vicious character. According to Legman, the laughter that greets the punchline of the sorts of jokes trolls prefer represents "the anxiety of all concerned over the taboos that are being broken."[2] This may have been true for some trolls, but there was no way of verifying, or in fact even asking, what trolls *really* felt about the X-rated, not safe for work (or arguably life) jokes they made.

What was clear, however, was the trolls' basic awareness of (and more importantly, interest in breaking) specific taboos. Also clear was the consistency of the trolls' comedic aesthetic, which was expressed through a highly distinctive vernacular described by folklorists as "argot." In addition to its fixation on transgression, the trolling argot I encountered was characterized by tortured, ungrammatical syntax and delight in improper spelling, inappropriate word choices, and bizarre anachronisms. For example, instead of saying please, trolls said "plox"; instead of saying masturbation, trolls said "fap"; "sauce" was shorthand for "where did you find that image?" while "inb4 an hero" meant "I expect you'll tell me to go kill myself, but I've already thought of that, so don't bother." Statements of fact were often followed up with nonsensical rejoinders like "then who was phone," everything in the past happened last Thursday, and so on.

In short, the more I immersed myself in the troll space, the more I realized that the behaviors emanating from and around 4chan weren't random acts of aggression. Quite the contrary—they were operating within a novel, though fully consistent, symbolic framework. To echo Dick Hebdige, whose 1972 study of British punks has had a lasting impact within cultural studies, trolls were characterized by a highly coherent, and highly subversive, subcultural style.[3] Just as Hebdige's punks were reappropriating existing cultural materials (most visibly in their style of dress) in order to undermine the existing economic order, so too were trolls reappropriating existing cultural material (most visibly in their linguistic style) in order to subvert, or at the very least tinker with, the existing moral order.

Furthermore, as Hebdige might have predicted, trolls' constant appropriation and recombination of cultural artifacts, from films to television shows to celebrity gossip to whatever else they deemed lulzy or exploitable, helped fortify participating trolls' shared sense of identity. This emerging "we" of trolling was, as previously discussed, both generative and magnetic, resulting in deeper subcultural meaning, stronger subcultural identification, and an ever-expanding nest of subcultural content. Had I approached this "we" with a clearer sense of what I was looking for, I almost assuredly would have missed important details. It would have been *my* system of meaning, not theirs. As it was, I had no clue as to what I was looking for (and in many cases, even what I was looking at), and therefore had no choice but to allow the contours of the space to unfold organically. Although initially intimidating, the process of slowly, painfully being led to my conclusions yielded a great deal of insight into the ethos and output of the community—insights I doubt I could have accessed as a presumptuous outsider.

Navigating Platforms

Just as certain cities are said to be supporting characters in the television shows, novels, and films for which they serve as backdrop—New York City comes to mind, in everything from *Seinfeld* to *Manhattan* to *American Psycho* to *30 Rock*—online platforms impart a similar flavor. Indeed, far from being empty, value-neutral spaces, platforms have a profound effect on how communities form and what community members are able to accomplish while online. Given this complicated interplay, I was forced to adapt my research methods not just to the particular group I was studying, and not just to the particular platform they frequented, but to the evolving interaction(s) between community, platform, and behavior.

For example it was nearly impossible, not to mention inadvisable, to court research subjects on 4chan's /b/ board. Almost everyone who posts does so anonymously, so even if I responded to a particular troll's post and requested an interview, and even if I managed to elicit a reaction, I would have had no way of verifying that the intended troll had indeed responded, to say nothing of knowing whether or not he or she was trolling me in his or her answers. Furthermore, on a purely practical level, there would have been no faster way to ensure a veritable trolling onslaught than to reveal my name and identifying information on the /b/ board. Because I would not have come away with much usable information, and because outing myself as a researcher would have subjected me to any number of unwanted advances (as curious as I was to see the inner workings of a raid, I was eager to avoid becoming a target myself), I focused instead on the "observation" side of "participant observation."

On Facebook, sustained contact with chosen collaborators wasn't just possible, it was in fact necessary; I quite literally had to "friend" trolls in order to observe their behaviors. The resulting (anti)social network into which I found myself thrust created a highly stable and at times even collegial research environment. Although I deliberately avoided collecting specific identifying information about the trolls I worked with and so couldn't be said to "know" them exactly (I discuss the implications of this choice in the following section), I did become quite familiar with their respective trolling styles, online personalities, and in many cases their voices, as this group of trolls preferred to communicate via Skype audio chat. The resulting research interactions would have been impossible to achieve on 4chan. Most significantly, I was able ask "my" trolls direct questions, initiate sustained conversations, make plans to meet up on Skype, and from time to time even shared drafts of chapters (they were, let's say, tough readers).

Although many of these trolls were initially wary of my motives, they eventually came to tolerate the researcher in their midst, and during the peak Facebook trolling years (2010 to mid-2011) provided absolutely invaluable information. Had I merely lurked on Facebook, none of this would have been possible. Conversely, had I attempted to socially engage with trolls on 4chan's /b/ board, I likely would have invoked their collective wrath and still walked away empty-handed. In short, despite the fact that a one-size-fits-all approach to data collection might have been more efficient, and although I would have preferred to have a clear plan of action going into my research, such a plan wouldn't have been all that helpful. In fact it may have been counterproductive, if not personally perilous.

The Problem of Anonymity

No matter the platform or the community, I deliberately restricted my analysis to trolls' online behaviors—a decision not without its drawbacks. As numerous academics, including cultural anthropologist Mizuko Ito,[4] digital media and race scholar Lisa Nakamura,[5] social media researcher danah boyd,[6] and many others have stressed, so-called real life necessarily bleeds into online life, and vice versa. Our raced, classed, and gendered bodies are encoded into our online behaviors, even when we're pretending to be something above or beyond or below what we "really" are IRL (in real life).[7]

That basic idea, that we mustn't overlook the terrestrial when we talk about the virtual, holds just as true for trolls. This is not to say that there exists a simple one-to-one relationship between the people behind the trolls and their trolling personas. But at a very basic level, terrestrial experiences—levels of education, access to media and technology, political affiliation or lack thereof—influence the choices users make while online, including (and most basically) the choice to go online at all.

Who and what trolls are, in other words, matters greatly. Unfortunately, precise demographics are almost impossible to verify. During my most active data collection years (2008–2012), trolls rarely if ever used their real names to troll, and were quick to shame or punish those who accidentally revealed identifying personal information. If and when they did decide to share certain details about their offline lives, there was no guarantee that these self-disclosures were in fact accurate. Many of the trolls I worked with would tell me all sorts of elaborate stories, often chronicling some childhood trauma, then would turn around and "lol jk" me (literally "haha sucker, I'm just kidding"). In these cases, I couldn't help but laugh—they were trolls, after all.

In this way, at least in the context of trolling, I've found myself in strange and at times uncomfortable alignment with anthropologist Tom Boellstorff, whose *Coming of Age in Second Life* bypasses discussion of terrestrial identity in favor of close anthropological examination of his subjects' online identities.[8] As danah boyd notes, Boellstorff's analysis implicitly acknowledges the significance of the "real" self yet refuses to consider the ways in which one self informs and complicates the other, in the process providing a limited account of a given set of behaviors.[9] Although I am in full agreement with boyd, it's simply not possible to analyze information that isn't there, or at least isn't verifiable. And so, for this project, I had to improvise.

Luckily, there was some precedent for this type of research. Anthropologist Gabriella Coleman has written extensively about trolls,[10] hackers,[11] and most recently the political arm of Anonymous,[12] and has successfully navigated many of the research hurdles my project faced. Like Coleman, I never knew exactly whom I was working with; like Coleman, I was constantly faced with the ever-present possibility that collaborators were, or at the very least could be, lying through their teeth.[13] Consequently, and like Coleman, I needed to adopt alternative vetting and analytic processes.

One approach was to eschew reliance on literal demographics and instead focus on symbolic demographics. Take, for example, the precise breakdown of race, gender, and class within the troll space. Given the anonymity of participating trolls, this information was empirically unverifiable; I couldn't know *for sure* whom I was talking to, or what their offline lives were like. This isn't to say that I didn't (and don't still) have my suspicions. After six years, dozens of interviews, and thousands of hours of participant observation, I have every indication that the vast majority of subcultural trolls—certainly the ones I interacted with—are relatively privileged white males for whom English is either a first or second language. And yet in terms of hard evidence, there isn't much to present. I don't have a trolling census to pull from, or reliable statistics to compile, or any way to confirm or deny individual trolls' demographic self-disclosures.

What is empirically verifiable, however, is the observable fact that trolling behaviors are gendered male, are raced as white, and are dependent upon a certain degree of economic privilege. As I discuss in subsequent chapters, the maleness of trolling inheres in the trolls' emphasis on dominance (along with other androcentric tropes), its whiteness on the trolls' universalizing assumptions, including the assumption that everyone else in the troll space is also white, and its privilege on the fact that trolling behaviors require robust technological and cultural access. This one can see, this one can prove, and so this is where I placed my focus (and also explains why I tend to use the male pronoun when describing the trolls I've worked with—not as a reflection of their biological sex, which I cannot verify, but as a reflection of their gender—that is, the socially constructed ways in which they present themselves as conventionally masculine).

A secondary implication of having little concrete, definitive data to work with was that I had no choice but to sidestep questions about the psychology of trolls. Not because I wasn't interested in their inner lives, not because I didn't think their thoughts and feelings mattered, but because I didn't have access to them. Even when speaking to reliable long-term collaborators, I couldn't trust their accounts, not entirely—for the same reason that I couldn't accept as unassailable fact any of the demographic information I collected. The best I could do was note how the trolls chose to present themselves to me, and extrapolate meaning from what was very likely a highly choreographed performance.

Of course, not all researchers have taken this approach. In 2014, Canadian psychologists Erin Buckels, Paul Trapnell, and Delroy Paulhus set out to test their hypothesis that trolling was a manifestation of the so-called Dark Tetrad of noxious personality traits, namely Machiavellianism, narcissism, psychopathy, and sadistic personality. To do so, they conducted two online surveys, the first focusing on 418 users of Amazon's Mechanical Turk crowdsourcing platform (through which self-selecting participants are paid small amounts of money for completing specific online tasks), and the second pulling from the responses of 188 Canadian psychology students and 609 United States Amazon Mechanical Turk users. In the first survey, individuals who indicated that they enjoyed trolling (5.6% of respondents, though it wasn't clear whether the self-identifying trolls were using the term in the subcultural sense or based on some other criteria) recorded high Dark Tetrad scores, with the exception of narcissism. The second survey focused more intently on the Dark Tetrad and yielded similar findings.[14]

Media coverage of this study could be summarized by Slate magazine's headline "Internet Trolls Really Are Horrible People: Narcissistic, Machiavellian, Psychopathic, and Sadistic,"[15] despite the fact that narcissism was not positively correlated with trolling enjoyment in either survey. Such a response was unsurprising, as the study seemed to confirm what many had long believed to be true about trolls. And it may well be that the individuals surveyed did indeed have Machiavellian, psychopathic, and sadistic traits. Then again, they may have been trolling for the researchers' cameras; it's impossible to know for sure.

Verifiability (or lack thereof) isn't the only problem with psychological approaches to trolling. Assuming it were possible to prove beyond a shadow of a doubt the specific damage of an individual troll, such information simply wouldn't tell us very much. It might confirm *that* certain trolls are narcissistic sadists (or whatever the diagnosis), but wouldn't provide context for *why* these traits are so common, both within trolling and nontrolling populations online and off. Consequently, I am much more inclined to direct my attention toward cultural—as opposed to individual—pathologies, and the ways in which trolling behaviors replicate and are imbricated in existing ideological systems.

Of course, I only arrived at this conclusion because I didn't have the luxury of an empirically verifiable dataset. I may have preferred to work with more concrete information, and may have preferred to extrapolate out to sweeping racial, gender, and class critiques of participating trolls. But given the populations I was attempting to study, that wasn't possible—at least not without forwarding theoretical and methodological inconsistencies, for example by emphasizing the unverifiability of trolling demographics in one section, then pivoting to analyses predicated on the literal demographics of trolling (i.e., objective statistics) in another. As a result, I chose to focus on what was and would always remain available to me—namely, the larger cultural flows operating within and reflected by these otherwise opaque groupings. In the process, I was able to establish not just the facts of trolling (who and what trolls target most frequently, where they congregate online, what kinds of artifacts they are inclined to create), but how these behaviors ultimately implicate far more people than the trolls themselves. What might have begun as an apparent research limitation, in other words, evolved into a theoretical backbone.

Moving Targets

My fourth major methodological roadblock—what I call the problem of verb tenses—took much longer to reveal itself, and posed what initially appeared to be an even greater challenge than questions about my research scope. Specifically, trolling subculture changed, and changed significantly, during the course of my research. From the time I started my project in 2008 to about 2010, I was writing in the present tense, as trolling subculture solidified. As time passed, however, I found myself describing certain trolling behaviors in the past tense, as something that had happened but was no longer happening, or was still happening, but not in the same ways. By early 2012 it was clear that the troll space had undergone a profound shift, one that required a complete reassessment of tenses.

Grammatical tense wasn't the only thing that changed during my research. The very category of trolling was in flux. Take, for example, my contribution to Henry Jenkins, Sam Ford, and Joshua Green's *Spreadable Media: Creating Value and Meaning in a Networked Culture*.[16] For my selection, written in 2010, I chose to discuss the ways in which trolls use the term "meme," focusing specifically on trollish engagement with hip-hop horrorcore duo Insane Clown Posse's 2011 "Miracles" video. In the video, rappers Violent J and Shaggy 2 Dope—who have made a career dressing as

evil clowns and rapping about various dark and often hyper-violent subjects like cannibalism and necrophilia—celebrate the miracle of rainbows,
giraffes, and household pets. Later, while chastising the scientific establishment for denying the existence of miracles, Shaggy 2 Dope asks "fuckin'
magnets, how do *they* work?"[17] Trolls had a field day with the video, particularly the magnets line, which I used as a case study for memetic creation within the troll space.

By the time *Spreadable Media* was published in 2013, however, I found
myself somewhat wary of my own essay, particularly my blithe framing of
the word "troll."[18] In 2010, when trolling was still somewhat underground,
and when the only people using trolling vernacular were people who self-
identified as trolls, I didn't need to qualify the term. By 2013, that was no
longer the case. As I describe in greater detail in chapter 8, references that
at one point could only mean that trolling was afoot were suddenly everywhere, making it extremely difficult to differentiate self-identifying trolls
from average Internet users.

Consequently—and I'd place this cutoff around early 2012, just as I was
heading toward my dissertation defense—it became painfully apparent
that I was no longer writing a study of emergent subcultural phenomena.
I was instead chronicling a subcultural life cycle. This may have complicated my writing process, but it confirmed the predictive and explanatory
power of my theory of cultural digestion. I was watching, in real time, as
trolls alternatively trailed and walked in lockstep with the dominant
culture, if only to exploit and repurpose existing materials. Yes I had to
rewrite section after section, and yes I spent many a sleepless night worried
that my dissertation would be outdated before I finished writing it, but
here was the proof I needed that trolls are in fact the strangest possible
canary in the most unexpected of coal mines.

Putting the "I" in Troll

A few months after I outed myself as a researcher to the RIP trolls I'd been
observing, I was scheduled to appear on a British radio program for a
segment on Facebook memorial page trolling. While waiting for my call
time, I opened Facebook chat. One of the trolls I knew—by that point
I was embedded within a loose group of high-profile Facebook trolls,
many of whom targeted memorial pages—was online, and I struck up a
conversation.

After a few minutes, the producer called with the segment panel lineup.
I told the troll that I would be afk (away from keyboard) while the producer

and I discussed the show. The troll said okay, and I answered my phone. The producer greeted me, thanked me for agreeing to the interview, then explained that I'd be talking to the father of a recent teenage suicide whose RIP page had just been attacked by trolls. The father was distraught and wanted to know why his son had been targeted. He also wanted to know just how evil a person had to be in order to engage in that sort of behavior. Before I had a chance to respond, the producer thanked me again and said to hold tight; he'd call back once the interview was live (for radio interviews, the producer usually calls twice, once to prep you for your interview, and again a few minutes later to patch you into the broadcast).

I hung up and returned to my Facebook chat. The troll I was talking to asked me what happened, and suddenly nervous—there is a big difference between having an academic discussion about trolling and being asked to speak on behalf of all trolls to a grieving father—I explained what the producer had said. The troll was quiet for a few seconds. "Just remember," he finally said. "It's not your job to defend us."[19]

The troll's reminder struck a nerve. One of the most consistent early critiques of my work was that I was an apologist for trolls, or at least that I wasn't critical enough. Initially, this line of criticism was a source of constant anxiety and defensiveness ("I'm not too close to my subject! I'm perfectly objective! You don't even know what a meme is! How dare you!"). Luckily I had the support of no-nonsense professors, mentors, and readers who constantly pushed me to think outside my own experiences, and who helped me realize that, actually, there was a kernel of truth in this criticism. Several kernels, in fact.

The first of these kernels had to do with the vast spectrum of trolling behaviors. As I quickly realized after starting my research, trolling takes many forms. Although I was unwilling to defend or apologize for the most problematic end of the spectrum, I was similarly unwilling to condemn all trolling outright, particularly when the behaviors in question draw attention to racial and/or class bias in news coverage, or corporate greed, or any number of things that certain trolls have deemed worthy of retribution (and which, it should be noted, align with my own feminist political ideals).

Put simply, I found certain forms of trolling funny, interesting, and in some cases justifiable, a position further complicated by my relationship to the trolls I was working with. These relationships were profoundly important to my research, and took a great deal of time to establish and even more energy to maintain. I worried that I would lose this access if I was too publicly critical, and that I would lose academic credibility if I was too publicly permissive. Finding the appropriate balance was a constant struggle, and especially at the outset of my research, I was a bumbling, insecure mess.

In hindsight, it isn't surprising that I was. After all, while I didn't set out to defend trolls, the goal was to understand them. In the process of learning their customs, their language, and when necessary, how to "pass" as a troll in order to facilitate better research interactions, the distance between myself and my research shrunk in ways that were often problematic. On the other hand, had I not developed an insider's understanding of trolling subculture, I wouldn't have been able to write a coherent argument about it. While I may have denied or at least taken offense at this idea during the first few years of my research, the fact that I sometimes teetered on the edge of being too close to my subject ultimately proved to be a necessary, if uncomfortable, step in my research process.

As this book (hopefully) attests, I found my footing eventually, due largely to the aforementioned professors, mentors, and readers who respected me enough to call me out, tell me no, and challenge my assumptions. Without this constant pushback, in fact without any of the research hurdles I've described, I shudder to think what kind of book I would have written. If I had been able to write a book at all. The resistance I encountered wasn't what one might call fun—it was often extraordinarily frustrating—but it was, without any doubt, necessary to my process. Not only did it force me to think critically about the relationship between trolling and mainstream culture and about my own relationship to trolling, it helped me articulate my overarching argument, particularly in relation to my theory of cultural digestion. I may have lost hundreds of hours to nervous pacing; I may have questioned myself and my work more times than I could count; but thanks to everyone who helped me think through my anxieties and the project's various shortcomings (and I am indebted to so many people for that), I learned what needed learning. And in the end, that's all any researcher can hope for.

II "The Golden Years," 2008–2011

Over the course of my research, the most common questions I've encountered have hinged on binaries. Are trolls good, or are they bad? Are they sociopaths, or are they politically motivated? Do they help catalyze online community formation, or do they hinder online community formation?

Although the impulse to frame trolling behaviors in black-and-white terms is understandable—it certainly would be easier if the issues were so straightforward—I have found these types of questions to be unhelpful at best and counterproductive at worst. For one thing, the answer to each binary is, and can only be, "yes." Trolls can be good, and they can be bad. Some appear to have sociopathic tendencies, others appear to be politically motivated, and many appear to be both (not an uncommon trait, even offline). In certain cases, trolls can help rally an online community around a common cause—namely, hating trolls—but can also weaken existing communities by instilling paranoia in community members. It really depends on the circumstance; consequently, it is simply not possible, or even advisable, to provide an overarching, universal answer to any question that attempts to sort trolls as *either* this *or* that.

A better and more fruitful question is the question I posed at the outset of this study. Specifically, how do trolls fit into mainstream culture? As I illustrate throughout part II, the answer to this question is "quite well." Not only do trolls scavenge, repurpose, and weaponize myriad aspects of mainstream culture (all the better to troll you with), mainstream culture normalizes and at times actively celebrates precisely those attitudes and behaviors that in trolling contexts are said to be aberrant, antisocial, and cruel.

It is at this juncture that trolls and trickster are most closely aligned. Much like mythological trickster figures, whose refusal to editorialize compels onlookers to make sense of what has happened, trolls' actions highlight the more ambivalent aspects of the dominant culture. Participating trolls might not be consciously aware of the ways in which their actions replicate mainstream tropes and behaviors, but they don't need to be. The important thing, and the point to which the chapters in part II will attest, is that trolls *reveal*.

4   The House That Fox Built: Anonymous, Spectacle, and Cycles of Amplification

In her profile of 4chan's infamous /b/ board, one of the Internet's most active trolling hotspots, Fox News reporter Taryn Sauthoff walks a very fine line. "Some see 4chan as a site filled with bored teenagers who like to push the limits on what they can do online," she writes. "Others see users as part of an 'Internet Hate Machine' filled with calls for domestic terrorists to bomb stadiums."[1] As evidence of the second claim, Sauthoff cites the board's highly transgressive content and misfit user base, whom Sauthoff describes as antisocial and foul-mouthed. In support of the claim that 4chan users are little more than bored teenagers, Sauthoff plays up users' social isolation and marvels at their love of cute pictures of cats.[2]

Using Fox News' well-publicized "some people say" rhetorical technique, in which a reporter editorializes by proxy,[3] Sauthoff thus manages to frame /b/ as a "surreptitious cultural powerhouse" populated by powerful misanthropes and an insignificant, "largely unknown" website filled with harmless, cat-loving computer geeks, a position she echoes in her profile of moot, 4chan's founder, whom she describes alternately as wily king of the Internet's underworld and hapless college dropout who lives with his mother.[4]

Sauthoff's take on 4chan is hardly unique. The vast majority of mainstream media accounts of 4chan, particularly the /b/ board, simultaneously portray users as both threatening and pathetic. By maximizing audience antipathy—namely, attacking whatever undesirable element from all possible angles, in Sauthoff's case, users' viciousness and implied effeminacy—the perceived (sub)cultural threat of 4chan is minimized, echoing Dick Hebdige's account of ideological incorporation.[5] Indeed, in their hostility toward and dismissal of 4chan, best summarized by the seemingly contradictory statement that 4chan is nothing to worry about and should be destroyed immediately, mainstream media outlets aim to neutralize a particularly counterhegemonic cultural space, one that, ironically enough, these same outlets helped popularize.

In addition to complicating subcultural trolls' origin story, the interplay between mainstream media outlets and the trolls who troll them highlights the striking overlap between trolls and their most vociferous opponents. As the following chapter illustrates, trolls and sensationalist corporate media outlets are in fact locked in a cybernetic feedback loop predicated on spectacle; each camp amplifies and builds upon the other's reactions, resulting in a relationship that can only be described as symbiotic. In this way, trolls loop sensationalist media outlets onto the same ethical hook from which they, the trolls, continuously swing—casting immediate aspersions over these same outlets' scandalized reactions to trolling behaviors.

The Internet Hate Machine

To reiterate a few details from chapter 1, 4chan is a simple image board modeled after Japan's Futaba Channel. It was founded in 2003 by then-fifteen-year-old Christopher "moot" Poole, who remains the site's head administrator. The day-to-day operations of the site are overseen by a handful of volunteer moderators and janitors. Moderators, generally referred to as "mods," delete posts and ban users when necessary, and occasionally interact with users and/or post content, though they must remain anonymous; as the FAQ page explains, there is no way to know who the mods are in real life, and/or when they may be policing a particular thread. Janitors, regular users who are selected by moot to keep an eye on specific boards, must also remain anonymous, though they cannot ban users and can only post as a regular anon. Those who reveal their true identities or who identify themselves as being a mod or a janitor while "on the clock" are summarily fired from the program.[6]

Currently the site houses dozens of content-specific boards, all of which cater to a particular subset of the 4chan population. The /a/ board, for example, is devoted to anime, the /x/ board to paranormal phenomena, the /v/ board to video games, and so on. The most popular board on 4chan—and the board to which I have restricted this chapter's focus—is /b/, the "random" board, which generates the bulk of 4chan's traffic.

As previously discussed, /b/ served as an incubator for early trolling culture, and over the years has earned the dubious distinction of being deemed the "asshole of the Internet," a characterization embraced by apologists and detractors alike. Matthias Schwartz elaborated on that characterization in his 2008 profile of the site. As he explained, "Measured in terms of depravity, insularity and traffic-driven turnover, the culture of /b/ has little precedent . . . [it] reads like the inside of a high-school bathroom stall, or an obscene telephone party line, or a blog with no posts and all comments filled with slang that you are too old to understand."[7]

Schwartz's association of /b/ with X-rated latrinalia is particularly fitting, as content—much like its bathroom stall equivalent—is almost always posted anonymously. Although users are given the option to populate the [Name] field, very few do, and even fewer provide identifying details (that is to say, actual names or pseudonyms the poster intends to use more than once). As a result, the vast majority of content is created anonymously and modified anonymously and downloaded, remodified, and attributed anonymously. Individual users are thus known as "anon," and the collective as "Anonymous."

Unsurprisingly, this arrangement poses a number of demographic hurdles. Anons who identify as male could actually be female; anons who identify as female could actually be transgender; teenaged anons could say they are thirty-five and twentysomethings could claim to be underage. There is no way to empirically verify exactly who is posting exactly what. It is however possible to identify a number of basic demographic indicators.

First, almost all threads on /b/ are written in English and engage American culture and politics, with the exception of various appropriated Japanese references (i.e., Japanese-produced cartoons such as *Pokemon* and *DragonBallZ*, as well as a number of popular anime, including *Azumanga Daioh* and *Gurren Lagann*). Occasionally other languages and nationalities are represented, but the overwhelming percentage of anons identify as middle-class suburban Americans.

Second, it is reasonable to assume that trolls on /b/ enjoy a certain degree of economic privilege. Over and above the leisure time required to engage in onsite antics and off-site raids, trolls must have a reliable Internet connection, a computer, and all the necessary software and peripherals. Although it is possible to troll on a shared computer, particularly with the advent of cloud computing (all the troll would need is a web browser to be able to access his or her files remotely), it would not be possible to do so without a basic knowledge of the systems he or she was using, and without a certain degree of physical privacy (i.e., a separate room or an office, somewhere the troll doesn't have to worry about prying eyes). Trolling requires tools, in other words, and these tools don't come cheap— at least, don't come without the expectation of existing technological know-how and/or the time and energy to learn.

Third, it is likely that most posters fall somewhere between eighteen and thirty, an assumption based on the proliferation of late 1980s and early 1990s pop cultural references, including a flood of "you nostalgia, you lose" threads in which posters wax nostalgic over shared childhood memories. Although attachment to a certain vintage of TV, movies, and toys doesn't guarantee a particular age range, it does suggest a preoccupation with a particular moment in American pop cultural history, a significant detail in itself.

In addition to suggesting a particular nationality, class, and age range, trolling behaviors on /b/ are strongly indicative of whiteness. First and most obviously, trolling on /b/ is frequently directed at people of color, particularly African Americans. While it is possible that certain trolls are African American (or any other ethnicity), the preponderance of racial humor directed at people who are not white suggests that, at the very least, participating trolls are either consciously or subconsciously *performing* whiteness.

The qualification that trolls might not actually be white but certainly act white harkens to Richard Dyer's analysis of the construction of whiteness in Western visual culture.[8] As Dyer explains, "actual" whiteness—that is to say, skin color—is a visible site of whiteness. But it is not the ultimate site of whiteness. The true power of whiteness resides in its symbolic power—specifically the power to automatically other (literally mark, make less white) anything that falls outside the norms of the dominant group.[9] Regardless of their offline race, trolls engage in precisely this sort of racialized boundary-policing. Indeed, even when engaging in racially neutral humor, anons on /b/ take whiteness, and the whiteness of their audience, for granted; on the rare occasion that an anon presents himself as a person of color (whether or not he's telling the truth), he must self-identify as such, that is, flag himself as being fundamentally different from the presumed norm. In this way, discourse on /b/ favors what Ryan Milner describes as "a white centrality" that is "premised on repressions of diverse voice[s]."[10]

Finally, although it is not possible to prove definitively that all trolls on /b/ are biologically male, the ethos of /b/ is unquestionably androcentric—that is, it privileges male-focused attitudes and behaviors—again pointing to why I tend to use the male pronoun when describing on-site behaviors. In addition to reveling in sexist tropes (one common response to female-presenting posters is "get back in the kitchen and make me a sammich") and deriding posters who come forward as female (the standard response being "tits or gtfo," i.e., "show us your breasts or leave"), the board presupposes the maleness of participants. Female anons, known on-site as "femanons" among other more misogynist terms, are therefore forced to "reify their outsider status,"[11] as Milner explains. Further emphasizing the androcentrism of the board is its seemingly endless supply of pornographic material, all of which is filtered through an explicitly male gaze. But not necessarily a heterosexual male gaze; a large percentage of porn on /b/ is gay, and trolls devote a great deal of energy to ostensibly homosocial (if not outright homosexual) behavior, including frequent "rate my cawk" threads, in which anons post and rate pictures of each other's penises.

The prevalence of the word "fag" further complicates this picture. Whenever anons joke about "an hero," a trolling term for suicide, wax poetic about drug use, or ask other anons for advice, the standard response is "do it faggot," often accompanied by a picture of someone or something (cartoon characters, dogs, bears, children) baring his, her, or its teeth grotesquely. The accusation of "faggotry" is rampant, from second-person claims that "your a faggot" to sophomoric discussions of "buttsecks." And yet when asked to self-identify, whether in terms of geography or college or major or interest, anons frequently affix "fag" to the end of self-reflexive nouns. Thus novice posters are "newfags," old hands are "oldfags," people posting in California are "Califags," posters claiming to be gay are "gayfags," and so on. Depending on the context, "fag"—whether used as a suffix or as a noun—can function as a homophobic slur, a term of endearment, or a mode of self-identification.

In addition to complicating the data collection process, anonymity within the troll space also has a profound behavioral impact. Most obviously, because there are no repercussions for posting racist, sexist, homophobic, or exploitative text and/or images, and because trolling is characterized by transgressive one-upmanship, /b/ is overrun by highly offensive and sometimes explicitly illegal content, including child pornography. 4chan's official policy is that it has zero tolerance for kiddie porn, and in 2008 moot claimed to have banned over seventy thousand IP addresses.[12] But mods can only work so fast, and can only oversee a certain percentage of threads. It is inevitable that even the most offensive content occasionally falls through the cracks.

As outrageous as some of the content on 4chan, and especially on /b/, might be, the site's traffic stats are even more so. In July 2008, *Time* reported that 4chan received 8.5 million daily page views and 3.3 million monthly visitors,[13] and in August of that same year, the *New York Times* clocked 4chan's monthly hit rate (a metric that includes both unique and nonunique users) at 200 million.[14] A 2009 *Washington Post* article cited moot's internal metrics at four hundred thousand daily posts,[15] and by March 2010 the *New York Times* reported that the daily post total had climbed to eight hundred thousand, with 8.2 million unique monthly visitors and six hundred million monthly page loads.[16] Later that year, moot ran a ChartBeat data tag that tracked the total number of eyeballs on 4chan and discovered that the site was host to sixty thousand overall users at any given moment and ten thousand on the front page of /b/ alone.[17] As a result, 4chan relies on five servers and processes the equivalent of twenty terabytes of data per day.[18]

In short, 4chan, particularly its /b/ board, is a cultural juggernaut, and would be categorized as such whatever its output. As it is, the content created on and disseminated by 4chan/b/ is so consistently outrageous that it may just be, as digital media scholar Finn Brunton suggested, "the single most broadly offensive artifact in the history of human media."[19] Whether or not this is in fact the case—I would argue that "legitimate" media outlets can be every bit as broadly offensive, a point I explore in this and later chapters—it is the case that 4chan has proven to be both massively offensive and massively appealing.

Anonymous Does Not Forget

Of course, 4chan didn't achieve cultural ubiquity overnight. The site needed a catalyst, and found one in the most unexpected of sources. Specifically, that great adversary, and, ironically, inadvertent champion of trolling subculture: Fox News. Fox certainly wasn't the only outlet to receive consistent trollish attention—during the "golden years" of subcultural formation, trolls targeted various Conservative radio programs (notably white nationalist Hal Turner),[20] Google (including one instance in which trolls "Google bombed" the site with a Unicode swastika, pushing the image to the top of Google's trends list),[21] and Time Magazine's Top 100 List (in a successful bid to vote moot to the number one position),[22] among many others.

That said, Fox was the trolls' most conspicuous and ultimately their most expedient media adversary. Not only was Fox's output (and the output of its various subsidiaries) reliably sensationalist, thereby furnishing trolls with a seemingly endless supply of trolling opportunities, it was also reliably (over)reactive, meaning that trolls would be provided with a steady diet of lulz. As a consequence, Fox holds a special place in trolling history.

Using Stanley Cohen's seminal account of moral panics, this section chronicles the development of these very strange but very well-suited bedfellows. As we will see, there was perceived aberration, reaction to the aberration, further reactionary aberration, reaction to the reactionary aberration, and so on, thus creating what Cohen describes as "circular and amplifying" cycles of disturbance[23]—in the process helping crystallize a discrete, highly recognizable, and increasingly influential behavioral and cultural category.

This analysis must begin with 4chan itself. As previously mentioned, 4chan was created in 2003 as a content overflow site for a Something Awful subforum called "Anime Death Tentacle Rape Whorehouse." In addition to adopting the nominative "troll," 4chan's early users embraced the emergent concept of lulz, which to reiterate chapter 2, indicates acute amusement in the face of someone else's distress, embarrassment, or rage.

With lulz as its behavioral rudder, the 4chan community began to coalesce. By 2006, and as an extension of their ominous refrain that "none of us is as cruel as all of us," trolls on /b/ had adopted a collective anonymous identity: specifically, the mass noun "Anonymous." Unfortunately, it is impossible to know exactly when the adjectival form of anonymous gave rise to Anonymous as mass noun; the infamously trollish Encyclopedia Dramatica wiki, which contained user-generated entries dating back to 2004, was unceremoniously deleted by its founder Sherrod DeGrippo in April 2011. A version of the ED wiki was saved, the result of emergency intervention on the part of the Web Ecology group,[24] and ultimately users were able to reconstruct the site—but not before seven years of edits were lost forever.[25]

Thanks to user-generated content on other sites, however, it is possible to estimate /b/'s basic timeline. In the case of Anonymous, and based on several Urban Dictionary entries that tag the term in relation to /b/ and 4chan, it is clear that the mass noun Anonymous was in circulation by 2006. These same entries also reveal that by 2007, Anonymous had already spawned the Anonymous Credo (variously, The Code of Anonymous), which has since undergone a number of iterations but initially opened with the somewhat ironic claim "We are Anonymous, and we do not forgive."[26]

At the time, Anonymous was personified by "greenman," a well-dressed avatar whose face is obscured by the phrase "no photo available." Rhetorically, this was no accident; from the very beginning, "Anonymous" was understood to be a loose collective animated by countless anonymous agents, described by trolls as "the hivemind." On /b/, the hivemind was, and still is, often described as having a rough sort of consciousness—a far cry from swarming behaviors found in nature, but which trolls take for granted as part of their collective trolling identity. When early anons would refer to Anonymous's exploits, they were thus referencing both the rhetorical power of the faceless collective as well as its behavioral effects.

Initially, greenman was confined to on-site interactions. Trolls referenced Anonymous (and individual anons) on /b/, and would use the moniker when contributing to off-site raid boards and Internet Relay Chat IRC channels (often used as staging areas for organized attacks), but rarely flashed this calling card in uninitiated circles. As the subculture grew, however, anons began crediting Anonymous on public forums, including Urban Dictionary and YouTube. Still, through mid-2007, knowledge of and interest in Anonymous was mostly confined to participating anons.

Then on July 27, Fox News aired its now infamous "Report on Anonymous" news segment. "They call themselves Anonymous," anchor John Beard begins. "They are hackers on steroids, treating the web like a real-life video game . . . sacking websites and invading MySpace accounts, disrupting innocent peoples' lives . . . and if you fight back, *watch out.*" Later in the clip, reporter Phil Shuman describes Anonymous as a "hacker gang" and "Internet Hate Machine" hell-bent on destruction. "I've had seven different passwords and they've got 'em all so far," one interviewee alleges. "I believe they're domestic terrorists," insists another, a proclamation followed by stock footage of an exploding service van.[27]

As Shuman explains, Anonymous is as merciless as it is clandestine. One mother faced constant telephone harassment and was forced to get a dog; a boy named David was dumped by his girlfriend when hackers posted "gay sex pictures" to his MySpace wall; several sports stadiums received bomb threats, now thought to be a hoax (an apparently unimportant detail). Later in the report, a former member of Anonymous—whose face and voice have been obscured, presumably for his own protection—accuses the alleged hacker gang of threatening to rape and kill him. In the following scene, the mother whose family was targeted, and whose identity is also obscured, pulls closed a pair of window curtains and offers a grim conclusion. "Would [the FBI] do something about it if one of us ended up dead?" she asks. "Probably."[28]

Fox's "Report on Anonymous" was posted to YouTube the same day the segment aired; as of 2014 the clip has received nearly 2.5 million hits and has amassed over twenty thousand viewer comments. A post made by DancingJesus94 captures the spirit of these responses: "Wow," he or she wrote. "Fox just fed the trolls, and did so in the lulziest way possible. I mean, what's a bigger ego boost than for Anon to be branded dangerous criminals who can hack your computer by closing their eyes and merely

Figure 4.1
The Internet Hate Machine. Accessed on 4chan/b/ on April 23, 2012. Thread since deleted. Original creator(s) and date(s) of creation unknown.

thinking about it."[29] This was, in other words, a windfall for Anonymous; the terms "hackers on steroids," "hacker gangs," and "the Internet Hate Machine" were immediately integrated into the trolling lexicon (figure 4.1), as was the image of the exploding service van, which was rechristened the 4chan party van and trotted out whenever law enforcement took interest in trolling raids ("getting v&" has since become shorthand for being arrested).

Not only did 4chan receive an enormous spike in traffic from Fox's coverage, trolls were outfitted with a sound branding strategy. Douglas Thomas describes a similar phenomenon in his study of hacker culture, particularly the "new school" hackers of the early 1990s. As Thomas explains, "The media, as well as the public . . . learned to expect the worst from hackers, and as a result, hackers usually offer that image in return, even if their own exploits are no more than harmless pranks."[30] By framing Anonymous and its constituent trolls as socially deviant, Fox News inadvertently furnished trolls with a behavioral blueprint, as well as an incentive to keep trolling.

Although Fox News didn't create Anonymous, the Fox 11 News Report gave Anonymous a national platform, upon which trolls built larger and ever-more conspicuous structures. What once had been an underground site, known only to the few thousand active participants, became a household name; "Anonymous" begin to show up in mainstream media reports only after the Fox 11 News Report aired.

Anonymous's next major catalyst came in January 2008, when Nick Denton at Gawker posted an embarrassing video of Tom Cruise lauding the Church of Scientology. Despite receiving a takedown notice from the Church, Denton refused to remove the video, citing it as "newsworthy."[31] In response to the Church's attempt to censor the video, some anon posted a comment to /b/ decrying the Church and its stranglehold on information. In the eyes of Anonymous, this was an unforgivable act and warranted immediate intervention.[32] Thus began Project Chanology (also known as Operation Chanology), Anonymous's most ambitious project to date—one spurred along, as Gabriella Coleman argues, by the near-perfect ideological inversion of Scientology, a tightly structured, painfully serious, obsessively proprietary organization, and Anonymous, a happily chaotic, wildly flexible, and obsessively open source collective. The two organizations were perfect antipodes, Coleman writes, and therefore perfect nemeses.[33]

Although Anonymous was hardly the first group to set its sights on Scientology,[34] it proved to be the most successful. A week after Denton published the Cruise video, Anonymous released its now-iconic Message to Scientology,[35] and on February 10, 2008, hundreds of protestors across the country gathered outside local Scientology centers. In order to maintain anonymity, participating anons wore plastic Guy Fawkes masks, a reference to what was then known on 4chan as "Epic Fail Guy," a stick figure drawing indicating failure and disappointment (the mask was also a reference to the Warner Brothers' 2005 film *V for Vendetta*, whose main character was loosely based on the historical figure of Guy Fawkes.[36] In 1605, Fawkes helped stage an ultimately failed campaign to blow up the British House of Lords, hence the "Epic Fail"). Images of the protesters, particularly those wearing Guy Fawkes masks, dominated the news. On February 12, 2008, two days after the first protests, Anonymous was given its own Wikipedia entry.[37]

As Anonymous—and its mothership, the /b/ board—achieved greater cultural prominence, media outlets became ever shriller in their coverage. This in turn generated greater opportunity for lulz, which courted more media coverage, which encouraged the production of additional outrageous content, which precipitated further media coverage. Fox News was the vanguard of sensationalism, with Bill O'Reilly leading the pack. After one anon "hacked" into (that is to say, guessed the password for) Sarah Palin's Yahoo account, O'Reilly denounced 4chan as "one of those despicable, slimy, scummy websites"[38] and urged the FBI to take drastic measures.[39]

Anonymous took this opportunity to declare outright war on Fox News, particularly O'Reilly. After the Palin hack, trolls raided O'Reilly's website and released users', as well as O'Reilly's, contact information.[40] Similar tactics were deployed in response to one Talking Points/Confronting Evil segment in which O'Reilly claimed that "a far-left website known as '4chan' is providing child pornography to Internet pedophiles."[41]

A year later, Anonymous initiated "Operation Bill Haz Cheezburgers," yet another attempt to disrupt his website. Unlike previous raids, however, this was designed to kill with kindness. "Try not to send him anything R rated," wrote the initiating anon (I happened to be online when the raid was first proposed). "That way when he rages on the air he'll have zero ammo and everyone will look at him like he's crazy for getting mad at kittens." For the next few hours, Anonymous spammed O'Reilly with hundreds of incoherent laudatory messages that participating anons would then "cap" (take screen shots of) and repost onto /b/, including numerous variations on the popular meme "[name] is a pretty cool guy, eh keeps us in line and doesn't afraid of anything." Anons also sent pictures of bunnies, ducks, and cats, with the caption "The Internet Love Machine." At some point during the raid, someone reposted O'Reilly's home address. Pineapple and pepperoni pizzas were subsequently sent, and one Anon captioned an image of O'Reilly's face with the question "What? I didn't order any pizza. I don't even like pineapples."[42]

In short, Fox's various responses to Anonymous, 4chan, and trolls generally helped fortify the borders of what at the time was a localized phenomenon but that soon emerged as a full-blown subculture. Not only did these stories augment the trolling lexicon—that is, provide trolls with additional memetic material—they helped legitimize the development of a discrete, deliberate, and highly recognizable trolling identity. Put another way, and with Fox News leading the charge, trolls were given a framework upon which to build their public face. They happily set up camp, and thanks to an increasingly incensed mainstream media, were furnished with a constant supply of food. Anonymous in turn grew stronger, and the media vacillated between feeding and decrying this most hideous progeny.

Keeping Up with the Does

The media wasn't the only catalyst in subcultural formation, however. The technological affordances of 4chan itself—literally, what the platform allows its users to do—also played a major role. Specifically, and as a consequence of not having enough server space to archive posted content, moot built 4chan to be ephemeral. Few threads remain on the site for more than a few minutes, and those that make it to the front page typically disappear within the hour. This frees up space for newer content, which essentially boots older threads from the server. Content does "stick," however—if enough users engage with a particular piece of content, either through reposting or remixing, it will enter the subcultural lexicon. It will, in other words, become a meme.

Trolls, particularly in the early troll space, took for granted that trolling culture was comprised of memes, and peppered nearly every conversation with memetic references, some of which were simplistic word swaps (e.g., "fap" for "masturbation"), and some of which were extremely involved, and demanded a high level of cultural literacy. The "shit was SO cash" meme provides an outstanding example of the latter and helps illustrate how recognizing a meme, remixing a meme, even simply referencing a meme helped fortify the troll space's burgeoning subcultural borders.

The original post from which "shit was SO cash" was taken was posted to 4chan's /b/ board sometime in 2007. It features an image of a stereotypical Italian American man (with orange skin, spiky hair, popped collar) holding a bottle of vodka. His arm is draped over a blond, similarly orange-hued young woman who easily could have passed as a cast member of *The Jersey Shore*. The text, which is unabashedly sexist, racist, ableist, and homophobic, reads:

Hey Faggots:
   My name is John, and I hate every single one of you. All of you are fat, retarded, no-lifes who spend every second of their day looking at stupid ass pictures. You are everything bad in the world. Honestly, have any of you ever gotten any pussy? I mean, I guess it's fun making fun of people because of your own insecurities, but you all take to a whole new level. This is even worse than jerking off to pictures on facebook.
   Don't be a stranger. Just hit me with your best shot. I'm pretty much perfect. I was captain of the football team, and starter on my basketball team. What sports to you play, other than "jack off to naked drawn Japanese people?" I also get straight A's, and have a banging hot girlfriend (She just blew me; shit was SO cash). You are all faggots who should just kill yourselves. Thanks for listening.
   Pic related: It's me and my bitch.[43]

This post quickly became "copypasta" on /b/, meaning that it was continuously copied and pasted into new threads (making the text's sexism, racism, and homophobia all the more significant—clearly the message resonated with participating trolls, a point to which I return in chapter 6). In addition to being frequently reposted, the original message and image underwent significant iterations. The text of John's message was repurposed into the following: a letter of apology from John, John's angry return, John's girlfriend Jenna's murderous plea, John's gay confession, and the introduction of Jack, who "likes every single one of you," to name a few. Some anon even created the following version featuring an image of two meatballs (an apparent nod to the Italian American stereotypes in the original post):

Hey meatballs, my name is Juan, and hatred each only of you. You are fat, slowed-down niggul no-lifes that spends every moment of its day that watches stupid pictures of the ass. You are all bad one in the world. Honest, anyone of you you have never obtained kitten? I mean, I conjecture it diversion of s that is refixed mnh of people due to its own insecurities, but everything take a whole new level. This is even worse than moving of a pull extinguished to the pictures in facebook. Don' t is a foreigner. Hardly golpeeme with its better shot. I'm rather much perfect. It was captain of the starter and football team, in my equipment of basketball. What sports do you play, except "he raised with the cat extinguished people" Japanese drawn naked;? Also with himself a 'rectum: s, and has a hot fiancée of I strike (she finishes blowing to me; the excrement was SO effective). You are all the meatballs that must as soon be killed. Thanks to listen. The pic was related; It's I and my dog.[44]

To outsiders, the image of meatballs coupled with the above (still sexist, still racist, still ableist, and still homophobic) text would have been meaningless, if not outright incomprehensible. To participating anons, however, "Hey meatballs" functioned as one of the troll space's countless subcultural litmus tests. The ability to recognize the original meme indicated that a particular anon was successfully keeping up with the Joneses—or perhaps more appropriately, keeping up with the Does.

Furthermore, once woven into participating trolls' collective experiences, memes like "shit was SO cash" directly connected to trolls' developing sense of collective identity. Trolls may have been individual people in real life, but as members of Anonymous they were subsumed by a thriving, and constantly evolving, online collective. Under this banner, individual cogitos—I think, therefore I am—was thus replaced by the cogitamus—we think, therefore we are,[45] an assertion that simultaneously established the normative center of the group and provided scaffolding onto which additional subcultural material could be affixed.

Over 9000 What?

Over 9000 Penises, a particularly outrageous nesting-doll meme—that is to say, a meme that emerged from an existing meme, which itself emerged from an even older meme—provides another, and even more striking, example of the world-building power of memes within the troll space. Not only does this example illustrate *how* these worlds were created, Over 9000 Penises highlights *what kinds* of worlds trolls were inclined to create—with specific focus on the role media interventions played in the world-building process.

Over 9000 Penises begins with Pedobear, one of /b/'s most durable images. Based upon Japan's "Safety Bear," the image of whom would accompany anime deemed inappropriate for children, Pedobear is a much more ambiguous figure. Sometimes drooling, sometimes sweating, sometimes featuring a sombrero or the words "DO WANT," Pedobear is always scrambling toward something (figure 4.2). It is not until one realizes precisely what Pedobear is chasing *after* that his form takes on new significance—"Pedo" is short for "Pedophile," making Pedobear the

Figure 4.2
Pedobear. Accessed on 4chan/b/ on November 7, 2010. Thread since deleted. Original creator(s) and date(s) of creation unknown.

unofficial mascot of child pornography (CP in the trolling world)—thus combining a fundamental icon of childhood with childhood's worst nightmare.[46]

This is not to say that use of Pedobear imagery necessarily represents offline interest in or support for child exploitation. More often than not, the image is used mockingly, as an implicit criticism of another anon's apparent predilection for young boys or girls, or in relation to some other meme, most notably the meme cluster surrounding *Dateline NBC*'s pedophile sting operation *To Catch a Predator* and its host Chris Hansen.

That said, the image of Pedobear sometimes does accompany child pornography, and sometimes does make light of, if not actively celebrate, sexualized images of children. Even this is slippery terrain, however, since child pornography is often deployed as trollbait against other trolls—it's one of the few things shocking enough to unsettle even the most jaded anon. Consequently, and despite the fact that posting child pornography onto 4chan is a permabannable offense (meaning that, if the site administrators encounter any child pornography, they ban the associated IP address from the site), posting child pornography, or as is usually the case, *threatening* to post child pornography, or making jokes about posting child pornography—which almost always appear alongside images of Pedobear—has become a meme in itself.

The second component of Over 9000 Penises is the phrase "over 9000," a nonsense numerical value taken from *DragonBallZ*, a popular manga series. Originally released in Japan in 1989, *DragonBallZ* premiered on American television in 1996 and became a cultural touchstone for a generation of anime fans and gamers. In one episode, heroes Vegeta and Nappa prepare to fight a villain named Goku; they consult their "scouter," a device that measures an opponent's power level. Nappa asks Vegeta what the scouter says about levels, to which Vegeta growls that it's over nine thousand, and smashes the scouter in his hand.[47] Someone posted this clip onto /b/, and perhaps due to nostalgia, perhaps due to the fact that "over 9000" was a mistranslation of "over 8000," thus providing built-in conversation (not to mention trolling) fodder, perhaps because of moot's subsequent implementation of a word filter that changed all instances of the number 7 to "over 9000," Anonymous adopted "over 9000" as the default answer to any question involving numerical value.

"Penises," the third and final component of the meme, can be traced to September 2008, when some anon decided to troll the *Oprah Winfrey Show* by posing as a pedophile on the show's message board. Winfrey, who had spent the previous week lobbying for legislation designed to crack down on online sexual predation, was made aware of the poster and decided to share what he had posted. "Let me read you something posted on our message boards," she gravely began, "from somebody who claims to be a member of a known pedophile network: He said he does not forgive. He does not forget. His group has over 9000 penises and they're all . . . raping . . . children."[48]

Within the hour, a second anon downloaded Winfrey's warning, which unbeknownst to her featured an iteration of the Anonymous Credo, and spliced the clip into a music video featuring Pedobear, Winfrey, the characters from *DragonBallZ* and Chris Hansen.[49] To the trolling community, this was a win on every front. In a 2008 edit of the Oprah Winfrey entry on Encyclopedia Dramatica, the corresponding videos and message board transcript were accompanied by an image of Winfrey sitting next to a man whose head has been replaced with a photoshopped troll face. But not just any man. In the May 2008 *Oprah* episode from which the image was taken,[50] the man seated next to Winfrey is none other than high-profile celebrity Scientologist Tom Cruise, whose leaked Scientology promotional video helped catalyze Project Chanology only four months earlier (figure 4.3). Pulling from the popular "[adjective] [noun] is [adjective]" meme, the photoshopped image is captioned with the phrase "Successful troll is successful."[51]

But why? What exactly was so successful about Over 9000 Penises? First of all, it is critical to address its transgressive appeal. It is no accident that trolls targeted this forum on this issue, nor is it insignificant that the resulting lulz continued long after the initial raid ended. Trolls would not have cared, or wouldn't have cared as much, if the issue hadn't been such a hot button for so many people. As it is, child exploitation, especially when sexual in nature, is one of the few taboos unaffected by political standpoint. As a result, whether deployed on 4chan or off-site, pedophilia (either threats of or references to) is one of the most exploitable tools in the trolls' arsenal. That the "joke" made it all the way to the *Oprah Winfrey Show* was profoundly amusing to participating trolls.

Even more amusing about Over 9000 Penises was its status as subcultural Trojan horse. Simply by uttering the phrase "over 9000 penises"—by uttering "over 9000" anything—Winfrey had marked the trolls' territory. Anyone even remotely connected to 4chan (or online culture generally) immediately knew that trolling had been afoot, and even better, that Winfrey was a pawn in the trolls' game. This in turn raised the online visibility of trolls, therefore lending even more infamy to an already

Figure 4.3
Over 9000 successful trolls. 2011. Image posted to Encyclopedia Dramatica by user
Angry Cosine on May 2, 2011. Accessed on April 24, 2012. Original creator(s) and
date(s) of creation unknown.

infamous (if nebulous) collective, and provided a catalyst for further
memetic creation.

Trolling in/and/as Détournement

In addition to highlighting the relationship between meme creation and
mainstream media intervention, Over 9000 Penises showcases trolls' facility with détournement. Loosely translated as "hijack" or "reroute," *détournement* is the process by which the existing meaning of a particular
statement or artifact is turned against itself. The term is most closely associated with the Situationist International and the Letterist International,
radical Marxist collectives founded in the 1950s. Prominent Situationist
Guy Debord and Letterist Gil Wolman theorized two basic types of détournement. Minor détournement is achieved when value-neutral artifacts are
placed alongside each other, thus reconfiguring the meaning of each, while

deceptive détournement subversively redeploys already-significant artifacts. Whether minor or deceptive, both forms of détournement challenge
dominant ideals through creative and often absurdist appropriation.[52]

While the Situationists and Letterists were explicitly political, trolls'
behaviors often have similar, if inadvertent, effects. Specifically, by *détourn-
ing* corporate media strategies for explicitly lulzy ends—angering Bill
O'Reilly by acting like Bill O'Reilly, for example—trolls "reinforce the real
meaning of an original element," to quote Debord scholar Anselm Jappe,[53]
thus allowing a particular statement or artifact to indict itself through
itself. In the process, trolls call attention to the striking similarities—
chronicled in what follows—between ostensibly aberrant trolling behaviors and behaviors normalized by mainstream media outlets.

First, trolls and the media are equally invested in *spectacle*, what media
studies scholar Douglas Kellner describes as the process through which
business and entertainment fuse.[54] Over 9000 Penises furnishes a textbook
example of this overlap. By reading the self-proclaimed pedophile's messages aloud (messages sent under user names like "lordxenu," a direct
Scientology reference, "josefritzel," an Austrian man who had recently
been convicted of imprisoning and raping his daughter, and "harpobear,"
a nod to Winfrey's production company Harpo Productions[55]) and framing
the poster as a spokesperson for all pedophiles (whom she strongly implied
was coming after her audience's children), Winfrey was courting spectacle
as insistently as her message board troll. Both were looking for eyeballs,
and what better way to attract eyeballs than by forwarding content most
likely to elicit audience engagement (and/or rubbernecking)?

A second conspicuous overlap between trolls and media outlets is their
respective push for *success*. Over 9000 Penises is also instructive in this
regard. For the trolls, Over 9000 Penises was successful because it harnessed
and exploited a particularly sensitive cultural trope, and in the process
generated a great deal of lulz. Trolls were not the only successful party,
however; the success of the trolling raid hinged on the success of the
show's producers. The ends diverged somewhat, in that the *Oprah Winfrey
Show* was courting a horrified yet sympathetic audience while trolls were
merely courting a horrified audience, but the means by which these goals
were achieved were in fact identical. Both trolls and Winfrey's production
team tugged at the audience's heartstrings, deployed emotionally loaded
language, and exactingly exploited the human-interest angle.

Finally, and building upon the previous point, both parties are motivated by profit. Of course, what qualifies as profit for trolls diverges from
what qualifies as profit for mainstream media producers. Winfrey, for

example, profited from Over 9000 Penises in the traditional sense. She delivered ratings, and therefore advertising revenue, a portion of which she eventually pocketed. Participating trolls may not have literally profited from their exploits, but they did amass their own form of currency, a connection not lost on participating trolls—not only is the pursuit of lulz explicitly described as "serious business," trolls frequently discuss their trolling options by forwarding a series of possible action steps, followed by the all-cap imperative "PROFIT!!!," a nod to a 1998 *South Park* episode in which a similarly structured business plan is forwarded by a pack of scheming gnomes eager to steal Eric Cartman's underpants (this same structure was used in the Jenkem copypasta included in the introduction).[56]

Given these similarities, it might be tempting to conclude that corporate media are vast institutions of trolling, or at least that individual media personalities are themselves trolls. This however would be a stretch, and furthermore isn't the issue. The issue is that, while trolls' exploitative behaviors are condemned as aberrational, journalists' similarly exploitative behaviors are accepted as being par for the capitalist course. Condemning one while giving the other a free pass doesn't just obscure the cultural conditions out of which trolling emerges, it almost guarantees that the most problematic behaviors will persist—and not just in the darkest corners of the Internet, but under the false flag of moral superiority, as the following chapter attests.

5 LOLing at Tragedy: Facebook Trolls, Memorial Pages, and the Business of Mass-Mediated Disaster Narratives

Building upon chapter 4, which posits a symbiotic and ultimately homologous relationship between early Anonymous and Fox News, this chapter considers the behavioral and rhetorical overlap between Facebook memorial page trolling and sensationalist disaster coverage. In addition to mapping the development of RIP trolling—in which online instigators post abusive comments and images onto pages created for and dedicated to the deceased—the chapter examines the highly contentious and ultimately parasitic relationship between memorial trolls and Facebook itself.

Recalling Elliot Oring's account of disaster humor,[1] the chapter goes on to suggest that, purposefully or not, RIP trolls highlight the exploitative and sometimes downright trollish underpinnings of mainstream disaster coverage. Rather than providing a snarling, sociopathic counterpoint to mainstream media, then, Facebook memorial page trolls (RIP trolls for short) enact a grotesque pantomime of precisely the corporate logic that transforms tragedy into a business opportunity—further blurring the ostensibly clear-cut line between those who troll and those who do not.

The Crunchy Side of Convergence

I first heard about Facebook memorial page trolling in March 2010. This introduction came via a troll named Paulie Socash, who was the Internet friend of an Internet friend familiar with my research. At Paulie's behest, I created a fake profile—I chose the moniker David Davison—and watched as my Facebook wall lit up with hundreds, maybe even thousands, of trolls, all of whom flagged themselves as such with profile names referencing well-known memes.[2] Although it was difficult to know exactly how many people were behind this initial onslaught (a single person could and usually would operate a number of profiles simultaneously), it was clear that whatever this was, it was big.

Almost immediately, troll profiles began friending other troll profiles (identifiable by handle and profile picture), forming an antisocial network of sorts. All one needed to do was log in and scroll through his or her news feed, which would show exactly what was being trolled by whom—perfect for research purposes. For the first few months of the project, I'd spend hours each day simply lurking, that is, quietly following trolls from public page to public page. Once Facebook began pushing back against trolling behaviors in late 2010, automatically banning profiles that were engaging in trollish-seeming behaviors (not posting anything on one's own wall, posting numerous messages to strangers' walls, frequently being blocked, sending far more friend messages than were ever accepted, constantly rotating between different profiles, often from the same IP address), this approach became increasingly difficult. In response, I begin reaching out to and interviewing individual trolls/groups of trolls, including Paulie Socash, Peter Partyvan, Wilson Mouzone, Soveri Ruthless, Frank Bagadonuts, and Pro Fessor, as well as a rotating cast of one- or two-time contributors, from whom I gathered invaluable and otherwise inaccessible data, including screencaps, gossip, and concrete timelines. Given how effective Facebook's anti-trolling measures proved to be, it would not be possible to replicate this study, making the trolls' contributions critical to understanding expansion (and retraction) within this particular troll space.

Digitally Mediated Mourning

In October 2009, Facebook employee Max Kelley addressed Facebook's changing attitude toward so-called memorial accounts.[3] Previously, Kelly explained, there was no way to deactivate a Facebook account once a person had died. Consequently, the deceased's profile would occasionally show up in friends' suggestion boxes ("Reconnect with Bill by posting something on his wall!"), prompting a number of users to complain.

After considering their options, Facebook decided to implement a new policy: friends and family members now had the option to permanently memorialize the dead person's account. Existing friends would still have access to their friend's wall but would not receive any messages regarding that profile. Additionally, only confirmed friends would be able to search for the profile, and no one would be able to log on as the deceased (a move that could be interpreted as a preemptive strike against mischief).[4] By implementing this policy, Facebook was deliberately positioning itself as a potential grief space, somewhere mourners could go, as Kelley stated, "to save and share their memories of those who've passed." After all, he continued, "when someone leaves us, they don't leave our memories or our social networks."[5]

In mid-February 2010, Lisa Miller of *Newsweek* praised these changes, arguing that "this is how we collectively mourn: Globally. Together. Online."[6] According to Miller, it was entirely appropriate that Facebook should provide networking support for mourners, an idea that reached full flowering with the seemingly overnight popularity of Facebook memorial pages. Unlike a memorialized account, which functions as a snapshot of a person's life just before he or she died, memorial (or RIP) pages allowed everyone, from those who knew the deceased to those who first encountered the story online or on television, to participate in the grieving process. Members could post condolence messages, communicate and grieve with other users, or simply keep track of group announcements.

What's more, involved parties—whether friend, family member, or sympathetic stranger—were able to link relevant news items (as well as the memorial pages themselves) onto their own Facebook profiles, thus directing even more traffic, and therefore attention, to an emerging story. If a particular story generated enough on-site buzz, media outlets would run a story about Facebook's engagement with the story, which would raise the visibility of the original story, as well as the associated memorial page(s). More exposure meant more page views, and more page views meant more Likes, and more Likes meant more group members; unsurprisingly, the biggest news stories generated the strongest reactions on Facebook.

A Series of Unfortunate Events

It was this perfect symbiosis between Facebook and corporate media that set organized, widespread RIP trolling in motion—a development that took a turn for the macabre during a particularly eventful two-week period in early 2010. The opening salvo came on February 25, when SeaWorld trainer Dawn Brancheau was killed by Tilikum, a 12,000-pound killer whale, as the two performed in front of a live stadium audience.[7] Within minutes of Brancheau's death, trolls began uploading macros onto /b/ featuring a homicidal whale as well as variations on rule 34, an unofficial rule of the Internet declaring that whatever "it" is, there is porn of it. With the invocation of rule 34, Dawn Brancheau the person was thus transformed into Dawn Brancheau the meme—that is to say, a dehumanized, sexualized object of lulz.

As frequently happens on /b/, the Tilikum/Brancheau family of memes began to incorporate additional memes, including references to the now-infamous "Epic Beard Man" video. The video, which was uploaded onto

YouTube ten days before Brancheau's death, captures an altercation between an older white man (of the eponymous epic beard) named Thomas Bruso and a fifty-year-old black man. The white man wears a shirt that reads "I am a motherfucker"; the black man, whose nose has been broken, repeatedly calls for an ambulance, which he pronounces as "amber lamps."[8] /b/ found the phrases "I am a motherfucker" and "amber lamps" particularly amusing, and when the RIP party spontaneously jumped from /b/ to Sea-World's Facebook page, an untold number of trolls flooded its wall with Epic Beard Man references and Tilikum macros, including one that read "Should Have Called the Amber Lamps."[9]

February 25 also marked the disappearance of Chelsea King, a pretty, blond white teenager from San Diego. In King's hometown, thousands of volunteers scoured San Diego County for clues, and community leaders organized candlelight vigils and prayer circles.[10] On the Internet, well-wishers from across the country utilized Facebook's networking platform to express sympathy and help cheerlead the search effort. The page "Chelsea's Light," for example, which was created by the King family almost immediately following King's disappearance, amassed over eighty thousand members within three days,[11] while unofficial pages like "Help Find Chelsea King: Missing California Teen"[12] pulled in tens of thousands of additional fans and group members, the vast majority of whom had never met King but nevertheless felt connected to the case.

Thanks to the media attention surrounding—and subsequent trolling interest in—the Dawn Brancheau case, trolls who otherwise might not have been paying attention were already plugged into the twenty-four-hour cable and online news cycle; consequently, they were some of the first responders when people began creating and, more importantly, making public, dozens of fan groups and RIP pages for King. For the next few days, trolls split their time between Brancheu's and King's respective pages, wreaking havoc with the admins of each and resulting in the first of many so-called trollercausts (indicating a high rate of profile deletion, a state of affairs easily remedied by the creation of new accounts).

Then on March 1, thirty-year-old John Gardener III was charged with the suspected rape and murder of Chelsea King as well as the murder of fourteen-year-old Amber DuBois, a local high school student who disappeared in 2009.[13] As soon as the news broke, Facebook users began creating scores of RIP Chelsea King and Amber DuBois pages, precipitating a renewed flood of trolling. Soon after, a San Diego man named Mike McMullen created the page "I Bet a Pickle Can Get More Fans than Chelsea King."[14] A play on "I Bet This Pickle Can Get More Fans than Nickleback,"

McMullen's page featured a picture of a scowling, underwear-clad cartoon pickle gripping a crudely photoshopped cutout of Chelsea's head.[15]

Almost immediately, Pickle was flooded with offensive images and statements as well as the impassioned condemnation of users who "liked" the page in order to defend Chelsea's memory. Not surprisingly, word spread quickly; a few days after it hit Facebook, an ABC affiliate in San Diego (10 News) ran a segment condemning the page and its creator. When confronted by reporter Joe Little in a Facebook message thread, McMullen seemed unfazed, choosing instead to speak as the pickle itself. In response, 10 News consulted Michael Mantell, a clinical psychologist, who concluded that there had to be something seriously wrong with McMullen.[16]

Although McMullen wasn't personally responsible for all the content posted to Pickle, he did provide a forum for a deluge of negative and X-rated comments. "Extreme butthurt," wrote poster Tyrone Dickinanot. "WU TANG CLAN AIN'T NUTTIN TO FUCK WIT," added George Everyman. Francis Bagadonuts posted a Google Earth image of the home allegedly belonging to one of the posters who objected to the page and whom posters Tracy Balls and Tasha Salad proceeded to torment; someone asked if there were any nude pictures of Chelsea King's body; someone threatened to rape the sister and mother of someone who had defended King's memory.[17]

As shocking as this segment might have been for 10 News' audience, these comments were comparatively tame—much of what was posted to Pickle was much too obscene to air, even if pixilated. Furthermore, the segment failed to acknowledge—indeed, seemed wholly unaware—that the real story extended far beyond a single fan page. This was not just about Mike McMullen; this was not just about Chelsea King. Contrary to 10 News' assumption that "I Bet a Pickle" was an isolated event, the behaviors exhibited on Pickle, as well as negative or otherwise ransacked Chelsea King pages, had already gone global.

Around the World in 80 Trolls

Indeed, similar patterns of behavior were unfolding in Britain and Australia, both of which were experiencing their own uptick in high-profile deaths. In Great Britain, and on the same day that Chelsea King's body was found, news broke that BBC presenter Kristian Digby had died of autoerotic asphyxiation.[18] Just as /b/'s response to Dawn Brancheau's death lent trolling momentum to the Chelsea King story, Digby's death breathed new life into organized attacks against British television personality Jade

Goody, whose ongoing and very public battle with cancer (which she finally lost March 22) had inspired a whole subgenre of British trolling.

In Australia, and nearly simultaneously, eight-year-old Trinity Bates and twelve-year-old Elliot Fletcher were both murdered.[19] Like their American and British counterparts, the ranks of Australian trolls exploded, sending the Australian media into a Facebook-bashing fury. Unlike American news outlets, however, which at the time conflated "cyberbullying" with "trolling," Australian bloggers, reporters, and even law enforcement knew precisely what they were up against, and incidentally were the first nation to take punitive measures against trolling behaviors—see the 2010 case of Paul Bradley Hampson, aka Dale Angerer, who photoshopped an image of a penis onto an existing photo of Trinity Bates, posted the image to Bates's Facebook memorial page (among other obscenities posted to Eliot Fletcher's page), and was subsequently arrested for child pornography.[20]

Despite differences in media representations and legal interventions, Australian trolls quickly began sharing resources with their American counterparts; from late February onward, American trolls were just as likely to raid Australian memorial pages as Australians were to raid American pages. Whatever a troll's nationality, he or she would blanket his or her friend lists with invites to RIP pages and groups, which would be forwarded down the chain to the friends of friends, and the friends of those friends, thus introducing local tragedy to a transnational audience.

During this initial period of global expansion, I was intrigued to discover that one could easily and accurately determine a Facebook troll's nationality simply by examining how they trolled. Their real names may have been withheld, but their cultural experiences bled through (and, once the trolls began to use Skype for group voice chat, could be confirmed). Australian trolls, for example, tended to be extremely aggressive, likely due to Australia's severe censorship laws—the logic being that if you're already flirting with illegality, you might as well go full force. British trolls were especially social, and often used trolling as an opportunity to make (and lose) online and offline friends. American trolls, by contrast, were simultaneously the most secretive and the most boastful, given the protections afforded by the First Amendment. So, while Australian trolls expected their government to prosecute, American trolls assumed their government would, ultimately, protect, and often cited civil liberties organizations like the ACLU as a legal failsafe (as one troll half-jokingly put it, the ACLU defends terrorists, so it wouldn't have a problem intervening on behalf of trolls).

In this way, participating trolls wore their nationalities like a World Cup soccer uniform, providing further (if unexpected) evidence for the theory of cultural digestion. These trolls were quite literally marked by the cultures that spawned them, so much so that even anonymity couldn't disguise where they were coming from.

The Antisocial Network

In addition to inadvertently spurring the popularity of memorial page trolling, Facebook's social networking platform helped engender a distinctive trolling style, one that hews fairly closely to "traditional" trolling but that differs both structurally and in overall tone. The following three sections chronicle these points of overlap, and illustrate just how imbricated Facebook is in the RIP trolling story.

The Technological Affordances of Facebook

The form and function of Facebook trolling was, from its very inception, predicated on the technological affordances established by Facebook's programmers. It was through the adoption of these affordances—which don't just encourage but engender user enmeshment—that trolling became a fundamentally *social* activity. This differed greatly from most forum trolling and certainly trolling on /b/, which was almost always blindly anonymous. Participating anons may have worked together during a particular raid, but they rarely stood still long enough to establish social ties and certainly didn't have a persistent online identity to which particular successes may be affixed.

Facebook trolling, by contrast, necessitated the creation of strong affinity networks. Most conspicuously, given their desire to maintain community ties after a profile had been deleted, Facebook trolls tended to stick with the same family of trolling names. This way, respawn accounts (new accounts created after an old account or set of accounts had been banned) would have an easier time finding and being found by other trolls, and would allow individual trolls to take credit for their on-site exploits. For example, every time my profile was banned, I would respawn as David, integrating this basic nominal building block into both first and last names regardless of gender (David Davison, Brittani Davidson, David Briggs). Paulie maintained two profile roots, Paul for male accounts and Leigh for female; Frank was Francis, Fran, François or Frankie; Ruthless was Ruth or Ruthie, etc. It might seem like an obvious point, but having stable names to call each other meant that trolls suddenly had persistent social identities to maintain, and could start making friends.

There is of course a flip side, since although persistent social identity helps engender community formation, it also encourages the development of stable personae with which to have persistent conflict. The ongoing war between trolls and anti-trolls is a case in point. To compress several years' worth of antipathy into a single paragraph, the seemingly overnight popularity of Facebook trolling caused a great deal of distress in average users; a number of anti-trolling groups began cropping up, including "I Think Internet Trolls Are Losers,"[21] "Stop the Bullying!"[22] "Army against Low Life Trolls"[23] and "These Cruel Facebook 'Trolls' Need to Be Locked Up for Attacking RIP Groups."[24] Although many of these groups were created in earnest, most if not all were swiftly infiltrated by trolls, who shifted their focus from trolling online mourners to trolling other trolls—hence the title "anti-troll" (and its corresponding objective, "anti-lulz").

The most infamous of these anti-trolls was Mike Lonston, who in 2010 set to work doxxing (i.e., revealing the real-life name, phone number, address, and/or workplace of) as many trolls as he could. Lonston's interventions spurred the creation of "Mike Lonston Week," an organized pushback in which dozens of trolls cloned dozens of Mike Lonston profiles ("cloning" a profile meant creating an unauthorized, identical profile) in order to gain access to anti-trolling groups and undermine Lonston's influence within anti-lulz circles.[25] Unsurprisingly, very little love was lost between "proper" trolls and antis; according to the "real" trolls, anti-trolls are tediously self-righteous at best and pathologically messianic at worst, often using the friends and families of the deceased as pawns in a war that, according to the trolls I've worked with, is more about ego and reputation than good-faith defense against the dark arts. Conversely, the antis' (public) position is that trolls are mentally ill social parasites who must be stopped at any cost.

Whatever the true motives of either side, the troll/anti-troll rivalry quickly escalated. Often spending weeks or months stalking their targets, antis amassed stockpiles of incriminating screencaps and handed identifying information, including any and all dox, over to the authorities. In the United States, such acts of anti-trollish vigilantism were for the most part ignored by law enforcement, a point over which stateside trolls frequently gloated. In Great Britain, however, the stakes were much higher—a point that antis, particularly Mike Lonston, were quite successful in exploiting. Again, it is critical to note the ways in which Facebook's platform influenced, if not outright determined, the behavior of its resident trolls, anti- or otherwise. You don't see these kinds of drawn-out and highly personal pissing matches on /b/, or on forums where identity is either fleeting or simply nonexistent; this was a Facebook-specific phenomenon.

Trolling and the Facebook Self

In addition to replicating the behavioral patterns of "legitimate" users, the Facebook trolls I worked with eagerly harnessed existing on-site sensitivities. Due to the knee-jerk sympathies they generated, RIP pages were an attractive, almost obvious, choice. This is not to say that all Facebook trolls engaged in memorial page trolling. Quite the contrary—from the trolls' perspective, Facebook was a smorgasbord of exploitable situations and people. One possible (and in my opinion highly likely) explanation is embedded within Facebook's basic architecture, which positions the user as the subject of every sentence he or she utters, indeed as the center of his or her particular social universe. Self-involvement, in other words, is built into the code; one is primed to take things personally. This is not to say that Facebook users are solipsists, exactly. But the relationship between user and content is, and is designed to be, solipsistic. After all, the "I"—and a carefully constructed, often fastidiously maintained "I" at that—prefigures every interaction and lends itself to a particular brand of ego investment and emotional sensitivity. The trolls I worked with were more than eager to take full advantage.

Furthermore, to the extent that Facebook's architecture encourages emotional investment in regular users, it encourages emotional divestment in trolls, thus ushering in increasingly outrageous and aggressive behaviors. After all, while "real" Facebook users are continuously reminded of and interpolated by their own "I," troll users are continuously reminded of and interpolated by the "I" they're *not*—an ongoing process of emotional repudiation that may explain why Facebook trolls during this period frequently shifted to the third person to describe their own actions. At first I was taken aback by this tendency. I'd be chatting with a collaborator, and suddenly he or she would mention some amusing thing his or her profile had done, as if the profile were somehow separable from the person whose profile it was. I eventually came to realize that, in the trolls' minds, their profiles *were* separable from their "true" selves. Theirs may have been the fingers pushing all the buttons, but they weren't the ones doing the damage, not exactly.

Obviously, the person behind the troll is explicitly and directly responsible for any and all trollish behaviors. They are the ones doing the trolling, regardless of what handle they're using. That said, while the person can be equated with the profiles he or she creates ("I am David"), the resulting profiles cannot similarly or necessarily be equated with the person ("David isn't *me*"); it is perhaps more accurate to say that trolling profiles, and trolling personas generally, fall somewhere between character and proxy—a sometimes-rupture sometimes-slippage between the offline and the online self that Facebook's encoded solipsism inadvertently reinforces.

Given the ease with which trolls on Facebook could find a seemingly endless stream of targets, as well as the ways in which the platform itself primed both subject and object of trolling for trolling, it is unsurprising that so many trolls regarded Facebook as an optimal stomping ground. During Facebook's period of trolls gone wild, it may have been the Internet's *most* optimal stomping ground. It was a perfect storm of technological and behavioral siphoning.

Facebook Responds

Needless to say, Facebook trolling generally and RIP trolling in particular proved to be a public relations nightmare for the Facebook brand, prompting the company to adopt increasingly strict anti-trolling measures.[26] In Britain, Facebook implemented the Child Exploitation and Online Protection (CEOP) application—also known as the "Facebook panic button"— which could be downloaded onto users' accounts to help protect children and track the behaviors of abusive Facebook users. In the United States, Facebook adopted a number of similar yet much less publicized policies, including "greylisting" certain profile names, analyzing users' IP addresses, and even blocking suspected trolls from sending friend requests, writing personal messages, and commenting on friends' walls.[27] Facebook also established a "Hate and Harassment Team" to help police the site, augmenting their already robust algorithmic defenses.[28]

This wasn't an entirely novel development. Even in the first few weeks of the RIP onslaught, before Facebook fully understood the scope of the problem, one's trolling profile could be deleted without warning. Around December 2010, however, and as a result of the aforementioned policy changes, profiles became almost impossible to maintain. Because my profiles frequently sent and received friend requests from users flagged for trolling, and because the majority of my interactions were restricted to these "greylisted" users, even I had a difficult time keeping accounts alive (I do admit to occasionally trolling Tea Party/Moral Majority-types, and was once banned from a group of white supremacists for complimenting a gun-toting, Confederate flag bracelet-wearing, hyper-masculine homo-phobe for his fashion sense and good taste in accessories. I was curious to see how the man would react to being accused of stylishness—a dangerous proposition for someone obsessed with traditional gender roles and even more obsessed with his own sexuality—and was amused by how quickly he reported me for abuse).

And yet trolls persisted. Many established off-site strongholds on YouTube or Skype, where groups could maintain ties even in the face of certain profile-death. Other trolls began dealing exclusively in kamikaze attacks, wherein a profile is created only to be destroyed—resulting in behaviors that were as disorganized as they were vicious (several collabora-tors decried this emergent trolling style as being sloppy and uncreative, both from a tactical and stylistic standpoint). In this way, Facebook trolling functioned as an environmental adaptation. Whenever Facebook made a move, trolls would immediately counter, creating a subset of troll that was particularly adept at harnessing and exploiting existing structures.

The Ethnographer Speaks

A few weeks after a massive round of bannings, I threw caution to the ether and outed myself as a researcher. Up to that point, I'd restricted my focus to information I could glean by digging through the public links and likes of several well-connected trolls. This was the first time I'd presented my real-life self to the twenty or so trolls who made up this particular cabal, and it was the first time I'd directly broached the subject of research col-laboration. By doing so, I hoped to gather more information about the trolls' relationships to and understanding of their own behaviors.

Anticipating that they would assume I was on some kind of doxxing mission, I assured potential research recruits that I was not interested in collecting identifying personal information, and that if somehow I were presented with any, say through the trolls' own disclosures, inadvertent discovery, or through idle gossip, I would lock that information down—wouldn't record it, wouldn't share the information with other trolls, and wouldn't include it in any published research. I even drafted a confidential-ity agreement, which I posted to every Facebook research page I created, and which I required all research participants to read and consent to before I would ask any interview questions.

Unsurprisingly, the reaction was mixed—and with very good reason. Trolls were constantly cloning each other or simply pretending to be some-thing else entirely. Paulie, for example, spent months undercover as a female Klanswoman ("all they do is play Farmville and send each other hugs"), and almost every troll I worked with had created at least one alternate persona. For example, Ruthless spent a summer as a kindly black grandmother named Ruthie, and Frank frequently trolled as Fran, who at some point adopted David as her only son ("Only on the interwebz," he later wrote, "can you have a man [me] posing as a girl [Fran Stepford] become the mom of a boy [David Davidson] who is actually a girl [Whit]").[29] Even I gave in to this impulse, inventing with my research profiles an entire nuclear family complete with strained marriage (it was "complicated" with Paul Lee) and dopey tagalong brother (David, of course). "Oh you can trust me I'm writing a book, now tell me about your feelings" would have been entirely par for this course.

My gender was also an issue, as Facebook trolling, like trolling generally, is explicitly androcentric ("absolute sausagefest" also works, and is how I chose to frame the space in the *First Monday* article on which this chapter is based[30]). Indeed over the course of two years of research, I encountered a mere handful of female Facebook trolls, only one of whom was willing (though not at all eager) to chat via Skype. Those who were female, and/or claimed to be female irl, were often just as sexist as their male counterparts, if not more so. The one female troll I spoke with enjoyed trolling Facebook support groups for rape victims, and bragged during a Skype interview about singling out, and in fact preferring, vulnerable female targets.

There was, however, no shortage of female-*presenting* trolls, most of whom were playing at femininity in order to accomplish any number of unholy objectives. As Ruthless, who at the time was trolling as Banme Anmarkzdies, explained, "I love trolling as a female, one of my favorite pastimes is making up some mock rape, abuse, neglect story that is my excuse for the way I am, and 9 times out of 10 they forgive me, and then I just LOL & JK them" (recall that in trolling parlance, "lol jk" means "haha you idiot I was just kidding").[31]

Consequently my claim that I was an academic, and a female academic at that, would have seemed doubly suspicious. Luckily, Paulie was willing to vouch for me and for my work, which helped—until an especially paranoid contingent accused me of *being* Paulie Socash, a suspicion that was given credence after someone using the handle "Paulie Socash" posted a few messages bearing the University of Oregon's IP address. Although regarded as a slam dunk by the paranoid contingent (at the time I was a PhD student and graduate teaching fellow at the University of Oregon), the Oregon IP incident could have indicated any of the following: that

Paulie/someone posing as Paulie had spoofed the IP, that Paulie/someone posing as Paulie was one of thirty thousand people who had staff, faculty, or student access to the University of Oregon wifi network, or that Paulie/someone posing as Paulie had acquired guest access to the UO network. Because I could neither prove nor disprove any of these scenarios (at least not without compromising my own confidentiality agreement), the controversy persisted and still occasionally surfaces (I can hear Peter Partyvan now, clucking at what he'll surely claim is a lame attempt to cover my tracks).

Regardless of the Paulie question (or perhaps because it made the prospect of collaboration more interesting), a number of trolls agreed to participate in my research, reasoning that if I *was* up to no good—for example, if I'd lied about who I was or what I hoped to accomplish—they'd eventually find out and would respond accordingly. I accepted these somewhat ominous terms, and over the next few months asked an inordinate number of questions both privately and in group chat settings.

The most consistent theme of these conversations was the seemingly natural and necessary link between trolling and the mainstream media. According to the trolls I interviewed, the media was indirectly responsible for the popularity of RIP pages, and therefore was the indirect target of organized trolling behaviors. By sensationalizing the "sexier" deaths (i.e., those guaranteed to bolster ratings), the media—or as Paulie Socash often called them, "tragedy merchants"[32]—essentially cattle-drove hordes of mourners onto Facebook. Already distressed and emotionally invested in the emerging story, these users were easy targets for trolls, who happily exploited their existing vulnerabilities. The media subsequently commodified these same vulnerabilities through advertising revenue.

In short, the oft-repeated (and reported) assumption that trolls devoted most of their time to terrorizing real-life friends and family members was not borne out by my experience. While certain RIP trolls did indeed attack real-life loved ones, and denied feeling any remorse no matter how traumatizing their behaviors ("I just hate everyone," Peter Partyvan once explained in a private message, his noncommittal shrug almost audible[33]), most of the trolls I worked with found "real" RIP trolling either uninteresting or downright distasteful and instead were more interested in exploiting media-induced fervor. As one troll named Wilson Mouzone bluntly put it, family members haven't done anything wrong and should be left alone. He, along with many trolls, might have thought that public outpourings of grief were "tacky," and might not have understood the impulse to create, let alone publicize, memorial pages for loved ones, stating that Facebook is never the right place and never the right time.[34] But most avoided, and some outright repudiated, attacks against loved ones.

That said, the same trolls who quietly avoided friends and family unabashedly reiterated the claim that "proper" targets of trolling deserved whatever they received. In the case of RIP pages, users "earned" their place in the trolling sun either by buying into existing media narratives or, ironically enough, by inserting themselves into other people's tragedies (of which all participating trolls were simultaneously guilty). As I found, the vast majority of trolls' RIP energies were directed at these "grief tourists," users who had no real-life connection to the victim and who, according to the trolls, could not possibly be in mourning. As far as these trolls were concerned, grief tourists were shrill, disingenuous, and, unlike grieving friends and families, wholly deserving targets. The much-ridiculed statement "I didn't know you but I'm very sorry you're dead" was therefore seen as a declaration of trollability, a point emphasized in Encyclopedia Dramatica's 2010 entry on Memorial Page Tourism.[35] "This isn't grief," Paulie once argued, echoing the spirit of the Encyclopedia Dramatica page. "This is boredom and a pathological need for attention masquerading as grief."[36]

Interestingly, trolls often courted this response in order to exploit users who were gullible enough to take the bait. Paulie was a master of creating and publicizing fake RIP pages for high-profile crime victims, particularly young attractive white women. As Paulie often insisted, the utter reverence grief tourists had for cute dead white girls ("they just *love* them") perfectly captured the absurdity of expressing grief via wall post. As he explained, few things were more amusing than creating a shrine to some dead stranger, allowing the group membership to swell, then ambushing the drive-by mourners with offensive content or other shenanigans, for example, by "flipping" the page from something innocuous ("RIP [insert name of dead white teenager]") to something outrageous ("Click 'Like' If You Think [dead white teenager] Deserved to Be Taught a Lesson").[37] To RIP trolls I interviewed, this was lulz at its most rewarding.

Take the Media Narrative and Run

Even when restricted to grief tourism, these less vicious forms of trolling remained fundamentally asymmetrical. Furthermore, they illustrated RIP trolls' deeply privileged (not to mention paternalistic) worldview, which the trolls subsequently used to justify what were still often quite destructive behaviors. At the same time, participating trolls provided fascinating insight into the business of mass-mediated tragedy. Not only did RIP trolling during the period from 2010 to 2011 reveal the mechanisms by which personal tragedy is transformed into a salable narrative, it harnessed and reiterated the media's most effective methods, and in the process challenged the efficacy and ethics of these same practices.

Trolls' reaction to Chelsea King's death (or perhaps more appropriately, trolls' reaction to the media coverage of Chelsea King's death) highlights trolls' talent for excavating and subsequently weaponizing mainstream media tropes. As discussed in the introduction, whether or not participating trolls were deliberately engaging in pointed media criticism, pointed media critiques were forwarded, providing fascinating (if distressing) insight into how the mainstream media sausage is made.

Trolling Racist News Coverage

First, the disproportionate frequency with which RIP trolls descended upon news about dead white young people—specifically murdered white teenage girls, white teenage suicides (with particular interest paid to gay white teenage suicides) and kidnapped and/or murdered white children—revealed the disproportionate frequency with which the mainstream media filed stories about these populations. Had there been more sensationalist, multiple news-cycle stories focused on nonwhite crime victims from 2010 to 2011 (the period of greatest RIP trolling activity), the statistics may have been different. But these stories rarely generated the level of moral panic typically assigned to young white victims, and so from the trolls' perspective weren't worth the time or effort.

A troll named Soveri Ruthless highlighted this point on his "Chelsea King Fans: Why Aren't You Helping to Find Jalesa Reynolds?" page. Reynolds, an African American high school student, went missing the same week as Chelsea King but hardly caused a blip on the media radar.[38] Chelsea was, to put it bluntly, a much more marketable victim: she was white, middle-class, and photogenic. Consequently hers was the story the nation, and subsequently users of Facebook, chose to embrace. True to trollish form, Ruthless was reluctant to attribute social or political significance to his Jalesa Reynolds page. As he explained during a Skype interview, he created the page primarily to bait self-righteous white people who were scandalized by the suggestion that they cared more about a missing white girl than a missing black girl.[39] Whatever his motives, the Jalesa Reynolds page called attention to disproportionate media coverage of white victims, and consequently revealed as much about the media organizations that perpetuate inequity as it did about the Facebook users who refused to acknowledge that such inequities exist.

Trolling the Human Interest Angle

Second, trolls' engagement with the grisliest or otherwise most upsetting aspects of a particular tragedy highlights the media's proclivity for focusing on just that, the grisliest and most upsetting aspects of a particular tragedy. Trolls were able to exploit certain details, in other words, because those were the details the media chose to present. In Chelsea King's case, trolls focused on her grades, her extracurricular activities, her religious orientation, what she was wearing at the time of her death, her killer's criminal and psychological history, how her friends reacted to her death on Facebook, how her friends reacted to the Pickle page on Facebook, her personal photographs (one of which was used for the Pickle page profile picture)—in short, anything and everything the media offered up. The second the rumor and detail mill stopped grinding, so too would trolls. But the detail mill kept churning, and so the trolls kept trolling.

Although it does not address RIP trolls specifically (or even trolls generally, or Facebook, or computers), Oring's "Jokes and the Discourses on Disaster" provides a brilliant model for precisely this interplay. As Oring discusses, the "tasteless and cruel" jokes that emerged in the wake of the *Challenger* space disaster—"Q: What color were Christa McAuliffe's eyes? A: Blue. One blew this way and the other blew that way."[40]—function as a counterpoint to hyperbolic media coverage, a suggestion that directly challenges the long-held assumption that such jokes *either* are evidence of human depravity *or* serve a critical therapeutic function. Oring is wary of both extremes, neither of which addresses the mainstream media's role in catalyzing disaster joke cycles.

In the wake of the *Challenger* disaster, for example, images of the explosion were played again and again, each time accompanied by a wide-eyed newscaster who reminded his or her audience that this was tragedy of the very highest order. And yet these same newscasters skirted the fact that, by playing and replaying the explosion, they were forcing their viewers to watch seven horrific deaths again and again. The emergent humor iterated this omission, calling attention to the uncomfortable truths that the media continued to exploit but refused to directly acknowledge.

Additionally, *Challenger* humor tended to poke fun at the "human interest" aspects of the story that the media did feel comfortable addressing (and consequently fetishizing)—McAuliffe's physical appearance, the astronauts' last words, what they had eaten just before their deaths, and so on.[41]

Just as trolls descended upon the most upsetting details of Chelsea King's death, so too did *Challenger* disaster joke tellers. The media made it difficult *not* to. At the very least, they supplied the raw materials, then decried the resulting structures as morally bankrupt.

Trolling the Business of Terrible News

Finally, and on a strongly related point, trolls' engagement with personal tragedy calls attention to just how good personal tragedy is for the business of media. As Oring explains: "Without imputing any malevolence to newspeople, it should be recognized that public disasters are media triumphs. They are what make the news. Indeed, our awareness of national or international disasters is dependent upon the media—particularly television news broadcasting. Furthermore, the frame for communication of information about a disaster is established by the media."[42]

During the height of RIP behaviors, trolls were quick to channel and even quicker to exploit this frame; in fact, they helped construct additional scaffolding. After all, in addition to benefitting financially from tragedy, mainstream media outlets benefited from trolls' fetishized engagement with the media's fetishized engagement. Trolls happily gamed this system, and were even happier to brag about having gamed it.

In response to a repost of 10 News' Pickle segment, for example, a group of collaborators—several of whom were mentioned by name in the original segment, including Frank Bagadonuts—were delighted. "LMAO," wrote Frank. "'THEY'VE ALSO THREATENED TO RAPE HIS SISTER AND MOTHER' LOLOL," wrote David Davidson (no relation to my David Davison account). "That part almost had me in tears," Leroy Freeman added, to which Frank responded, "Oh American media, how I adore your melodrama."[43] Apparently forgetting that a young woman had in fact been raped and murdered, the trolls instead focused on 10 News' willingness—if not downright eagerness—to keep the Chelsea King story alive. Despite the fact that the trolls made little to no effort to hide the fact that they were trolling (they used explicitly trollish names, including "Tyrone Dickinanot," "Tracy Balls," and "Tasha Salad," and dropped troll reference after troll reference), 10 News took everything posted to the page literally, either because they couldn't be bothered to slow down and consider the source, or because they had considered the source and decided to move forward anyway. Participating trolls were banking on the media to take this bait, and in the end 10 News came through.

What's more, both 10 News and the participating trolls benefited from this arrangement. 10 News was able to keep the Chelsea King story alive, and the trolls were able to bolster their own reputations. Recalling the relationship between early Anonymous and Fox News, then, the relationship between RIP trolls and the mainstream media was simultaneously symbiotic and homologous. Trolls needed the media to become hysterical, and the media needed trolls to terrorize; more often than not, each side lived up to its end of the bargain, and each side benefited from the overreaction of the other.

Never have these parallels been more conspicuous than in the wake of the 2010 outbreak of teen suicides. In the United States and in Great Britain, close to a dozen teenagers—all of whom were white, many gay or otherwise outcast—took their own lives. Given the common thread of social media (like most middle-class teens in the developed world, the decedents had engaged in some form of online activity in the lead-up to their deaths), the emerging narrative, and subsequent moral panic, cited "cyberbullying" as the reason our white teenagers kept dying.[44]

Adding to the moral panic surrounding cyberbullying was the increasingly popular trend of creating Facebook memorial pages for the deceased, a trend that, as previously discussed, resulted in a sharp uptick in trolling behaviors. Mainstream outlets in the United States and Great Britain embraced this angle, pouring over every hateful thing trolls—which the American media still subsumed under the term "cyberbullying"—posted to Facebook. In many cases, this coverage merely reinscribed the language of trolling in order to maximize reader outrage—all the while condemning trolls for exploiting other people's grief for personal gain.

Consider *The Today Show*'s coverage of Alexis Pilkington's death. Lexi, a white seventeen-year-old high school student from Long Island, hanged herself in March 2010. Due in part to the rumor that Lexi had been a victim of cyberbullying (a rumor her parents denied), and that her death was the result of autoerotic asphyxiation (a rumor likely started by trolls), trolls descended upon her official memorial page and created several pages of their own, including one titled "Alexis Pilkington Hang in There!" In response, *The Today Show* produced a segment featuring interviews with her parents, home videos of Lexi during happier times, and proclamations of the teen's bubbly all-American beauty—all of which was sandwiched between images and statements posted by trolls, including a screencap from the "Alexis Pilkington Hang in There!" page as well an accompanying picture of Lexi's head photoshopped through a noose. Later in the segment, three of Lexi's high school friends were seated in front of a computer monitor. They proceeded to read a series of hateful comments off one of Lexi's memorial pages, which the

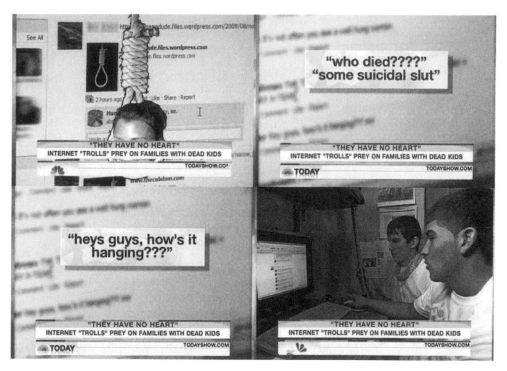

Figure 5.1
Stills from *The Today Show*'s "They Have No Heart" segment compiled by the author.
First aired on March 31, 2010. Accessed on MSNBC.com on July 3, 2012.

producers helpfully transcribed for the audience (figure 5.1). Near the
end of the segment, *Today* reporter Jeff Rossen wondered what kind of
people would engage in such behaviors, a question more pointed (and
ironic) than he seemed to realize.[45]

Great Britain's *Daily Mail*—affectionately described by trolls as the *Daily
Troll*—was just as quick to condemn trolling, and just as quick to harness
its distressing tone. For example, in an article devoted to the suicides of
fifteen-year-olds Tom Mullaney and Natasha MacBryde, reporter Beth Hale
interviewed the teenagers' parents and asked them to describe how they
felt when they first realized the trolls were attacking their children's RIP
pages. According to Tom's father Robert, the troll-made images were "so
distressing" he "[couldn't] describe them," an impediment Hale bypassed
by describing one of the grislier images herself—specifically, Tom's head
photoshopped through a noose (clearly a popular RIP trolling trope).[46] In

a similar *Daily Mail* article titled "'Help Me, Mummy. It's Hot Here in Hell': A Special Investigation into the Distress of Grieving Families Caused by the Sick Internet Craze of 'Trolling,'" reporter Tanith Carey directly quoted a number of trolling macros, including "Help me, Mummy. It's hot here in hell," which one troll used to caption an image of Lauren Drew, a deceased fourteen-year-old. In the article, this phrase appears almost directly above Drew's photograph, mimicking the form and content of the very image Carey was decrying.[47]

Given the demonstrable correlation between media coverage of suicide and subsequent increases in suicide, this sort of coverage wasn't just sensationalist, it was outright irresponsible. As Phillips and Carstensen argue in the *New England Journal of Medicine*, teenagers are especially vulnerable; not only do teenage suicide rates go up following reports on suicide, but the more widespread the coverage, the greater the increase.[48] Subsequent research published by the American Foundation for the Prevention of Suicide (AFPS) supports this conclusion. In their "Recommendations for Reporting on Suicide," presented in collaboration with the Annenberg Public Policy Center, Centers for Disease Control, and UCLA School of Public Health, and other public policy organizations, the AFPS cites over fifty research studies corroborating the phenomenon of "copycat suicide" and urges news organizations to exercise caution. As the recommendations section stresses, "Risk of additional suicides increases when the story explicitly describes the suicide method, uses dramatic/graphic headlines or images, and repeated/extensive coverage sensationalizes or glamorizes a death."[49]

Whether or not the individual journalists and editors responding to the teen suicide stories were aware of these risks, whether or not they actively chose to privilege page views over public health, sensationalist media outlets provided breathless coverage of every suicide, often including precisely the sorts of details and emotion-laden language decried by health care professionals. Hale, for example, discussed the exact placement of Tom Mullaney's body in the wake of the teenager's "sudden and apparently savage act of despair," and made sure to mention that Natasha MacBryde "died under a train on Valentine's Day," a morbid and unnecessarily poetic detail.[50] In their segment on trolls, *Today Show* reporters discussed how and when and under what circumstances Lexi's parents found her body, all while showing images of a smiling, happy, dancing teenager.[51] Other news outlets also lingered over the specific details of her death, some going so far as to frame her suicide as a clear case of "bullycide," despite her parents' insistence to the contrary.[52]

Although trolls were often framed as the snarling, misanthropic villains of the RIP trolling story, sensationalist news outlets were just as invested in harnessing audience distress, and just as guilty of profiting from the resulting panic. As with the relationship between Fox News and early Anonymous, the trolls' motives may have diverged from that of mainstream media, but their rhetorical and behavioral strategies were strikingly similar. The difference, of course, is that trolls didn't stand to benefit financially from additional tragedy.

In the spring of 2011, I found myself smack in the middle of this storm. Because I'd already appeared in an article about the Facebook memorial page phenomenon, Beth Hale from the *Daily Mail*—the same Beth Hale mentioned earlier—sent me an interview request. According to Hale, a troll named Pro Fessor had been posting nasty pictures with captions to Natasha MacBryde and Tom Mullaney's memorial pages. She wanted to know if she could talk to me about the pictures, and/or if I could arrange for her to talk to a real-life troll, preferably Pro Fessor himself.

I agreed to the interview, and through my troll collaborators Peter and Wilson was able to get in touch with Pro Professor. After the standard expressions of wariness (was I really a researcher/was I really female), Pro Fessor agreed to an interview, both with me and with Hale. Over the next few days, he sent me some of his favorite macros and explained how he got involved with trolling; like many of the trolls I've worked with, he was pleasant and polite and seemed somewhat nervous about providing "good" answers. Also like many of the trolls I've worked with, he shrugged off the presumption of sociopathy and stated that his behaviors were the result of boredom and unemployment as much as anything.[53] In his interactions with Hale, however, he reverted to his trollish tauntings, boasting about his lack of remorse and playing up his perceived villainy. In other words, he gave Hale exactly what she wanted.

Two weeks later, Hale responded in kind. Although she'd avoided sensationalist language during our conversations, she ended up publishing the highly sensationalist piece described (and criticized) above. More notable than the tone of Hale's article, however (she did have a job to do), was the parallel between my interpersonal interactions with Hale and my interpersonal interactions with Pro Fessor. First, while both parties were thoughtful and affable in private (perhaps because they really were thoughtful and affable, perhaps because they were performing for my proverbial camera), both slipped into character—Pro Fessor as the unapologetic troll, and Hale as the uncompromising journalist—the second the curtain rose. Second, just as Pro Fessor was banking on Hale to file a sensationalist report, Hale was banking on Pro Fessor to provide sensationalist responses. Both parties gave the other party precisely what was needed—namely, sensationalism, which is the best thing that could have happened to either.

In the subsequent months, an increasing number of media outlets began covering RIP behaviors. Because of Hale's *Daily Mail* article (I had the dubious distinction of being Google search indexed alongside RIP trolling), many of these outlets would get in touch with me, often asking for referrals to "real life" trolls who might be interested in talking. I would take the requests to the trolls, who would decide who to humor and who to shoot down. By and large, the American contingent of the trolls I've worked with were greatly amused by this attention, particularly articles in the "Help Me, Mummy" vein, which they felt only created greater trolling opportunities. British trolls had more to lose, and were much more likely to bristle at these requests. Despite the risks, however, they continued trolling, and in many cases were spurred to troll harder and smarter, often as retribution for what the trolls half-jokingly described as exploitive media practices.

Gesturing toward a Conclusion

Like so many trolling behaviors, RIP trolling between 2010 and 2011 was a study in media-fueled amplification. With each new death, Facebook trolls would feed on and exploit the ever-shriller media coverage, and the media would in turn feed on and exploit the ever-fiercer trolling response. Facing pressure from all quarters, Facebook was forced to take drastic measures, which trolls promptly subverted. The cries for Facebook to do something thus grew ever louder, giving both reporters and trolls further grist for their respective mills. It was, in other words, a monument to symbiotic noxiousness.

It was also a deeply troubling business. Because unlike previous iterations of mass-mediated disaster humor—for example, the jokes that followed the *Challenger* space disaster—RIP trolling was public, searchable, and infinitely more damaging than rolling one's eyes during a newscast or telling a horribly insensitive joke in the privacy of one's living room. Whether friend or family member or sympathetic stranger to some unlucky victim, *real* people were *really* affected—in real time, no less—by RIP trolling, complicating any analysis that focused exclusively on context.

It was extremely easy, for example, to place Tom Mullaney in an abstract category of British teen suicides, and to talk about trolls' defacement of his memorial page as representative of a feedback response loop between trolls and sensationalist corporate media. That is indeed what happened. But it proved to be much more difficult to say so to Robert Mullaney, Tom's father—which was precisely what I was asked to do during the British radio segment discussed in chapter 3. My "expert" analysis of the situation— namely, that what happened on Tom's page wasn't about Tom personally— suddenly felt flat and inconsequential. Tom was someone's child, and now he is dead, and whether or not the trolls intended for his parents to see those images they *did*, and they were devastated, and there is no theoretical framework that can make that okay.

Even Paulie Socash, one of the most committed trolls I've encountered, and whose standard response to criticisms of trolling is an emphatic *hey guys the power button is right here*, has at times struggled with this ethical dilemma. He is, as he has explained, a normal enough guy who also happens to be a troll, and the normal enough guy side of the equation doesn't always align with his trolling persona. So when he messaged one afternoon to say that the inevitable finally happened, that he stumbled upon an RIP page dedicated to someone he knew in real life, I knew he—and not the troll he plays on the Internet—was genuinely concerned. I asked him what he was planning to do. "Monitor it," he answered, adding that if the trolling got out of hand (so far, "real" fans of the page were ignoring the trolls, the fastest and most effective way to stop a raid in its tracks) he would create a new profile and send the admins of the page a personal message. He would warn them, suggest they make the group private—which, he continued, the trollishness returning to his voice, is what they should have done in the first place.[54]

I share this anecdote to call (admittedly ambivalent) attention to the often-confounding *danse macabre* that is RIP trolling. It would be easy to say—as many members of the media have said, to a flourish of attention, page views, and ad revenue—that all forms of RIP trolling are objectively bad, and that all RIP trolls are objectively evil. But such a conclusion flattens the behaviors, and the people who engage in these behaviors, into one monolithic category. And in the process shuts the conversation down before any of the political stakes or precipitating economic circumstances can fully be considered.

Furthermore, and much more problematically, reductive conclusions about RIP trolling obscure the symbiosis between Facebook, mainstream media outlets, and the trolls who help line everyone else's pockets. Of course, the fact—and it is a fact—that memorial page trolling echoes routine corporate engagement doesn't and shouldn't mitigate the emotional impact of RIP behaviors. It does, however, call attention to the cynicism, hypocrisy and irresponsibility of routine corporate engagement with personal tragedy. Ultimately, this is the—again, highly ambivalent—legacy of Facebook memorial page trolling. By reenacting the grotesque extremes of mainstream behavior, RIP trolls force their audience to wallow in what passes for the norm.

6 Race and the No-Spin Zone: The Thin Line between Trolling and Corporate Punditry

According to cultural theorist Stuart Hall, there are two basic categories of racist expression: overt racism and inferential racism. Overt racism is just that—unapologetically, unequivocally bigoted. Inferential racism, on the other hand, is a subtler, though arguably more insidious, form of racist expression. It is the kind of racism that doesn't explicitly declare itself as such, yet still forwards damaging racial stereotypes—stereotypes that are made all the more damaging by the casualness with which they are forwarded, and by the speaker's unquestioned assumption that their statements couldn't possibly be racist because they are, at least according to the speaker, *true*.[1]

The following analysis focuses on the overlap between trolls' overtly racist expression and mainstream media's inferentially racist expression, with particular attention paid to the 2008 U.S. presidential election, the 2009 Obama as socialist Joker poster controversy, and Fox News' engagement with 2009's Birther movement. In so doing, the chapter provides yet another example of the breakdown between trolling and the mainstream. As I argue, trolls gleefully exploit racial tensions wherever they go, and they engage in language and behavior that is so outrageously offensive it almost defies categorization. That said, the conversation doesn't, and shouldn't, end with a simple condemnation of trolls. Just as one should place trolls' exploitative behaviors in the context of corporate exploitation, one should also consider the ways in which trolls' racist behaviors reflect and are reflected by mainstream prejudice.

The Everyday Racism of Trolling

Although the trolling collective precludes analyses of constituent anonymous members—for the very basic reason that constituent anonymous members cannot be differentiated or identified—it essentially functions as a self-contained upvoting system (on websites that utilize upvoting systems, users express interest in a particular piece of content by clicking any number of on-site approval indicators; content with the most likes/votes/ clicks floats to the top of a given thread or post, providing a real-time snapshot of the most popular stories, comments, or content). Harkening to Henry Jenkins's claim that if content doesn't spread it's dead, what resonates with the group will "live on" through reposts, remixes, and conspicuous group engagement, and what doesn't resonate with the group quietly fades away.[2] Thus by examining the types of content most frequently engaged by the so-called trolling hivemind, it is possible to posit a very basic profile of what the collective finds interesting, amusing, and worth engaging.

In the trolls' case, and as evidenced by the preponderance of explicitly racist humor within the troll space, it is clear that trolls enjoy racist expression. This is not to say that trolls are themselves racist. That particular point is unverifiable, and therefore moot. What is verifiable is the observable fact that trolls revel in explicitly and unapologetically racist language. Not only do trolls relish the opportunity to use race as trollbait within civilian (i.e., nontrolling) populations, they also deploy racist content in the presence of other trolls, as a form of racist one-upmanship.

Trolls' engagement with "nigger," particularly on 4chan's /b/ board, provides a striking example of this impulse. Save for a brief reprieve in 2011, during which time 4chan implemented a word filter that replaced all instances of the word with the still-offensive "roody-poo," this most toxic of epithets has appeared on the /b/ board with such frequency for so many years that its use has taken on an absurd, almost Dadaist feel. Trolls on /b/ use it as a pronoun. They use it as a verb. They use it as an adjective, as a conjunction, and as a standard one-word response to yes/ no questions. In many ways, trolls treat the word like a floating, meaningless signifier.

On the other hand, trolls are fully aware that this word is the furthest thing from a floating, meaningless signifier. In fact, they depend on its political significance, just as they depend on the political significance of all the epithets they employ. Echoing Judith Butler's analysis of hate speech, which posits that racial epithets always already gesture toward their own history regardless of what a person *means* when he or she uses hateful language,[3] trolls need their language to contain a kernel of hate. From the trolls' perspective, this is a purely practical point. If the epithets in question weren't politically contentious, they would be useless as trollbait.

Although trolls are aware of and in fact are dependent upon the power of racist language, they are often outright dismissive of their role in replicating racist ideologies (the same racist ideologies, it must be noted, they gleefully and unapologetically seek to exploit). In this way, trolls are imbricated in what anthropologist Jane Hill describes as the everyday language of white racism, which adheres to the following line of reasoning:

I am a good and normal mainstream sort of White person. I am not a racist, because racists are bad and marginal people. Therefore, if you understood my words to be racist, you must be mistaken. I may have used language that would be racist in the mouth of a racist person, but if I did so, I was joking. If you understood my meaning to be racist, not only do you insult me, but you lack a sense of humor, and you are oversensitive.[4]

Trolls forward a similar line of reasoning. Racist language might flow through them, but according to many of the trolls I've interviewed, they aren't being racist. They're *trolling*, which to them is a different thing entirely. In this way, and echoing Hill's analysis of perpetrators of everyday white racism,[5] trolls frame themselves as sole authority over what their words mean. What's more, the fact that the target failed to realize and/or simply accept that the troll was "just trolling" only justifies the attack. If the target hadn't been so oversensitive about "harmless" words (words trolls use because they do indeed cause harm), he or she wouldn't have been trolled; therefore, it is the target's fault.

Of course, trolls don't have a monopoly on racist expression. As the following analysis of 2009's Obama as socialist Joker controversy shows, trolls' racist output is often surprisingly similar to, if not outright indistinguishable from, content unapologetically disseminated by mainstream media outlets. The question is, which is worse? Racist statements forwarded as "truth," which have institutional, corporate backing, or racist statements forwarded by people whose stated goal is to be as racist and upsetting as possible? It is my basic contention that, while both forms of racist expression are unquestionably ugly, at least trolls advertise. The same cannot be said for mainstream media outlets, whose racism is often buried deep within the lede.

Obama as Socialist Joker

On August 3, 2009, the *Los Angeles Times* reported that a mysterious poster had begun appearing on Los Angeles freeways and on-ramps.[6] Sectioned into four discrete cells, the poster recalls an Andy Warhol print and features a photoshopped image of Barack Obama as Heath Ledger's Joker (figure 6.1). His mouth a ghastly, blood-stained grimace, Obama's skin is white-washed and his eyes black-rimmed; the word "socialism" cuts across his chest, suggesting that whatever this poster is trying to say, it isn't a compliment.

Despite the fact that the Obama as socialist Joker story had been quietly circling the web for several months,[7] the blogosphere descended upon the *Los Angeles Times* article. Suddenly, everyone was scrambling for answers. Who was responsible for the poster? Why hadn't the artist come forward? Was he or she afraid to be outed as a secret Republican? Was he or she lying low in order to shield him- or herself from the wrath of an Obama-worshipping art world?[8] Or was it something else, something more sinister?

Figure 6.1
The Obama as socialist Joker poster. Accessed via 4chan/b/ on August 4, 2009. Original creator(s) and date(s) of creation unknown.

One possibility the media didn't consider was the role trolls on 4chan's /b/ board played in the creation and amplification of the Obama as socialist Joker story. Understandably so—unless a person was already familiar with trolling culture, and therefore could recognize the image's memetic origins, it would have been difficult, if not impossible, to decipher the source of the image. This near-universal oversight was unfortunate. Not only does the connection between the Obama as socialist Joker poster and trolls help explain the origins of the controversy, it also illustrates just how similar trollish output was to corporate media output during the summer of 2009. After all, this was the summer of the Tea Party (initially "Teabaggers"), the Birthers, and the Deathers. The Obama as socialist Joker poster fit right in.

The Joker Treatment
The first piece of the Obama as socialist Joker puzzle is trollish engagement with Christopher Nolan's *The Dark Knight*.[9] Not only did the publicity surrounding Heath Ledger's death—the actor overdosed shortly after the film wrapped—imbue his Joker character with an acute, almost ironic morbidity, trolls on /b/ identified with his character's seemingly motiveless pursuit of chaos. They were so taken by Ledger's Joker, in fact, that they collectively adopted him as /b/'s unofficial mascot.

Further fueling the trolls' interest was the film's perceived memetic exploitability, which resulted in an explosion of Batman-related memes. In one meme family, stills of Batman and the Joker are stacked on top of each other—forming what are called "verticals"—and captioned with increasingly absurd invented dialogue, including one exchange in which Batman proclaims that he just "accidentally a [*sic*] whole Coca-Cola bottle" (a play on an earlier, unrelated meme) and asks the Joker if is this bad. Another popular meme offsets a particularly unflattering shot of Batman in full regalia with any number of bizarre captions, including the lamentation "This is why we can't have nice things."[10]

Trolls had the most fun with the film's first official advertisement, in which the Joker traces a bloody outline of the now-infamous catchphrase "Why so serious?" Echoing the trolling maxim that nothing should be taken seriously, "Why so serious?" quickly entered the trolling lexicon and inspired a slew of spin-offs (figure 6.2). Everyone from Sarah Palin to then-candidate Barack Obama was given the "Joker treatment," and jokerized images of cats, babies, and cartoon characters abounded. Depending on the context, the phrase "Why so serious?" was altered to read "Why so curious?" (attached to jokerized images of Curious George), "Why so cereal?" (in reference to an infamous gaffe in which Al Gore mistook the word "cereal" for "serial"), "Why so basement?" (in homage to Josef Fritzl, the Austrian man who imprisoned and repeatedly raped his own daughter), and "Why so dead?" (a question often attached to images of Ledger himself).[11]

As early as the 2008 presidential election, and in response to Republican hysterics over Obama's alleged socialism, trolls began photoshopping the phrase "Why so socialist?" onto images of Obama, and sometime after that, "socialism" became the caption of choice. On August 29, 2008, an Encyclopedia Dramatica user uploaded an image that brought the two tropes

Figure 6.2
Examples of "jokerized" portraits compiled by the author. Images accessed on Encyclopedia Dramatica on September 3, 2013. Image creator(s) and date(s) of creation unknown.

together—Obama made up to look like the Joker, with "socialism" scrawled across his chest.[12] In other words, Joker and socialism (and even Obama *as* socialist Joker) imagery was well established on /b/ by the time the Obama as socialist joker poster story first broke. But this is only half of the Obama as socialist Joker story.

Teabag Patriots

The trouble started the previous April, when right-wing bloggers introduced (or more accurately, reappropriated) the concept of "teabagging" in order to protest Obama's tax policy, the Troubled Asset Relief Program (TARP) bailout of struggling financial institutions (signed under President Bush), and the Obama administration's overall economic agenda. The idea was simple: conservative voters were encouraged to send bags of tea, or photocopied images of tea bags, to their local representatives.[13] These online protests gave way to local protests, which ostensibly provided a forum to discuss economic issues but more often than not served as a sympathy circle for anti-Obama sentiment.

The movement peaked on April 15, 2009, when thousands of protesters participated in local "Tea Party Tax Day" demonstrations. By this point, the movement had lost track of its original message, and protesters, who were almost exclusively white and lower middle-class, descended into "if we disagree with X, then X equals Hitler" territory, a sentiment echoed by the staggering number of angry, violent, and often downright bizarre protest signs. "The American Taxpayers Are the Jews for Obama's Ovens," read one. "Barack Hussein Obama, the New Face of Hitler," read another. "Guns Tomorrow," read a third. In Florida, a six-year-old child waved a sign that promised "We Will Not Go Quietly into the Socialist Night," while a well-dressed businessman obscured his face with the message that Obama is a "SOCiALiST PIG." "Hang 'em high!" read another sign, which offered a list of "Traitors in Congress," including Nancy Pelosi, Harry Reid, Barney Frank, and Ted Kennedy.[14]

The Teabaggers (who around this time quietly rebranded as the Tea Party, perhaps because someone finally Googled the term "teabagging" and realized that it is slang for dipping one's testicles into another person's mouth) introduced this rhetoric into the public sphere; the Birthers, a contingent unconvinced of Obama's U.S. citizenship, brought it to critical mass. Lead by Orly Taitz, an Israeli lawyer-cum-dentist, and encouraged by right-wing political pundits like Rush Limbaugh, Lou Dobbs, and Glenn Beck, the Birthers argued that Obama was born outside the United States, and is therefore ineligible for the presidency. Obama had supplied a birth certificate and is an American citizen, but that wasn't the point. The point was that, to a Birther, Obama was Other, un-American, dangerous. Indeed, as Taitz explained in an interview with faux conservative Stephen Colbert, nothing would convince her of Obama's legitimacy—he'll always be questionable, because his father was from Africa.[15]

Given that Taitz is a lawyer-dentist, it is highly doubtful that she'd never encountered the term "natural-born citizen." But regardless of what Taitz did or did not know about the law she practiced, her statement revealed the inescapable subtext of the Birther movement. It was angry. It was xenophobic. But it was smart enough to keep its racism inferential. Instead of directly addressing the president's race, protesters deployed more TV-friendly allegations, most notably challenges to his citizenship and associations with Hitler and socialism. Because unlike other epithets, you can still say "Hitler" and "socialist" in public.

These not-so-subtle dog whistles were particularly loud during the summer's series of town hall meetings. Designed to provide a public forum for Obama's proposed health care plan, the meetings became a breeding ground for further dissent. As Paul Krugman wryly noted, however, and as illustrated by their oft-shouted invective to "keep your goddamn government hands off my Medicare"[16] (which, for the record, is a government program), the vast majority of these protestors seemed uninterested in having a substantive, issue-driven debate. So what were the protestors actually protesting? According to Krugman, the angry mob was less concerned with what Obama was doing and more concerned with who Obama is.[17] Simply put, he's not like *us*—the "us," here, carrying profound racial and socioeconomic implications.

While many of these town hall meetings were subject to a fair amount of Astroturf—that is, manufactured and often corporate-backed anger (as opposed to legitimate grassroots activity)[18]—the Tea Party and Birther movements represented a very real sense of outrage and helplessness. They even courted a new contingent—the "Deathers," those who swore that Obama was planning to create so-called death panels designed to exterminate every elderly, sick, or disabled person in the country. "Such a system is downright evil," former vice presidential candidate and reality TV star Sarah Palin stated in a Facebook note,[19] and there were plenty of people who strongly agreed.

The Deathers' morbidity was on full display at Obama's August 11 town hall meeting in Portsmouth, New Hampshire. Protesters waved a number of threatening signs, including "Abort Obama (care)," "Obama's Nazi

Death Care Plan," "Government 'Care'=Murder" and "Stop the Trojan Horse of Islam." One sign even featured the Obama as socialist Joker image, although in this particular version the caption merely read "Joker" and was accompanied by a separate printout compelling its audience to "cash this clunker."[20] Fortunately, only one town hall attendee remembered to bring his gun.[21]

A Poster for All Seasons

In other words, it was a particularly ugly summer. So, when the *Los Angeles Times* Obama as socialist Joker story hit in August, the blogosphere was primed for a strong reaction. Conservatives, who have sometimes uncomfortably (and, as evidenced in the U.S. 2010 midterm and 2012 general elections, against their better interests) aligned themselves with the Tea Party/Birther/Deather crowd, were more than happy to take credit. From their perspective, the poster confirmed precisely what they'd been saying for months: Obama was trying to destroy the country with socialism, just like the Joker tried to destroy Gotham City. Granted, the Joker failed, but that was beside the point—to a conservative hell-bent on discrediting the Obama administration, the image was perfect.

Furthermore, because the image was plastered all over Los Angeles, right-wing bloggers were quick to attribute the image to an organized, grassroots effort to contest Obama's allegedly socialist agenda. Conservative radio host Tammy Bruce, for example, tagged the photo with an almost audibly giddy caption that proclaimed "You know B. Hussein is in trouble when . . . ,"[22] while on the right-wing blog Atlas Shrugs, the photo was filed under "The Worm Turns," complete with smiley-face emoticon.[23] Despite the lack of supporting evidence, this was the narrative conservatives chose to adopt.

Similarly, after months of racially charged attacks against the president, liberals couldn't help but see racism in the Obama/Joker image. Philip Kennicott of the *Washington Post* argued that the poster equated Obama with everything that is dangerous and unpredictable within the urban landscape, and by extension, linked the president to all those dark bodies that threaten the purity of some Palin-approved "real" America. Forget the ghoulish whiteness of the Joker's makeup; forget the apparent claim that Obama is a socialist; forget the fact that the Heath Ledger's Joker was an avowed anarchist, making his association with or endorsement of socialism fairly unlikely. According to Kennicott, the take-away point was that, racially speaking, Obama is a wolf in sheep's clothing.[24] *LA Weekly*'s Stephen

Mikulan agreed, claiming that "the only thing missing is a noose,"[25] while Jonathan Jerald of *Bedlam* magazine highlighted its "sort of malicious, racist, Jim Crow quality."[26]

Fear and disgust were not the only emotions on display. Shepard Fairey, the artist responsible for the then-ubiquitous "Obama/Hope" poster, admitted that the Obama/Joker artwork quickly conveyed that Obama was up to something very bad, and in that sense was successful. Still, he explained to *Los Angeles Times* reporter Mark Milian, "I have my doubts about the [artist's] intelligence," since the underlying meaning of the image seemed to contradict the image itself, and suggested a less-than-thorough grasp of the issues.[27] This sentiment was echoed by David Ng at the *Los Angeles Times*, who wrote that the image is "especially disturbing because it is completely devoid of context—literary, political, or otherwise," though he still assumed that the image was borne of malicious, and likely conservative, intent.[28]

Then, on August 17, something unexpected happened: the Obama/ Joker artist was revealed. Much to everyone's surprise, however, he wasn't a rabid conservative. In fact he wasn't a rabid anything. The harshest thing Firas Alkhateeb, a college senior at the University of Illinois, had to say about Obama was that "there wasn't much substance to him," and that he hadn't bothered to vote in the presidential election because, as he explained, his vote wouldn't have mattered. Indeed, this "breaking news" was shocking only in its banality. Seven months earlier, the story went, Alkhateeb decided to test out his Photoshop skills. Using what reporter Mark Milian described as a "tutorial he had found online to 'jokerize' portraits," Alkhateeb downloaded Obama's *Time* Magazine cover and spent half a day tinkering with the president's face. Once finished, he uploaded the image onto his Flickr page.[29]

And this was where things got fuzzy. At some point between January and August, someone saw Alkhateeb's work, downloaded it, and removed the *Time* Magazine typeface. From there, it's anyone's guess as to when the "socialism" tag was added, or who decided to transform the image into street art. "It really doesn't make any sense to me at all," Alkhateeb admitted to Milian. "To accuse [Obama] of being a socialist is really . . . immature. First of all, who said being a socialist is evil?"[30]

Over the next few days, a number of online newspapers and blogs published articles profiling Alkhateeb and his now-infamous image. As is the case with most high-profile stories, a series of talking points emerged: *Firas Alkhateeb, typical college student, didn't mean any harm. He avoided the press as long as he could, for fear of liberal backlash. He doesn't know who altered his file, and doesn't know who posted the posters.* No matter how this information was organized (some started with the image, some started with Alkhateeb), no matter what angle the reporter might have taken (many explored Flickr's role in the controversy, which deleted Alkhateeb's file due to "copyright infringement," while others explored the human-interest angle), every last article mentioned and then brushed aside a major point—with the lone exception of Alkhateeb, everyone associated with the Obama Joker poster image remained anonymous.

This Article Is Part of a Series on Trolls

Remained anonymous. Or more likely, remained Anonymous. Indeed, it is possible to establish links between the nebulous trolling collective and the person or persons responsible for the Los Angeles posters, thereby impeaching the idea that the story began and ended with Alkhateeb.

The most tenuous connection between Anonymous and the Los Angeles poster spree is Alkhateeb himself. As previously discussed, the "Why so serious?" Joker meme was first popularized on 4chan's /b/ board. Consequently, even if Alkhateeb really did visit a how-to website devoted to "jokerizing" images (no one seems to know exactly which website he meant), his photoshopped image contained a trace of the original meme, and therefore gestured toward the culture out of which the urtext emerged. Whether or not Alkhateeb recognized the memetic trace is less important than the fact that there was a trace to recognize.

And this is precisely what trolls did. In fact the Obama/socialism image was so recognizable, and its deployment so characteristically trollish, that Encyclopedia Dramatica cross-linked its "Firas Alkhateeb" article with its long-running series on trolls.[31] This isn't to assert that Alkhateeb had been trolling, or that he ever even set foot on /b/; he could have encountered the Obama/Joker/socialism meme on any number of online forums. It is, however, worth noting that trolls posited this connection and embraced the Los Angeles poster controversy as a collective trolling success.

Alkhateeb wasn't the only link between the Obama/Joker image and Anonymous. As a commentator on *Bedlam Magazine*'s Obama/Joker discussion board explained a few days after the initial story broke, "I don't know about the original creators, but regarding the spread of the poster, I've seen chatter about it on /b/ as early as two weeks ago, with anons claiming to have posted many posters and encouraging others to do the same . . . Some there seem into it as an irreverent joke, others have discussed it as a prank to taunt liberal commentators into accusations of racism."[32]

Given the ephemerality of content on 4chan, it's not possible to verify the *Bedlam* poster's account, nor is it possible to sift through the edit history of Encyclopedia Dramatica (as previously mentioned, all pre-2011 edits to the site were lost). But given the history of the meme, and the fact that the final product fits so perfectly within Anonymous's ethos, it is highly likely that the people responsible for the Los Angeles posters were anons themselves or, at the very least, had a working knowledge of trolling subculture.

Of course, at some point in the evolution of the image, a right-wing activist could have stumbled upon Alkhateeb's file and could have added the word "socialism" as a protest against Obama's health care plan. If the image had been the work of right-wing grassroots activists, however, one would have expected the group to take credit, or at least take advantage of an entire summer's worth of free publicity. As it was, not a soul came forward, and even the furthest far-right blogs were unsure about the poster's origins. Additionally, and as many commentators have noted, the image/word combination is nonsensical at best, bolstering the claim that only someone familiar with the meme would have arrived at that particular message.

But even if rightwing activists had intervened—and I have every reason to believe that the Obama/Joker poster was at the very least amplified by trolls—there would be much more to the story than the Photoshop tinkerings of an apolitical college student. But that was the story the media chose to report. As soon as the basic question was answered—namely, "who did this?"—the conversation stopped. No one knew who modified Alkhateeb's original file, no one knew who posted the posters, no one knew why they may have done so. In fact, the media knew *less* after Alkhateeb's outing than before he came forward. That, however, was only details. It was Firas Alkhateeb, in the computer lab, with his Adobe creative suite.

Ultimately, this was a fortuitous choice—for members of the media, anyway. After all, by attributing authorship to a single, and highly oversimplified, source, the media wouldn't need to examine the ways in which their own coverage fed into and proliferated precisely the sort of racist discourse the poster inspired. They wouldn't need to grapple with the fact that, during this period, there was almost no discernable difference between racist trolling content and racist corporate media content. Alkhateeb's outing shut that conversation down before it could begin.

Outfoxed or Out-Trolled?

Had this conversation not been quashed, Fox News would have proven to be the most consistent, and consistently unapologetic, offender. This is not to assert that individual pundits at Fox or anywhere else are themselves racist. Just as the contents of the trolls' hearts are impossible to verify, so too are the contents of pundits' hearts. I will therefore make no attempt to determine whose racism is real and whose is an act ("I'm not a racist, I just play one on TV"). Not only is this information unverifiable, it's unimportant; regardless of whether or not a person really means the racist things he or she says, the fact that he or she says them has a real and measurable affect on those forced to listen. My argument, then, isn't that the racism deployed by Fox News—again, or anywhere else—is more earnest than racism expressed by trolls. My argument is that it is more toxic.

That caveat writ loud and clear, consider Fox's coverage of the Birther controversy, which first emerged during the 2008 presidential election. In May, a month after Hawaii's Department of Health spokesperson confirmed the authenticity of Obama's Hawaii birth certificate, Fox News' morning show *Fox & Friends* invited right-wing author Jerome Corsi onto the program to discuss the alleged controversy. Corsi proclaimed that online analyses of Obama's birth certificate revealed that the document had Photoshop watermarks—which according to Corsi proved that the document was fake.[33]

Nearly a year later, Fox was still peddling the same nonstory. As Media Matters reporter Eric Hananoki noted,[34] one particularly telling Fox Nation headline read "Should Obama Release Birth Certificate? Or Is This Old News?" Of course, by that point the story *was* old news—this story ran a full nine months after Obama had released all the necessary documents. And yet some people remained unconvinced, a point White House Press Secretary Robert Gibbs was forced to address during a May 2008 briefing, and which Fox Nation subsequently posted under the headline "Gibbs Finally Fields Birth Certificate Question." "This question in many ways continues to astound me," Gibbs said, before once again confirming what had already been confirmed. "I certainly hope, by the fourth year of our administration, that we'll have dealt with this burgeoning birth controversy."[35]

As it turned out, Gibbs's timeline wasn't that farfetched. Fox continued spinning throughout the summer, and in July descended upon a story of a U.S. soldier who—under the counsel of Dentist-at-Law Orly Taitz—refused orders to go to Afghanistan on the grounds that Obama wasn't a "real" American. During his July 14 show, Fox newscaster Bret Baier suggested that the story was one of dozens of legal challenges to the president's citizenship, a statement he failed to qualify with the apparently unimportant detail that none of the challenges had any legal merit. Sean Hannity presented the same story in similar fashion, and described the soldier's claims as merely "controversial" (as opposed to "baseless"). Not only did Hannity not question the soldier's accusations, he failed to indicate that by the time of his broadcast, Georgia's *Ledger-Inquirer* (the source that initially broke the story) had already reported that the Army had revoked the soldier's deployment for unspecified reasons.[36]

Even this wasn't the end of the Fox-fueled Birther craze. That same week, Fox Nation ran an image of Obama wearing traditional Somali clothing alongside an article questioning his citizenship. On July 14, the image was captioned with the headline "Obama Birth Certificate Challenge Wins Small Victory" (without mentioning that the "victory" was in fact part of normal procedural process, i.e., the case had yet to be thrown out). Six days later, on July 20, the same image was re-captioned "Retired Two-Star General Joins Obama Birth Status Suit."[37]

A week later, FoxNews.com published an article claiming that the entire dustup was Obama's fault—for not releasing his birth certificate. "You have to admit," Fox News writer Tommy De Sano mused, "even if you are a devout Obama-bot, Obama's refusal to release any original documents makes for a newsworthy story by itself."[38] Then in August, *Fox & Friends* invited Mark Williams, a professed Birther and organizer of the Tea Party Express (which was funded by the Republican PAC Our Country Deserves Better), onto their program. In the segment teaser, co-host Brian Kilmeade framed the Tea Party Express as an opportunity for citizens to voice their health care concerns, and promised information on how viewers could sign up.[39]

Although Fox never came right out and said that Obama was a dangerous brown foreigner, that was the implied talking point. In addition to cherry-picking evidence (for example in the "Should Obama Release His Birth Certificate" article) and providing the Birthers with a sympathetic platform, Fox unabashedly gave equal face time to unequal positions. Namely, paranoid speculation was not equivalent to the fact that Obama was born in the United States. By placing unfounded assertions alongside verifiable facts, as if one were just as credible as the next, Fox legitimized— and therefore implicitly endorsed—the Birthers' expressly xenophobic and racist concerns.

The Birther controversy—which was controversial only in so far as the story was amplified by conservative media outlets—wasn't the first time Fox's coverage of Obama engaged with and amplified existing racist discourse. In the lead-up to the 2008 election, Fox sounded a number of racist alarms, including concern over Obama's name, particularly his middle name ("Barack *Hussein* Obama" was a common Fox soundbite during this time),[40] as well as his alleged Muslim leanings. Despite the fact that Obama had been very public about his Christian faith, Fox pounced on the possibility that Obama was a "secret Muslim," and when news broke that Obama had attended a madrassa (translation: school) while living in Indonesia as a child, Fox went into overdrive. *Fox & Friends* co-host Steve Doocy reiterated the fact that Barack Obama's father (a foreigner!) had given his son the middle name "Hussein"; that young Obama had attended a madrassa; that madrassas were financed by Saudis and were aligned with the Wahhabism, an ultraconservative sect of Islam; that Wahhabism teachings probably weren't on the curriculum back them but could have been; that Obama reportedly attends a Christian church in Chicago, but was raised as a Muslim; and in case viewers missed it the first time, that Obama attended a madrassa.[41]

Doocy repeated the sentiment during a later broadcast, twice asserting that Barack Obama had been raised as a Muslim, and intimating that this revelation was (or should be) a game-changer.[42] When the Obama camp pushed back against the erroneous claim that he had attended an extremist school, Doocy countered not by correcting his original statement, but by saying that the Obama camp had *said* Obama hadn't attended an extremist school.[43]

Speculation over Obama's rumored Muslim roots and brown skin generally reached a fever pitch in June of 2008, when Obama clenched the Democratic presidential nomination. Following his victory speech, he and his wife Michelle celebrated with a gesture Fox News contributor E. D. Hill flippantly described as a "terrorist fist jab."[44] Hill's comment received a great deal of blowback, and later that week Fox replaced her show with another (though Hill was not fired from the network). Specifically, Hill was replaced by conservative pundit Laura Ingraham, who two months later would tell Bill O'Reilly that there was something sinister and off-putting about Michelle Obama.[45] One year later, Glenn Beck echoed that very point when he speculated that Obama might hate white people or white culture, he wasn't sure which. When pressed, Beck backpeddled (somewhat) and explained that he wasn't suggesting that Obama didn't *like* white people, just that he believed Obama was a racist.[46]

Fox News image   Troll image

Figure 6.3
Comparison of two racist images, one troll-made and another Fox-made, formatted by the author. Screencap from The Fox Nation taken and posted to Media Matters on July 20, 2009; troll-made image posted to Encyclopedia Dramatica on November 7, 2009 (site since deleted). Image creator(s) and date(s) of creation unknown.

During this same period, trolls on 4chan/b/ and elsewhere latched onto and eagerly *détourned* the most outrageous pages in Fox's campaign playbook, resulting in troll-made content that was at times almost identical to Fox's content. For a striking example, consider the following comparison between two contemporaneous images: one that was featured in the aforementioned Fox Nation Birther articles, and one that circulated the /b/ board before being posted to Encyclopedia Dramatica (figure 6.3).

The turban featured in both images was hardly the only visual, political, or rhetorical point of overlap between troll-made and mainstream content. During this time, participating trolls fixated on Obama's middle name, eagerly amplified concerns over his secret Kenyan and/or Muslim and/or Socialist roots, and decried his alleged anti-white leanings. They photoshopped Obama's head onto the bodies of black men with exaggerated genitalia, many of whom were having sex with white women. They placed the president alongside watermelon, buckets of fried chicken and food stamps, and created a slew of images likening him to Stalin, Hitler, and, of course, the Joker.

Troll-made content may have been extreme, but its underlying themes—Obama is other, dangerous, un-American, inferior—echoed the spirit not just of Fox's coverage, but of coverage on more ostensibly neutral outlets. Indeed, longtime CNN anchor Lou Dobbs, who in 2007 weathered criticism for his anti-immigration rants and willingness to host white supremacist leaders on his program,[47] spent the summer of 2009 fretting about Obama's "missing" long-form birth certificate. Dobbs's coverage was so persistent and so egregious that it prompted Phil Griffin, resident of rival news network MSNBC, to state bluntly: "It's racist. Just call it for what it is."[48] Then-President of CNN/U.S. Jon Klein disagreed, insisting that Dobbs's coverage of the story was "legitimate" (although he himself acknowledged that the story was "dead").[49]

But even those outlets and programs that avoided forwarding overtly racist content were guilty, at the very least, of providing bigots a national audience, and for further normalizing racist discourse and stereotypes (a criticism from which Phil Griffin isn't immune, as his network was a longtime employer of lightning rod conservative Pat Buchanan, who was ultimately suspended from the network for the racist, anti-Semitic, and homophobic undertones of his 2012 book *Suicide of a Superpower: Will American Survive to 2025?*).[50] Again, this is not to say that network employees, even those most complicit in perpetuating racist coverage, were themselves racist. That information is unverifiable and beside the point. The point is that racist hysterics over Obama's birthplace, middle name, religion, and brown skin had indeed become "legitimate" news, to borrow Klein's framing—not because any of it really was legitimate, but because racism directed at Obama was *profitable*, and was therefore regarded by corporate media outlets as being worth repeating, and repeating, and repeating, perhaps to further a white supremacist agenda, perhaps to further a capitalist agenda, perhaps some combination of both. Whatever the motivations might have been, the outcome—namely, grotesque racist caricature—remained the same.

Why So Serious, Indeed

Given the swirl of direct and inferential racism surrounding the early years of President Obama's first term, it is therefore unsurprising that the Obama as socialist Joker image would be taken seriously (and in many instances, actively embraced) both within the troll space and by sensationalist media outlets. This sort of racist expression was par for the trolling course. It was just as common in mainstream media circles, with dishonorable mention going to Fox News.

The following example further illustrates just how fuzzy the line between racist trolling humor and "legitimate" punditry could be. Directly following Obama's presidential victory, an unflattering image of rapper Lil Wayne began circulating the /b/ board. His face covered in tattoos and his teeth studded with diamonds, Lil Wayne can't seem to focus on whatever it is he's attempting to observe. "WE PRESIDENT NOW," the caption reads.[51]

Though clearly and unabashedly racist, the WE PRESIDENT NOW macro echoes a public statement made by Tammy Bruce, the archconservative blogger who first adopted the Obama as socialist Joker image for the Republican cause. Laura Ingraham, the Fox News correspondent who replaced Hill following the "terrorist fist jab" controversy, and current official guest host of *The O'Reilly Factor*, asked friend-of-the-show Bruce to guest-host her March 23 radio program. "You know what we've got?" Bruce stated on-air. "We've got trash in the White House." She quickly backpedaled—again, as only political pundit can—and insisted that "trash" was "color blind" because it crosses all "eco . . . ecosocionomic [*sic*] kind of categories . . . Trash are people who use other people to get things, who patronize others, and who consider you bitter and clingy."[52]

Using this logic (to the extent that it can be described as such), the Obamas are "trash" because they haven't earned what they have; they are successful only because they've taken resources and opportunities away from those who truly deserve them; and because they are condescending toward others. Put more explicitly, the Obamas are affirmative action hires, are uppity, and look down on "bitter and clingy" white folk—an accusation that only makes sense in the context of a 2008 speech made by then-candidate Obama, in which Obama suggested that people from small, economically devastated areas of the country "get bitter [and] cling to guns or religion or antipathy to people who aren't like them or anti-immigrant sentiment or anti-trade sentiment as a way to explain their frustrations."[53]

Rather than tempering her statement, then, Bruce's somewhat bizarre qualification belies its ugly racial implications. Her basic argument is that the current occupants of the White House are fundamentally unfit for the job—because they are different from, and inherently less than, what she implicitly refers to as "us"—namely, "real" Americans, namely, white people.

I would argue that ultimately, Bruce's statement is no less offensive, and no less racist, than WE PRESIDENT NOW. The difference is that Bruce—like so many conservative media figures, particularly those affiliated with Fox

News—was engaging in inferential racism, while the trolls were trafficking in unambiguous, unapologetic, and undeniably *overt* racism. Whatever their real-life political affiliations, whatever their true attitudes toward Barack Obama's candidacy or people of color generally, trolls were shouting from the rooftops precisely the attitudes that were being communicated via dog whistle in more ostensibly "civilized" forums. So condemn the trolls' behavior, absolutely. But don't forget that trolls are not the only guilty parties. In fact their actions are merely the tip of the cultural iceberg—the full depth of which is the focus of the following chapter.

7 Dicks Everywhere: The Cultural Logics of Trolling

One of the 1980s' most recognizable anti-drug public service announcements features a heated confrontation between a father and his teenaged son. The father brandishes a box of drug paraphernalia, apparently discovered in his son's closet, and demands an explanation. "Who taught you how to do this?" the father asks, his voice shaking. The son looks up. "You, alright?" he admits. "I learned it by watching *you*." The camera lingers on the father's stunned face. "Parents who use drugs have children who use drugs," the announcer warns.[1]

Despite the ad's melodramatic tone and questionable assumptions, the argument that parents should consider the repercussions of their own actions (thereby impugning the hypocritical "do as I say, not as I do" parental imperative) is directly applicable to analyses of trolls. Specifically, knee-jerk condemnation of trolling does not and cannot account for the fact that trolling behaviors run parallel to a host of culturally accepted logics. Trolls may push these logics to their furthest and most grotesque extremes, but ultimately trolls' actions are imbricated in the same cultural systems that constitute the norm—a point that casts as much aspersion on the systems themselves as it does on the trolls who harness and exploit them.

The Mask of Trolling, Revisited

Building upon my previous discussion of the mask of trolling, this section will consider the cultural circumstances by and through which the mask of trolling was forged. It will also explicate the ways in which trolling behaviors mirror—and therefore shine an uncomfortable spotlight on—conventional behaviors and attitudes. Three discrete factors will be considered: the relationship between mass mediation, emotional distance, and off-color laughter; the ways in which trolling behaviors replicate the logic of social media, particularly its celebration of the end user; and the behavioral implications of political upheaval.

Rubbish Rubbish Everywhere

The first factor undergirding the mask of trolling is the relationship between mass mediation and dissociative humor. Christie Davies posits this connection in his essay "Jokes That Follow Mass Mediated Disaster in a Global Electronic Age." Davies argues that, rather than merely expressing callousness, laughter in the face of violent or otherwise tragic events bespeaks a particular set of historical and technological conditions.[2] As Davies explains, "sick" humor has been around since people began writing down jokes. But even the sickest jokes did not, as far as anyone can tell, take the form of the modern disaster joke. Moreover, while people certainly commented upon gruesome news, this commentary never evolved into traceable joke cycles (clusters of jokes that emerge, evolve, and eventually plateau in response to specific tragedies). Significant historical events have inspired quite a bit of retroactive joking—for example, the sinking of the Titanic or the assassination of Abraham Lincoln—but Davies contends that this humor didn't become prominent until after the events were widely theatricalized.[3]

As Davies explains, the first major disaster joke cycle followed President Kennedy's assassination and coincided with what he describes as the "total triumph of television."[4] Davies presents three causes for this connection. First, he argues, disasters in the television age are followed and preceded by "rubbish," creating an incongruous package to respond to, therefore complicating or outright undermining normal expressions of human empathy. Second, television blurs the line between reality and fantasy, fact and fiction. Live disasters are thus conflated with fictional representations of disasters, precluding the viewer from truly believing that the event has taken place, and mitigating the impact of real tragedy when it really strikes. Finally, the experience of watching a televised tragedy is mediated by space, time, and geography, facilitating and sometimes even necessitating emotional detachment, and therefore cynical or comedic responses.[5]

Although Davies's analysis is focused on the ways in which television spurs disaster joke cycles—he does address the Internet, but writing in the early 2000s sees the web more as an infinite bulletin board than an actively generative social space[6]—his underlying argument is directly applicable to the contemporary Internet. In fact, I would argue that today's Internet, which is more incongruous then the most scattered variety show, which collapses the boundaries of reality and fantasy even further, and which posits ever-greater distance between viewer and that which is viewed, handily outmediates television.

Of course I want to avoid the assumptions, with which Davies seems to flirt, that technological advances singlehandedly bring about the emergence of novel behaviors, and furthermore that consumers of mass-mediated content are so gullible and so devoid of agency that in response to the slightest corporate prodding they lose the ability to distinguish fiction from reality. But Davies's basic point, that mass mediation engenders emotional distance, and that emotional distance lends itself to detached, fetishistic humor, is extremely illuminating, especially in the context of trolling.

Consider trolls' highly fetishized engagement with the attacks of September 11, 2001. The most popular photoshopped images and GIFs include World Wrestling Federation wrestlers smashing the towers to bits; Will Smith as the Fresh Prince of Bel-Air tap dancing as the first tower falls; Kanye West scolding both towers ("Yo al Qaeda, I'm a really happy for you, and I'mma let you finish . . .but the war of 1812 was the best attack on US soil of all time!"); Nyan Cat at the moment of impact ("Nyan 11: Nevar Forget"); Where's Waldo careening out of the dust clouds wearing a troll mask; the Kool-Aid man emerging from the rubble; Obi-Wan Kenobi making racist jokes about "sand people"; the just-stricken towers crudely animated to look like two stick figures smoking a joint, the list goes on. In other images, actual news stills are superimposed with all kinds of bizarre captions, including vague memetic references (of the planes themselves: "no you are a plane, you can't work in an office, you don't even fit"; "do a barrel roll"), deliberately bad wordplay ("9/11 jokes are just 'plane' wrong"; "9/11 Americans won't understand this joke"), and assertions of ironic detachment (of a jumper: "Maybe that was a little dramatic").

Although the trolls' engagement with 9/11 might seem particularly callous, it provides a striking example of the complimentary relationship between trolling humor and mass—and in this case, digitally—mediated disaster coverage. After all, once uploaded onto the Internet, clips and images of the attacks were cast into a whirlpool of incongruity, from animated movie stills to videos of cute cats to hardcore pornography. And then there are the advertisements. A single webpage may host a dozen ads, some of which flash, some of which are embedded with audio, and all of which both frame and detract from whatever it is the viewer thinks he or she is focusing on. If television broadcasts of the attacks would have been emotionally alienating—thus courting detached comedic responses, as folklorist Bill Ellis chronicled in his study of joke cycles directly following the September 11, 2001, attacks[7]—then digitized reposts of the attacks would have been infinitely more so.

Trolls' ability to transform existing artifacts into visual jokes further widens this affective gap. Unlike viewers who watched live analog coverage of the attacks, trolls have had nearly fifteen years to manipulate facsimiles of the attacks to suit their particular needs, most notably their impulse to juxtapose death and destruction with pop-cultural iconography. As Davies would have predicted, the more decontextualized these images became, and the more cluttered their audience's field of vision (figuratively and literally), the more likely it was that these images would become fodder for further memetic variation, further affective distance, and further troll-ish engagement.

That trolls have harnessed the September 11 attacks for their own troll-ish ends isn't just unsurprising, then; it may be the direct result of the kind of clutter and emotional splitting necessitated by the present media land-scape—what might be described as the "total triumph of the Internet." From this perspective, trollish play with tragedy is what happens when current events become *content*, a term frequently (and cynically) used in the blogosphere to describe the various bits of digital stuff that may be shared, remixed, and of course monetized through advertisements.

Trolling for Filter Bubbles

Incessant disjointed multimediation isn't the only condition out of which the mask of trolling emerges. The mask is also forged from the cultural logic of social media, which values, and in many cases directly commodi-fies, transparency, connectedness, and sentimentality. Trolls don't just reject these values; they deliberately target their most conspicuous propo-nents. That said, and simultaneously, trolls embody and in fact are the grimacing poster children for the more ambivalent aspects of socially mediated web culture, namely objectification, selective attachment, and pervasive self-involvement, all of which fuel the desire for and amassment of lulz *and* constitute "proper" engagement with social networking technologies.

Consider the difficulty of establishing and maintaining context online, and the ways in which context, or lack thereof, feeds into detached emo-tional responses (and therefore detached unemotional laughter, echoing the previous section). As Henry Jenkins argues, online content, whether in the form of home-brewed videos or family photos or remixed sound bites ripped from the local news—really anything that can be uploaded—is always one hotlink away from becoming unmoored from its original context.[8] If one looks hard enough, it is usually possible to trace most artifacts back to their original source. After all, everything online comes from somewhere, whether or not a particular viewer has the ability or inclination to conduct such a genealogy. That said, online content is rarely presented in full political, material, and/or historical context. More often than not, content functions as the visual equivalent of a sound bite—a few interesting seconds clipped from a much longer conversation.

Just as offline sound bites can present a skewed picture of what was actually said (as if one sentence could ever capture the spirit and nuance of an hour-long speech), problems arise when the things people do, share, and create are appropriated by an unintended and often unwanted audience. See Star Wars Kid (a chubby high school student who recorded himself clumsily reenacting a scene from the latest *Star Wars* film, the video of which was uploaded by a classmate and began amassing tens of millions of views), Scumbag Steve (a Boston-based rapper whose image was posted to reddit and quickly became the meme de jour), Goatse (whose gaping asshole has become a cultural icon, at least within certain Internet circles[9]), Rebecca Black (whose unintentionally funny 2011 vanity music video catapulted the teenager into the national spotlight), Antoine Dodson (who was featured in a local news report responding to the "bed intruder" who attempted to rape his sister), and so on. All found themselves thrust under the online microscope, and all made the often uncomfortable, and necessarily objectifying, transition from person to meme.

Despite the fact that each story represents a very real person navigating a very real set of social circumstances, the people behind the memes were immediately reduced to grotesque caricatures—a transformation that is perfectly in line with the logic of social media. Because content is so easily severed from creator, and because information spreads so quickly online, often in reverse-snowball form (in that contextualizing information is lost over time, not accrued), it is inevitable that real people would be reduced to fictionalized things. Not in spite of or incidental to the architecture of the web, but as a direct result of the ways in which its constituent content is created, spread, and engaged.

Specifically, Internet users are free, if not actively encouraged, to engage only the content he or she chooses, and to avoid the content he or she might find objectionable or otherwise uninteresting. Rather than functioning as the ultimate democratizing and pluralizing force, then, the web is, and is designed to be, a portal for what Eli Pariser calls "online filter bubbles"—personalized monads fortified not just by individual choice (frequenting only those blogs you agree with, hiding the posts of Facebook friends you hate, blocking undesirable followers on Twitter or Tumblr) but also by algorithmic interventions by superplatforms such as Google and Facebook, whose robots note the things you seem to like and the things you seem to avoid, and quietly begin stacking the deck with the former.[10]

According to Facebook CEO Mark Zuckerberg, such bubbles are a blessing to the user. As he once noted, "a squirrel dying in front of your house may be more relevant to your interests right now than people dying in Africa."[11] In other words, if you don't want to engage with certain content, you shouldn't have to. Outside Facebook and Google's walled gardens, users even have the option to preempt offending content, a concept Greg Leuch has explored through his numerous self-censorship plug-ins—for example, his "Shaved Bieber" project, which blocks all references to the ubiquitous Canadian teen,[12] and his "Olwimpics browser blocker," which does the same for any and all references to the 2012 Olympics.[13]

It should go without saying that picking and choosing online, not to mention being picked and chosen for, is an enormous privilege, one that risks normalizing selective emotional attachment. Trolls take this privilege to the extreme, choosing to engage with only the content they find amusing and ignoring everything they deem irrelevant to their interests (e.g., their target's feelings). Their resulting lulz fetishism may appear foreign to average Internet users, but they are in fact subsumed by the same cultural logic that undergirds "normal" online engagement.

"Now Watch This Drive"

In August 2002, just before teeing off for his morning game of golf, President George W. Bush held an impromptu press conference. He'd just gotten word that a Palestinian suicide bomber had killed several Israeli citizens, and he wanted to send an unequivocal message to terrorists around the world. His eyes steely, Bush looked directly into the camera. "We must stop the terror," he urged. "I call upon all nations to do everything they can to stop these terrorist killers. Thank you. Now watch this drive."[14]

Bush's comments did not go unnoticed. On *The Daily Show*, Jon Stewart featured the clip in the closing "Your Moment of Zen" segment,[15] and Michael Moore included it in a pivotal scene of *Fahrenheit 9/11*.[16] In both cases, the clip was used to highlight the Bush administration's heavy-handed and often dizzyingly inconsistent post-9/11 tone. On the one hand, Americans were told to remain vigilant against further terrorist attacks. On the other hand, Osama bin Laden was dismissed as a nobody by the very president who vowed to capture him dead or alive. This was an era in which citizens were urged by the Department of Homeland Security to prepare for possible anthrax attacks by stocking up on plastic wrap and duct tape, and were told by the president that the best way to fight terrorism was to relax, have fun, and take a family vacation to Disneyland.[17]

America was at war, and then wars, and the justification for the larger of these two wars kept changing, and at a certain point the talking heads stopped bothering to offer any reason, and the looming terrorist apocalypse was assigned a color-coded alert system, which miraculously would be raised whenever an election or important congressional vote loomed, and torture was deemed A-OK so long as it was conducted for democracy's sake, and patriotism trumped rule of law, and the president made jokes about looking for weapons of mass destruction under his Oval Office desk,[18] and the Geneva Conventions were suddenly "quaint" (at least according to then-White House Chief Council Alberto Gonzales),[19] and sometimes the only thing you could do to keep from crying was to laugh.

It was in this political climate that subcultural trolling and its constituent mask first emerged, a statement reflected in the following Encyclopedia Dramatica entry on lulz: "Lulz is engaged by internet users who have witnessed one major economic/environmental/political disaster too many," the entry reads, "and who thus view a state of voluntary, gleeful sociopathy over the world's current apoplectic state, as being superior to being continually emo."[20] This attitude was common among many of the trolls I worked with, who argued that it was better to have a trollfest than a bawwfest (in trolling parlance, bawwing means crying, and is often used alongside or in the context of the term "butthurt"; for example, the accusation that a person expressing a strong negative emotion is a "butthurt bawwfag").

Let me be clear: I am not implying that the September 11 attacks—including fallout from the wars in Afghanistan and Iraq—caused trolling subculture to coalesce, or caused the mask of trolling to fall pre-forged from the heavens. As discussed in earlier chapters, geeks and hackers had been causing mischief online for years, decades in some circles, and the term "troll" had long been in circulation on Usenet. Trolling was not, in other words, the sole creation of 4chan's platform, nor could it be.

Henry Jenkins explores a similar point in his analysis of YouTube's cultural ascendency, in which he argues that successful platforms rarely if ever engender entirely new categories of behavior. Rather, these platforms provide users with more efficient ways of doing the things they were already doing. YouTube's success, for example, wasn't derived from its ability to spur participatory/remix culture(s), but from its ability to court and provide a forum for existing communities and participatory remix culture(s). Without a built-in audience for home-brewed content, YouTube would not and could not have been such an overwhelming success.[21]

The same basic argument could be made about 4chan. The message board didn't and couldn't *create* the impulse to engage in trolling behaviors as much as tap into and provide a forum—and later, point of amplification—for existing energies. And there was plenty of energy to go around. The young web was swirling with mischief, pranks, and what would become known as "ultra-coordinated motherfuckery," to borrow a term from Coleman.[22] The difference between these behaviors and subcultural trolling behaviors was that early proto-trollish energies were for the most part confined to early adopters, primarily hackers and geeks. 4chan changed all that; 4chan, particularly the /b/ board, brought a very particular understanding of the term "trolling" to the wider Internet. Not because there was anything inherently new or even all that special about these particular behaviors. It was simply the right time and right place for something like 4chan/b/—and something like subcultural trolling—to reach critical mass.

The fact that it was *this* place and *this* time matters, and must be taken into account when considering not just how and when trolling subculture emerged, but why it caught on with so many people. Of particular importance is the fact that, during this period, Americans were unmoored, and were encouraged by the mainstream media and the Bush administration to remain unmoored—from history, from war, from the suffering of others, from the suffering of fellow citizens.

Of course, for New Yorkers and those who lost friends or family members in the attacks, September 11 was and remains a flesh-and-blood nightmare. The same holds true for returning veterans, as well as the loved ones of those deployed. For the vast majority of Americans, though, 9/11 was experienced as an endless loop of the same forty-five seconds of film, particularly the horrific spectacle of the second plane crashing into the South Tower. Similarly, for millions of Americans, both wars were only ever experienced remotely (i.e., via the news or online), making them no less real and no less upsetting but eerily removed from day-to-day life—a disconnect compounded by the Bush administration's insistence that unless Americans went about their daily lives as if nothing was wrong, the terrorists would win.

In short, Americans were asked to dissociate. They were asked not to dwell on the consequences of the wars, of torture, of the resulting economic bloodletting. They were asked to go on vacations, and to shop, and not to ask too many tough questions. Is it any surprise, then, that trolls—who essentially function as cultural dung beetles—would choose to hold the tragedy of others at arm's length? Is it any surprise that trolling, which crystallized into a discrete subculture immediately following a series of massively mediated tragedies, would be explicitly and unapologetically fetishistic? Furthermore, is it any surprise that instead of crying, these trolls would have chosen to laugh, not just *with* other self-identifying trolls, but *at* those who fail to keep their emotions similarly in check?

Whether or not there exists an alternative explanation or nest of explanations for the development of trolls' dissociative behaviors, the uncomfortable truth is that trolls weren't the only group to disengage from social or political consequences, nor were they the most likely to harness tragedy for personal gain. This is particularly true during the period of subcultural origin, roughly between 2003 and 2007, during which time September 11 became its own sort of fetish—at least for the politicians who mined the attacks for votes (I am reminded of then-presidential candidate Joe Biden's assertion that former New York City Mayor Rudy Giuliani's presidential campaign platform could be summarized as "a noun and a verb and 9/11"[23]).

To summarize, regardless of how aberrant (and/or abhorrent) it may appear, trolling makes a great deal of sense within the context of contemporary American media. Trolls make expert use of the creative tools provided by the Internet. Their attitudes toward and use of social media is often in direct alignment with the interests of platform marketers, CEOs, and their corporate shareholders. They harness the contours of the historical and political landscape, and the corporate media systems therein. In a lot of ways, trolls do everything right. But that is hardly the extent of the connection between trolls and dominant cultural logics.

Dicks Everywhere

In addition to operating within mainstream media logics, trolls and trolling behaviors replicate and are animated by a number of pervasive cultural logics. Not only is trolling predicated on the "adversary method," Western philosophy's dominant paradigm,[24] it is characterized by a profound sense of technological entitlement born of normalized expansionist and colonialist ideologies. Furthermore, trolling behaviors are undergirded by precisely the values that are said to make America the greatest and most powerful nation on earth. In other words, there is ample cultural precedent for trolling; that anyone is subsequently surprised by the ubiquity of trolls is itself surprising.

Your Resistance Only Makes My Penis Harder

First, trolls' privileging of cool rationality over emotionalism, coupled with their emphasis on "winning," that is, successfully exerting dominance over a given adversary, represents a logical extension of androcentrism, what cultural theorist Pierre Bourdieu describes as the "continuous, silent, invisible injunctions" that naturalize a phallocentric (male-focused) worldview. Though androcentrism may manifest itself as violent sexism or misogyny, it is in fact most potent when its effects are taken to be natural and necessary, something that could not be otherwise.[25]

Trolls' alignment with androcentrism is most conspicuously apparent in their replication of the adversary method, described by feminist philosopher Janice Moulton as the defining feature of the Western philosophical canon. As Moulton explains, the goal of this method is to be cool, calm, and unflinchingly rational; to forward specific claims; and to check those claims against potential counterarguments, all in the service of defeating or otherwise outmaneuvering one's opponent(s).[26] Although seemingly unassailable (how else might we hope to argue things, one might ask), the adversary method provides a textbook example of androcentrism and in the process exemplifies the subtle ways in which male-focused thinking is naturalized. Specifically, in addition to establishing the ground rules for "proper" argumentation, the adversary method presupposes the superiority of male-gendered traits (rationality, assertiveness, dominance) over female-gendered traits (sentimentality, cooperation, conciliation). In the process, it privileges and in fact reifies an explicitly androcentric worldview while simultaneously delegitimizing less confrontational discursive modes.[27]

Arthur Schopenhauer's *The Art of Controversy*, also translated as *The Art of Being Right*, perfectly embodies the adversary method.[28] Though by no means the only example one could cite (Schopenhauer's arguments pull from and expand upon a well-established rhetorical tradition, most notably Aristotelian logic), *The Art of Controversy* is unique in that many trolls regard it as a blueprint for modern trolling. In fact this text was recommended to me by one of my troll collaborators, with the promise that I would find in Schopenhauer a kindred spirit for trolls.

And indeed I did, particularly Schopenhauer's understanding of the Controversial Dialectic, "the art of disputing, and of disputing in such a way as to hold one's own, whether one is in the right or the wrong."[29] As

Schopenhauer explains, what something really means, and more importantly, what someone really feels, is less important than one's ability to win a particular argument. In other words, truth is nice, but victory is better; to help ensure the latter, Schopenhauer offers thirty-eight axioms essentially designed to hack the Dialectic.

For example, in order to win an argument, or perhaps more appropriately phrased, in order to defeat one's opponent, one strategy is to carry his or her opponent's claim "beyond its natural limits,"[30] thereby forcing the opponent to accept responsibility for a straw man, which may then be refuted by a series of counterarguments. Another is to deliberately court the anger of an opponent "by doing him repeated injustice, or practicing some kind of chicanery, and being generally insolent,"[31] since an angry opponent is often a frazzled and therefore sloppy opponent. Other tips include replacing the language used by an opponent to describe his or her position with terminology that exaggerates or casts aspersions upon that position and, consequently, its proponents (i.e., referring to abortion as baby killing), or personalizing arguments by demanding that the opponent practice what he preaches (i.e., during a discussion of assisted suicide, encouraging one's opponent to go kill himself if he thinks it's such a good idea).

Most trollishly, Schopenhauer urges his readers to push against any and all resistance, since anger almost always indicates insecurity and therefore argumentative weakness. The goal is to aim for the lowest possible personal blows, not just in relation to an opponent's argument but in relation to his person, family, friends, income, race, or anything that might appeal to what Schopenhauer calls the "virtues of the body, or to mere animalism."[32] Regarding this last tip, perhaps the sharpest tool in the rhetorician's arsenal, Schopenhauer warns that an opponent is likely to respond in kind and begin hurling his own insults. If and when that happens, one must remind one's opponent that personal insults have no place in a rational discussion and request that he or she consider the issue at hand—at which point one may return to one's own insults and prevarications.[33]

Trolls take a similar approach, explicitly eschewing the pursuit of truth— typically by bracketing "real life" from the adversarial play space—in favor of victory, and more importantly, dominance. Furthermore, trolls take active, gleeful measures against rhetorical others—namely, "soft," feminized thinkers. For trolls, softness implies anything emotive, anything less than perfectly rational; they see strong negative emotions like sadness, frustration, or distress (referred to collectively as "butthurt") as flashing neon target signs. Ironically, trolls court the very modes of thinking they subsequently attack. They poke and prod their targets until they draw metaphorical blood—note the popular trolling declaration and current section header "your resistance only makes my penis harder"—then point to this blood as proof of the troll's inherent superiority, and the target's inherent weakness.

Not only does "knowing how to rhetoric" (as I've heard many trolls describe their discursive methods) serve as a point of pride for trolls, it provides a built-in justification for their antagonistic behaviors. After all, if cool rationality is in fact superior to "softer" modes of thinking, then denigrating and attempting to silence the feminized other isn't just warranted, it is the trolls' cultural duty (in response to their target's distress, "you're welcome" was an attitude frequently expressed by the trolls I worked with). Ultimately, then, the primary difference between "normal" manifestations of the adversary method and modern subcultural trolling is that participating trolls make absolutely no attempt to sugarcoat the ideological implications and inherent sexism of their behaviors.

Trolls' eagerness to align themselves with adversarial rhetoric—and by extension, the Western tradition—is further exemplified by their obsession with and adoption of the figure of Socrates. As the editor(s) of the "Socrates" entry on Encyclopedia Dramatica explain, "Socrates was a famous IRL troll of pre-internets [sic] Greece credited with inventing the first recorded trolling technique and otherwise laying the foundation of the science of lulz. He is widely considered to be the most irritating man in history."[34] Accompanying this statement is a quotation from *The Apology* in which Socrates proclaims, "I am that gadfly which God has attached to the state, and all day long and in all places am always fastening upon you, arousing and persuading and reproaching you," and that is captioned with the statement "Socrates explains trolling." Later in the article, the editor(s) explains "the famous Socratic Method of Trolling," which replicates the well-known trolling meme template discussed in chapter 4:

*Ask a bunch of questions about shit nobody cares about
*Be blatantly condescending while pretending to agree
*Raep your victim with logic
*Pretend to be objective and ignorant
*Put forth a batshit insane position for lulz
*???
*Profit

In a final flourish of reclamation, the author(s) of the post claim that Socrates's last words were "I did it for the lulz," and the entry itself is tagged as part of a series on trolls.[35]

In a 2012 segment filmed for Huffington Post live, notorious troll weev—the once-president of the trolling and hacking collective known as the GNAA ("Gay Nigger Association of America"), who was sent to prison in 2013 for his role in Goatse Security's AT&T data breach before being released in 2014 after the conviction was overturned on a venue technicality—elaborated on this sentiment. "Socrates would be a troll," weev argued. "He was confrontational. He was specifically trying to provoke a reaction and was trying to undermine the existing establishment."[36] In short, Socrates "raeped" with logic—"raep" being the preferred misspelling for "rape," which according to many trolls is the best of all possible trolling outcomes.

For an example of why trolls would be so inclined to adopt Socrates for the trolling cause, consider Socrates's comportment throughout *Meno*, which begins with an examination of the nature of virtue.[37] Meno, Socrates's interlocutor, asserts knowledge; Socrates professes ignorance; Meno forwards an explanation; Socrates proceeds to beat Meno over the head with his own words, stopping only to berate Meno for rhetorical chicanery and to lob strange, backhanded compliments. Midway through the onslaught, Meno seeks a reprieve. "I think you are bewitching and beguiling me, simply putting me under a spell, so that I am quite perplexed . . . my mind and my tongue are numb, and I have no answer to give you."[38] Meno has, in other words, given up. But Socrates isn't finished. He calls Meno a rascal and accuses him of deception, propelling the conversation forward despite Meno's objections, and despite having already proven his point—a point he immediately undermines by pivoting to divine intervention, a move many classicists read as ironic.[39]

Socrates might not assert a singular answer to the question of virtue, or any question for that matter. But by policing the borders of "correct" philosophical engagement, Socrates reifies a particular discursive mode—namely the Socratic method (not that he would have called it that himself), which isn't a position as much as it is an attitude toward the pursuit of answers. In their efforts to extract the greatest number of lulz from the most "deserving" online targets, trolls take this approach to its most antagonistic conclusions. Furthermore, while both camps refuse to forward a particular politics, and in fact target those who appear too emotionally invested in their ideals, both impose and are subsumed by a rigid rhetorical model, one that privileges and universalizes a male-focused worldview. In others, such rigidity would be unacceptable. But as long as they're the ones tossing off the philosophical or emotional imperatives, the problem of attachment is apparently moot.

It is therefore no surprise that trolls would be inclined to adopt Socrates as one of their own. But even for those resistant to the idea that Socrates was indeed "a famous IRL troll of pre-internets Greece," the fact that trolls have chosen as their intellectual mascot one of the most venerated and fetishized figures in the Western tradition, whose rhetorical method is taught to every college undergraduate in the United States, is significant in itself. Also of significance is the fact that, while trolls and trolling behaviors are condemned as aberrational, similarly antagonistic—and highly gendered—rhetorical methods are presumed to be something to which every eighteen-year-old should aspire. This is, to say the very least, a curious double standard. Trolling might be more conspicuously outrageous, offensive, and damaging than traditional discursive modes, but what does it say about the cloth if misogyny can so easily be cut from it?

Go Forth and Conquer

In addition to embodying the adversary method, trolling is animated by the same cultural logic that normalizes the drive for discovery and progress. To go further, to go faster, to go where no one (well, no one deemed important enough to count) has gone before—this is, at least is said to be, the defining feature of Western culture, a point Robert Nisbet iterates in his expansive *History of the Idea of Progress*.[40] Indeed, the assumption that one should go where one can, regardless of precedent or apparently minor details such as who currently occupies a given territory, undergirds everything from the myth of the American West to the desire to put a man on the moon.

It is also often cited—though much more indirectly—in early conversations about the Internet. Once the brainchild of the United States Department of Defense, the Internet generally, and later the World Wide Web specifically, was embraced and subsequently reclaimed by a wave of what early Internet researcher Howard Rheingold described as "digital homesteaders," users eager to stake their claim within the emerging world of cyberspace.[41] The landless land grab that swept the early web even inspired John Perry Barlow, an early Internet activist, cofounder of the Electronic Frontier Foundation, and later a research fellow at Harvard University's Berkman Center for Internet and Society to write "A Declaration of the Independence of Cyberspace,"[42] which asserted the political and moral sovereignty of "the new home of Mind." "I declare the global social space we are building to be naturally independent of the tyrannies you seek to impose on us," Barlow wrote. "We believe that from ethics, enlightened self-interest, and the commonwealth, our governance will emerge."[43]

Regarding the emerging encroachment of terrestrial law within cyberspace, Barlow attested the following: "These increasingly hostile and colonial measures place us in the same position as those previous lovers of freedom and self-determination who had to reject the authorities of distant, uninformed powers [i.e. American Revolutionaries]. We must declare our virtual selves immune to your sovereignty, even as we continue to consent to your rule over our bodies. We will spread ourselves across the Planet so that no one can arrest our thoughts."[44] Barlow's utopian and decidedly libertarian message thus functioned not just as a Declaration of Independence, but also as Manifest Destiny version 2.0. To these early adopters—the vast majority of whom were white males—the Internet was a land of endless opportunity, something to harness and explore, something to *claim*.

Trolls' attitudes toward the web echo Barlow's utopian vision—albeit its dark underbelly. Just as Barlow declares independence from the tyrannies of corporate and governmental encroachment, trolls regard the Internet as their personal playground and birthright; as such, no one, not lawmakers, not the media, and certainly not other Internet users, should be able to dictate their behavior. Trolls are, at least according to trolls, wholly sovereign to everything but their own will.

It's not just a strong libertarian streak that connects trolls and early Netizens (at least, early Netizens as conceived by Barlow). It's also their entitled attitude toward the virtual space. Recall Howard Rheingold's aforementioned framing of the "digital homesteader," which harkens to those rough and tumble, bootstrappy American frontiersmen who chose to stake their claim westward. But instead of heading west, digital homesteaders are on a virtual course. Trolls take this concept to its furthest and most grotesque extreme, which in fact is closer in spirit to "real" homesteading than early cyber-utopians' starry-eyed idealizations. Homesteading, after all, is the act of declaring that this plot of land is now *my* plot of land, regardless of whose land it might be currently. Whose plot of land it might be currently doesn't matter. That's just details, and is nothing a musket or ten can't fix. And that is precisely what trolls do. They homestead.

Take for example the infamous Habbo Hotel raids of 2006, in which trolls from /b/, goons from Something Awful, and several other motley trolling crews planned and executed the first of several massive raids against the eponymous Habbo Hotel, a strictly moderated social media platform catering to tweens and teenagers. After creating an army of identical avatars—black men in black suits with huge afros—nearly two hundred trolls, each operating multiple avatars, swarmed the American hotel (Habbo is an international chain, boasting virtual branches in thirty-two countries). The troll army immediately began spamming public chats with various obscenities, essentially shutting down the hotel's public spaces. Simultaneously, a few dozen trolls formed a human blockade in front of the hotel pool. "Pool's closed due to AIDS," they insisted, a line that immediately entered the trolling lexicon.[45]

Habbo Hotel was hardly the first and hardly the last time trolls set forth and conquered. Trolls have applied the same basic model—show up, turn a website's social networking platform and community against itself, lol—to countless online spaces, as if lulz were a natural resource to be extracted. Encyclopedia Dramatica, for example, began as an archive for LiveJournal drama (hence the name), but was soon overrun by trolls—much to the chagrin of its founder Sherrod DeGrippo.

As discussed in chapter 5, trolls' largest land grab came in 2010, when trolls harnessed Facebook's social networking platform for their own trollish ends, making the site an unwitting and unwilling pawn in subcultural formation. Unsurprisingly, Facebook was not amused, and their admins did everything they could to repel the trolling onslaught. Trolls took this resistance as a call to arms, and began devising increasingly clever work-around strategies. This was *their* space, and no one was going to take it away from them; just as Barlow had done twenty years earlier, trolls declared their virtual selves immune to Facebook's sovereignty, and vowed to spread the lulz across the Planet so that no one could arrest their thoughts. And for these self-evident truths, they were more than willing to fight.

In short, through raids, forum hijacking, and platform repurposing, trolls tease out the trace of violence and exploitation that is so often effaced from discussions of progress and expansion, particularly within an American context. Again, though, while trolling behaviors are regarded as inherently problematic, the cultural tropes with which trolls' behaviors are aligned are either celebrated or, more frequently, rendered invisible, as if expansionism were as natural as the air Americans breathe.

I Can, Therefore I Should Be Able To

Not only do trolls' acts of entitlement mimic expansionist ideology, they also, and simultaneously, exhibit a culturally proscribed relationship to technology. Internet historian Jason Scott provides a framework for understanding this relationship in his 2008 ROFLcon talk "Before the LOL." As Scott argues, tinkering, playing, and otherwise hacking existing systems for one's own edification or amusement is simply what people will do when confronted with new technologies, a point he illustrates through an examination of the nineteenth-century telegraph network, the HAM radio network in the 1960s, and copy machines in the 1950s and 1960s, each of which generated a great deal of (often transgressive) play.[46]

Although seemingly simple, if not outright commonsensical, the assumption-cum-conclusion that "this is what people will do" with emergent technologies is far more ideologically loaded than one might expect. First, the claim teeters at the edge of Hume's Law, also known as the is-ought fallacy. People can play with technology, and so they do, and so they *should*, or at the very least one mustn't be surprised when the inevitable comes to pass. The "is" of ludic engagement, in other words, is reframed to an "ought," thus naturalizing and universalizing the impulse to play with new technologies. The problem with this framing is that, while the ludic impulse may be strong in some, it is not, and cannot be, strong in everyone, for the simple reason that not all people have access to the technologies in question, the time to devote to learning the ins and outs of specific systems, or the energy to play with the tools they've been given.

Consequently, Scott's claim warrants reassessment. A much more accurate claim would be that "this is what privileged people will do" with technology, since those in positions of privilege—whether derived from racial, gender, and/or class position—have the inclination, access, and most importantly, the internalized sense of entitlement that it isn't just acceptable to play with whatever toys one has been given, but in fact is one's right to do so.

This issue of rights echoes the tone and overall spirit of the hacker ethic, which was first articulated by Steven Levy in his foundational 1984 account of early hackers.[47] According to Levy, the hacker ethic consists of the following interrelated axioms: access to computers should be unlimited, one should always yield to the hands-on imperative, all information should be free, authority should be mistrusted and routed around if necessary, hacking skill matters more than "bogus" real-world criteria like race, gender, or degrees, and computers can change the world for the better.[48]

One particularly relevant outcrop of the hacker ethic, and which undergirds Scott's assertion that "this is what people will do" with new technologies, is hackers' celebration of creative appropriation. To hackers, technologies were *made* to be played with (hence the hands-on imperative). Consequently, attempts to block or restrict hackers' perceived right to do what they want with the technologies in front of them is met with profound umbrage.[49]

While it would be a mistake to lump all hackers under the same banner—in her study of free and open software production, Gabriella Coleman is careful to highlight the often-conflicting branches in the hacking family tree[50]—Levy's formulation of the hacker ethic, particularly his emphasis on the impulse, and some hackers might even argue, the obligation, to unlock closed doors and to reappropriate available technologies, has endured as a behavioral ideal for nearly three decades. And not just in hacking circles—the impulse to push existing technologies to their limits, in short to do *what* you can *because* you can, is explicitly celebrated by the tech industry (whose best and brightest, it is worth noting, were raised on the hacker ethic, the most notable examples being Microsoft's Bill Gates and Apple cofounder Steve Wozniak).

The technologically privileged assertion that one can play with technologies and therefore should be able to provides yet another example of the ways in which trolling behaviors run parallel to dominant tropes. Trolls, after all, are champions of the idea that the practical ability to accomplish some goal ("I am able to troll this person") justifies, if not necessitates, its pursuit ("therefore it is my right to do so"). Nontrolls are quick to reject this line of reasoning on the grounds that it is callous, solipsistic, and exploitative. In other contexts, however, "I can, therefore I should be able to" is taken for granted, and in some circles is explicitly fetishized. It certainly has made a lot of white men a whole lot of money.

Land of the Free, Home of the Trolls

The logic of privilege that undergirds trolls' relationship to technology is itself undergirded by the ideals Americans are taught to hold most dear: namely, that all men are endowed by their Creator with certain unalienable Rights, among them Life, Liberty, and the pursuit of Happiness, and furthermore, that Congress shall make no law abridging the freedom of speech. American trolls in particular embrace these ideals, and when pressed on the ethics of their behavior, often cite what they presume to be their constitutionally protected right to irritate strangers on the Internet. For these trolls, the iconic line from the Declaration of Independence might be revised thusly: "All trolls are endowed by their Internet with certain unalienable Rights, among them Anonymity, Impunity, and the Pursuit of Lulz." On this view, and gesturing toward hackers' general abhorrence of locked doors, American trolls regard any form of online censorship, including on-site moderation policies, as a basic infringement on the their civil liberties.

During the aforementioned Huffington Post segment, weev—who was framed by the host as both godfather of trolling and free speech warrior—echoes this position. As he explains, he has "the right, and perhaps even the moral obligation, to drop your dox." For weev, doxing someone (i.e., publicizing the target's personal identifying and/or financial information) is a "consequence of pissing off the community," essentially imbuing trolling behaviors with a kind of implicit pedagogy. "That's the great thing about free speech, about the First Amendment," he continues. "Not only does Violentacrez [an infamous reddit moderator responsible for creating and moderating "jailbait" and "creepshot" subreddits[51]] have a right to be a prick on the Internet, we have the right to punish him! That's beautiful. Our Constitution is beautiful."[52]

Initially, the impulse to wrap trolling in the American flag might seem counterintuitive, particularly when one considers its most destructive forms. In response to coordinated attacks against the parents of recent teenage suicides, say, I can't think of a less convincing justification than "free speech." Nor can I think of a more myopic framing of behaviors designed to humiliate, frighten, or intimidate, a particular and well-publicized specialty of weev's. In a 2008 *New York Times* profile, for example, weev boasted about doxxing and libeling technology writer Kathy Sierra,[53] who felt so threatened by the resulting onslaught that she was forced to retreat from the Internet entirely.[54] In another more recent example, weev's bullying and attempted extortion of a slander victim was presented during his 2013 AT&T sentencing hearing.[55] In these types of cases, particularly cases where the behaviors in question meet the legal definition of harassment (which, for the record, is *not* protected by the First Amendment), the idea that what trolls are actually doing by tormenting strangers is "fighting for free speech" is absurd, and might itself be an act of trolling.

Regardless of how unlikely the connection between trolling and free speech might appear, however, and regardless of what message they intend to send by embracing such a cherished American ideal, trolls' more extreme actions call attention to the ugly side of free speech, which so often is cited by people whose speech has always been the most free—namely straight white cisgendered men (i.e., men whose gender identity aligns with cultural expectations for their biological sex)—to justify hateful behavior towards marginalized groups. In these cases, claims to protected speech are often less about the legal parameters of the First Amendment and more about not wanting to be told what to do, particularly by individuals whose perspective one doesn't respect.

Just as it places assumptions about free speech in a new and perhaps uncomfortable light, trolling also reveals the destructive implications of freedom and liberty, which, when taken to their selfish extreme, can best be understood as "freedom for *me*," liberty for *me*," with little to no concern about how these actions might infringe on others' freedoms. American history is littered with moments in which freedom, liberty, self-determination, and of course the push for westward expansion— everything that is said to make America great—have been deployed with positive consequences for some and absolutely devastating consequences for others. The idea that a person has a right, and perhaps an obligation, to take advantage of others for their own personal gain is the American dream at its ugliest—and is exactly the dynamic the most offensive forms of trolling replicate.

As this chapter, and in fact the entire second section of this book illustrates, trolls are hardly anomalous. They fit comfortably within the contemporary American media landscape, and they effortlessly replicate the most pervasive, and in many cases outright venerated, tropes in the Western tradition. In that sense, trolls are model ideological subjects. The question is, then, what exactly are people criticizing when they criticize trolls? I would suggest that criticisms of trolling behaviors are indirect (if inadvertent) criticisms of the culture that spawns them, immediately widening the scope and significance of the so-called troll problem. I will expand upon this basic, if somewhat disturbing, point in the conclusion. First, however, we must consider just how far trolling has come, and where it might be going.

III   The Transitional Period, 2012–2015

At the outset of this study, I argued that trolls are agents of cultural diges-tion. Scavengers to their core, they have the time, the energy, and the inclination to scour the landscape for exploitable materials, which they subsequently weaponize into lulz extraction tools.

In the earliest phases of my research (and much to the chagrin of my various professors), I framed this relationship in terms of actual digestion. Specifically, if you want to know what food sources are avail-able to, say, a bear, then find a pile of its excrement and figure out what it's been eating. Similarly, if you want to understand the contours of the contemporary media environment, then study the content trolls adopt, the jokes trolls make, and the groups trolls most frequently target. In short, there is a great deal of cultural information embedded in the shit trolls produce; it is not arbitrary, and in fact can be quite predictive of approaching trends.

I forwarded this theory in the last two sections of the introduction ("The Political Significance of Trolling?" and "Trolls as Tricksters"), and provided methodological context for its development in chapter 3's "The Problem of Anonymity." As I explained in that later section, I was seeing a great deal of change within the troll space, which initially seemed to threaten my entire research project—until I realized that trolling was evolving alongside mainstream culture, thereby providing real-time evidence for the fundamental relationship between the troll space and dominant institu-tions. The following two chapters chronicle these changes, and in so doing shine a final spotlight on the political, cultural, and behavioral overlap between trolling and the mainstream.

The study closes with a reexamination of trolls as trickster. Like trick-ster, trolls are woven into the very fabric they seek to unravel; like trickster, trolls have a great deal to teach. Not because trolls or their behaviors are themselves instructive, but because the messes they leave behind *are*. Specifically, they unearth the biases, hypocrisies, and deep inconsistencies that compose mainstream culture—and in the process, handily blur the boundary between where the troll mess ends and the mainstream mess begins.

8 The Lulz Are Dead, Long Live the Lulz: From Subculture to Mainstream

As agents of cultural digestion, trolls are subject to and directly reflect shifting political, historical, and economic sands. It would stand to reason, then, that changes in mainstream culture would result in corresponding changes in trolling subculture, a critical point when considering the differences between the emerging troll space of the mid-2000s, the established troll space of 2008–2011, and the scattershot troll space of 2012–2015. This chapter chronicles two factors contributing to these changes: the mainstreaming of participatory meme culture and profound shifts within the mass noun Anonymous. Not only does this analysis provide an account of trolling in the contemporary moment, it further emphasizes the inextricable relationship between trolling and the mainstream.

Mainstreaming the Web

As I explained in chapter 1, a significant percentage of popular memes (LOLcats, Advice Animals, and rage comics, to name a few) originated within or were amplified by subcultural trolls, particularly those associated with 4chan's /b/ board. In fact, the act of trolling and the act of making memes were so interconnected during the subcultural origin period that the existence of memes on a given page or forum almost guaranteed that trolling was or had been afoot. As memes became increasingly prominent, so too did many aspects of trolling culture, to the point that the existence of memes (even visibly trollish memes like the ubiquitous "you mad bro?" trollface comic) no longer guaranteed the existence of trolls. Instead, they merely indicated that participants had some spent some time, but not necessarily much time, on the Internet—a development I chronicle in the following section.

Meme Factory

The overall shift from subculture to mainstream was a slow one; for years, trolls and the memes they shared (and made, and remixed) didn't just fly under the corporate radar, they avoided the corporate radar entirely. 4chan proved particularly impervious to corporate commodification. Given its much-deserved reputation as the "asshole of the Internet," it's not difficult to see why. As Nicholas Carlson of *Business Insider* explains, "The reason 4chan can't make any money . . . is that it is the dark, disgusting underbelly of the Internet. For every LOLcat, there's a dead cat. For every photo of a cute girl in punky clothes, there's seven of people with no clothes. It's content no advertiser would ever put its brand near."[1]

4chan's FAQ page addresses this issue specifically, providing answers to questions about donations and the overall solvency of the site. Not only do online payment processors like PayPal refuse to do business with 4chan, individual donations cannot be securely processed; the best way to support the site, the FAQ insists, is for users to enable all cookies and click on all relevant advertisements.[2] It should therefore come as no surprise that during a question and answer session at the 2010 TED conference, moot admitted that "the commercial picture [of 4chan] is that there really isn't one."[3]

Anonymous—which at the time was essentially synonymous with 4chan's /b/ board—was even more difficult to commodify. In its first few years of existence, there were only two instances of attempted corporate encroachment. The first came in November 2010, when retail giant Hot Topic began selling "rage face" t-shirts on its website. Rage comics—especially the eponymous rage face, which features a grimacing cartoon captioned with the invective "FFFFFFFUUUUUUUUUUUU-"—had been a mainstay on 4chan since 2008. Anons were none too pleased that Hot Topic was selling "their" content and quickly devised what came to be known as Operation Black Rage. "This is only the beginning," the Operation flier explained. "If this is allowed to continue then it'll only be a matter of time until /b/ starts getting raped of every meme to be turned into the next I Can Haz Cheezburger? And before long? */b/ will die*." The proposed operation was straightforward: anons would flood Hot Topic's Facebook page with messages alerting the company to the image's racist undertones, and create as many racist iterations of the meme as possible. By doing so, "everyone learns a valuable lesson, stays the fuck away from trying to sell memes."[4]

A few months after Operation Black Rage, Old Spice also attempted to harness this hitherto untapped market. "Hello Anonymous," spokesman

Isaiah Mustafa began. "I'm glad that some of most of you are liking my new Old Spice commercials." Although this was one spot in a series of viral advertisements produced for Old Spice by advertising agency Wieden and Kennedy, the Re: Anonymous ad was the first time Anonymous had been hailed *by name* by a major brand.[5] Trolls responded to Old Spice's shout-out with a combination of incredulity and derision. In threads devoted to the Old Spice ad, anons on /b/ posted hundreds of pornographic, bestial images, including constant reposts of a man being fellated by a cow. On YouTube, they flooded the comments section with obscene posts and racist attacks against Mustafa, an African American.[6] Needless to say, Old Spice made no further outreach efforts.

This however wasn't the only reason trolling subculture—and memes generally—had been left undisturbed. A secondary but no less significant reason was the fact that the early troll and meme space(s) were all but inaccessible to outsiders. While certain members of the media and even some advertisers (Wieden and Kennedy being the most conspicuous example) were plugged into trolling and participatory meme culture, the relative obscurity of memetic references minimized the salability of troll or meme-themed ad campaigns. In other words, marketers didn't commodify such content because they *couldn't*, either because there was little interest outside trolling and/or meme circles or because the marketers themselves were outside the circle and therefore couldn't decipher what was being communicated.

And then came Know Your Meme, which quickly established itself as the go-to resource for everything memetic. Unlike Encyclopedia Dramatica, which defined trolling references using other trolling references (making it a profoundly NSFW experience), Know Your Meme (KYM) was written with the novice in mind, with detailed, almost clinical explanations of the Internet's most popular participatory content. KYM thus helped democratize a space that had previously been restricted to the initiated—inadvertently codifying what once had been an evolving repertoire of shared experience.

With increased accessibility came increased visibility, and with increased visibility came marketability. This point was emphasized in a 2012 marketing strategy posted to HubSpot, an online marketing blog. In it, marketer Pamela Vaughan describes "memejacking," the process by which marketers appropriate existing content for branding purposes, and cites Know Your Meme as an excellent resource.[7] As Vaughn's directive indicates, memes were suddenly *worth* something to outsiders. As former Know Your Meme editor and community moderator Chris Menning explained, "We simply wanted to help explain the cultural artifacts of what was, at the time, indecipherable to the uninitiated. Granted, that translation sped up the process of bringing this culture to larger audiences; (we accidentally made our punk rock turn into pop-punk, if you will)."[8]

KYM's response to Operation Black Rage provides a perfect example. Initially, Hot Topic bowed to the manufactured backlash, releasing a statement apologizing to those who had been offended by the FU T-shirt's racist connotations and vowing to discontinue the shirt's sale. After speaking to a Know Your Meme employee, however, Hot Topic reversed its decision, and the following day resumed selling the shirt.[9]

During the "Mainstreaming the Web" keynote panel at the second ROFLcon (an Internet culture conference) in 2010, moot from 4chan, Ben Huh from the LOLcat heavy Cheezburger network, Kenyatta Cheese and Jamie Wilkinson from Know Your Meme, and Greg Rutter from Wieden and Kennedy grappled with precisely this tension—tensions that, ironically enough, the panelists were indirectly complicit in propagating.[10] "It's an interesting group we have up here," moot began, "because essentially . . . I run the site that produces memes, you all study it, Greg kinda collates it, and Ben, essentially you profit from it," a statement met with affirmative hoots from the audience.[11]

Later in the talk, moot revealed the source of his frustration with Huh's million-dollar Cheezburger empire. "The problem I have with your model," moot began, "is that you're essentially an oil tower—it's milking and milking and extracting, but it doesn't really return much. And you can say we're giving people tools to create LOLcats, and that's great and all, but more or less you're giving people those tools so you can post them on your site because you monetize them with display ads. Do you feel that you put something back? Because I don't."[12]

moot's basic criticism echoed the increasingly common complaint among meme enthusiasts (incidentally the very demographic for whom the ROFLcon series was created) that memes were being hijacked by corporate interests—a chorus that only grew louder when Huh's Cheezburger network bought Know Your Meme in 2011.

In addition to ushering in waves of corporate encroachment, the mainstreaming of the web resulted in a dizzying influx of novice users. As a consequence, the period between 2011 and 2012 saw a marked uptick in discussion of and pushback against what many meme-centric communities believed to be cursory, superficial engagement, particularly on slick safe-for-work aggregators like 9gag and anything under the mostly safe-for-work Cheezburger umbrella.

These frustrations reached their peak in early 2012, when American universities began creating "meme pages" on Facebook. Students were encouraged to make memes about their specific institution, which they could then post to the school's page. Users possessive and protective of meme culture, notably those based out of reddit and 4chan, balked at this development. It wasn't just that increasing numbers of people were suddenly making and sharing memes, although that was certainly a major complaint. It was that people were *doing it wrong*, including how they were using the term meme. For meme purists, a meme can refer to any bit of content, so long as it is passed along though a community-vetted, collectively constitutive creative process. On Facebook meme pages, in contrast, the term was being used to describe one distinct family of memes—namely, Advice Animals.

This was another point of contention. Advice Animals had been a staple on /b/ for years, and had long been a source of trollish amusement. The format was simple: an animal—beginning with Advice Dog, but eventually branching out to include Courage Wolf, Insanity Wolf, Foul Bachelor Frog, Technically Impaired Duck, Philosoraptor, and Socially Awkward Penguin—was centered against one of several radiant color-wheel patterns (each animal corresponded to a specific background). Text—the standard font being white Impact, with a slight shadow (though in the early years Arial was also used)—would then be placed at the top and bottom of the image (figure 8.1).

The joke was predicated on participants' knowledge of the standard format, as well as previous iterations of the meme. As one might expect, all the animals provided some form of advice, the focus and tone of which depended on which animal it was.

Advice Dog, for example, offered satirical, absurd, and at times outright psychotic life tips (figure 8.2); Foul Bachelor Frog, suggestions for hygiene-challenged bachelors; Courage Wolf, hypermasculine inspiration; Insanity Wolf, rape-related inspiration (Insanity Wolf was a slightly hyperbolized version of Courage Wolf, which was a slightly hyperbolized version of Advice Dog); Philosoraptor, ironic pontifications; and Technologically Impaired Duck, terrible IT suggestions. Socially Awkward Penguin followed a slightly different format, in that it was less about giving tips and more about lamenting the apparently common experience among trolls of being socially anxious and awkward offline, especially around girls. Though not all early Advice Animals were explicitly misogynist, a large percentage was, and a large percentage of that percentage ended with a "joke" about rape (a point that casts a great deal of aspersion over their subsequent

Courage Wolf

Insanity Wolf

Foul Bachelor Frog

Philosoraptor

Socially Awkward
Penguin

Technologically
Impaired Duck

Figure 8.1
Advice Animal examples compiled by the author. Images accessed on Encyclopedia
Dramatica on July 3, 2012. Image creator(s) and date(s) of creation unknown.

Figure 8.2
Advice Dog examples compiled by the author. Images accessed on Encyclopedia Dramatica on July 3, 2012. Image creator(s) and date(s) of creation unknown.

mainstream popularity; the origin of this particular species is steeped in violent sexism).

Initially, Advice Animals required some basic technological skills. Finding the appropriate blank template was easy enough, but in order to do the caption correctly, one needed to know how to outline the text with a 2–5 pixel shadow, a three-step process in Photoshop, and even more involved process in GIMP, Photoshop's open source equivalent. Hardly an impossible task for someone well-versed in photo editing, but not something an average user would be likely to figure out without help. By making an Advice Animal, one was therefore asserting both subcultural knowledge and technological competence.

Meme generating platforms, most notably Meme Generator (created in 2009) and Quickmeme (created in 2010) changed all this. Suddenly, the means of production shifted from individual to platform. All a user needed to do was choose which image he or she wanted to caption, and the formatting work would be done automatically. This resulted in an explosion of participation, as well as an ever-expanding pantheon of templates, many of which found their way onto Facebook—much to the chagrin of trolls and others invested in the "purity" of memes. Also to the chagrin of these users was the increasing number of "bad" memes, that is, memes that deviated significantly from the established subcultural format of years past, or worse, memes that didn't even attempt to abide by the established subcultural format, for example, Pedobear opining about chicken sandwiches (figure 8.3).

Figure 8.3
Pedobear gets handed a vegan pamphlet on the way to get a chicken sandwich. Image accessed via email on February 11, 2012. Image creator(s) and date(s) of creation unknown.

Needless to say, trolls and other meme enthusiasts were incensed. Before memes became the hottest new trend on Facebook, they were as much an expression of identity as they were discrete images or jokes. Furthermore, they required quite a bit of homework; a person couldn't just start using memes. After memes went mainstream, however, what once had functioned as a highly specialized subcultural marker no longer performed the same subcultural function. Meme purists regarded this shift as unnatural and argued that Facebook like button-based engagement ran counter to how the Internet was "supposed" to work.

Back in My Day, Trolling Really Meant Something

During his solo panel at the third and final ROFLcon in 2012,[13] moot echoed precisely this sentiment. According to moot, people aren't investing as much time or energy in content creation and community formation because these days no one needs to, because their online networks are already established, because content is untethered to specific communities and is instead free-floating and devoid of all but the most basic context. "Back in my day, we walked five miles to school," the twenty-four-year-old lamented, "and were more predisposed to be producers of content, instead of just consumers."[14]

Although he was discussing memetic creation generally, moot's statements reflected the increasingly dour mood on /b/. By 2012, seasoned anons were constantly railing against the flood of "newfags" and "summerfags," users ignorant of trolling culture ("summerfagging" implies that an anon just discovered the site, likely during summer vacation). The designation of new/summerfaggotry was hardly novel behavior; self-identifying oldfags had for years decried what they describe as "the cancer." That said, and up until this latest flood of noobs, new anons were outnumbered by established anons, and were therefore compelled to conform— allowing for the possibility of subcultural upgrade. On /b/, the consensus was that the experienced troll population was dwindling and that "the cancer" had taken over.

One anon posting in a thread devoted to the perceived changes between "old /b/" and "new /b/" explained this position as follows:

sure, [old /b/] wasn't anything special, but back then we did things for the lulz. we conducted raids, pranks, and trolls for the sake of having fun; and gaining a laugh. now, despite having more people than ever, we are limited to trolling each other with the same shit we see every hour of every day for months at a time. we don't even bother having fun fucking with the unsuspecting. the only raids we conduct

. . . have a moral basis. it is no longer about having fun, but about seeing justice. it fucking disgusts me.[15]

Even the admins at 4chan seemed to agree, and in February 2012 they posted the following (highly trollish) message to the front page:

/b/ has changed.
it's no longer about original content, epic GETs and win
it's an endless series of reposts, perpetuated by newfags and trolls
fail [sic]—and its consumption of /b/ has become an unstoppable cancer.
/b/ has changed.[16]

To help restore /b/ to its former infamy, the admins reenabled "forced anon," a mechanism that disallows pseudonymous posting. Users who had been posting using "tripcodes," on-site ID numbers, would once again be forced to post anonymously. "Let's see if this helps curb shitposting and return /b/ to its roots," the admin wrote.[17]

The response was overwhelming. "kindly GTFO and go back to 9fag," one anon wrote, "where you can live in an eternal bucle [sic] of lamejokes and fail."[18] "This is now some bastardized version of Reddit," wrote another. "Apparently, very few people appreciate chaos and spontaneous forms of communication. The desire to conform is too strong for most of the sheep."[19] "I'm no oldfag," added a third, "but threads nowadays are just weak and disgraceful compared to a few years back . . . people who truly want /b/ for what it once was deserve the chance to have it back . . . I don't normally rage like this, but given the opportunity I'll express my views for the greater good of /b/."[20]

Though perhaps oxymoronic, concern for "the greater good of /b/" became a common topic of trollish conversation post-2011 (and, ironically, was grounds for immediate accusations of newfaggotry; caring about anything, including trolling itself, is regarded by many self-described oldfags as inherently cancerous). Trolls might not have understood exactly why their world was changing, but they did know that it had—changes due in no small part to the shifting reputation of Anonymous itself.

Anonymous's Perfect Circle

I begin this section with a basic, increasingly self-apparent assertion: the faceless collective subsumed by the mass noun Anonymous ("Anonymous" for short, though the prefatory qualification is critical to acknowledge) has undergone a dramatic transformation. Previously framed by the media as

the Internet Hate Machine, post–Wikileaks Anonymous has become synonymous with so-called hactivism and is frequently lauded as a progressive
force for good. Or if not a force for "good," then a force for *something*—that
is, some political position or ideal. The precise reasons for this shift are
difficult to pinpoint, though it is reasonable to assume that changes in the
American pop cultural landscape (changes described in the previous
section) have played a large role. It is also reasonable to assume that changing media coverage has had a profound impact on the Anonymous brand,
including its move toward political activism.

The Lulz/Cause Divide
First, it's helpful to consider the longstanding tension between "lulzfags"
and anons variously known as "causefags" or "moralfags." As one might
expect, anons designated as lulzfags are motivated primarily by lulz. Anons
designated as cause/moralfags, on the other hand, deliberately target
groups or individuals who have committed (what is perceived to be) some
form of injustice. They are also known as "White Knights" based on the
impulse to protect those who have been wronged.

An early, but by no means the first, clash between the two camps
occurred in 2009, when Anonymous was still in the throes of Project Chanology, Anon's first organized attack against the Church of Scientology.
Some anons were irritated by the seriousness with which certain anons
were approaching the operation, particularly so-called causefags who took
legitimate issues with church doctrine and practice. As Julien Dibbell
chronicled in his article "The Assclown Offensive," many anons worried
that this influx of seriousness would have irrevocable consequences.
Namely, if they were to establish too coherent a message, and too
many clear ethical objectives, Anonymous risked pigeonholing itself
as a *movement*, something the media could easily wrap their heads around,
and which would in turn attract the wrong sort of element: namely
activists.[21]

In an effort to silence the activist wing of Anonymous, an anon calling
himself Agent Pubeit strolled into the New York City Scientology Center
in January 2009 covered in a thick coating of petroleum jelly mixed with
pubic hair and toenail clippings. To the undoubted horror of the reception-
ist, Pubeit slimed the waiting area with clumps of jellied hair and humped
the side of an office cart before fleeing the scene with his two accomplices,
one of whom had filmed the whole ordeal.[22] Operation Slickpubes, as it
came to be known, essentially reclaimed Project Chanology for the lulz,
and was therefore hailed by the lulzfag contingent as a resounding success.

It also proved to be inadvertently prescient. As the moral objectives of particular raids became increasingly apparent, the gulf between lulz and activism widened. Initially, these two categories weren't mutually exclusive. When Anonymous initiated Operation Payback in 2010, a multipronged operation in protest of antipiracy measures, explicitly political rhetoric existed comfortably alongside more traditionally trollish behaviors—for example, when Anonymous redirected staunch copyright advocate Gene Simmons's website to bitTorrent site The Pirate Bay.[23]

The widening gulf between chaotic lulz and focused activism became increasingly apparent in the wake of the 2010 WikiLeaks scandal. WikiLeaks, an activist collective designed to facilitate political whistleblowing, had gained access to and subsequently published thousands of incriminating diplomatic cables. Julian Assange, WikiLeaks' founder and spokesperson, faced an increasing amount of pressure from governments around the world, particularly within the United States. He was finally arrested in December 2010 on sexual assault charges. Assange's supporters, as well as Assange himself, denounced the arrest, arguing that the charges were politically motivated. In response, Anonymous initiated Operation Avenge Assange, which was quickly subsumed under Operation Payback.

Although there was some trollish play on /b/, the bulk of Anonymous's activity during this period—which was organized on and executed from any number of anon-specific IRC channels—was devoted to DDoSing (conducting distributed denial of service attacks against targeted websites) and otherwise wreaking havoc with organizations deemed unfriendly to Assange and to Wikileaks, including Visa, Mastercard, and Paypal.[24] These efforts were certainly effective, but not particularly lulzy, a point reflected in the media's subsequent coverage of the group's "hactivism."

The political arm of Anonymous was further strengthened by the 2011 Arab uprisings, notably Operation Tunisia, an effort to help Tunisian dissidents organize anonymously, and the similarly focused Operation Egypt and Operation Libya. Anonymous—that is, anons working under the Anonymous banner—explicitly aligned themselves with what Al Jazeera reporter Yasmine Ryan described as a "global push for freedom of speech and freedom from oppression,"[25] a position the American media frequently echoed. Lulz played almost no role in the Arab uprising, and 4chan (particularly the /b/ board) was rarely if ever mentioned in mainstream accounts. If it was, /b/ was never more than an aside, something to offset with dashes. 4chan/b/ wasn't the story; Anonymous was the story. For the first time, the latter didn't immediately implicate the former.

A Tale of Two Anonymouses

As a result of this shift, it soon became necessary (at least within Internet research circles) to specify exactly which Anonymous one meant when one talked about Anonymous. "Big-A Anonymous" was a quick and easy way to indicate the political arm of Anonymous, while "little-a Anonymous" referred to trolling behaviors on or based out of 4chan's /b/ board. Although lulz were still common within the ranks of little-a, they were becoming increasingly scarce within Big-A. Not entirely extinct, however; as Gabriella Coleman notes, Big-A anons experienced a brief resurgence of lulz in the wake of Operation HBGary, a retaliatory attack against an online security firm that publicly bragged about having doxxed top Anonymous opera-tives.[26] However, the fact that lulz were regarded as a remarkable result, something outside the operating norm, was itself quite telling. Lulz used to be a given; lulz and Anonymous, just like Anonymous and 4chan/b/, used to be synonymous. By 2011, this was no longer the case.

The division between Big-A and little-a was further complicated by the rise of LulzSec, a small hacker collective responsible for a series of increas-ingly brazen security breaches, including attacks against the Sony PlaySta-tion network.[27] Although the group was trollish in aesthetic, they were hackers in deed—their targets weren't individual Internet users but rather large corporate websites and the data contained therein. For this reason, LulzSec was associated—and associated itself—with the hactivist arm of Anonymous, and throughout the summer of 2011 propelled Anonymous to the top of the news cycle. Invigorated by all the attention, Big-A con-tinued growing, while little-a was more and more relegated to the fringes.

Interestingly, the anons Dibbell interviewed in 2009 anticipated and in fact took active preventative measures against precisely this outcome—of which Operation Slickpubes was the most conspicuous. Just as Agent Pubeit and company had predicted, the more recognizably political the operation was, the more positive the subsequent media coverage became. This, in turn, attracted a particular sort of new recruit (and/or activated political sentiment within existing anons) who would then push for increasingly political action, which would generate further media buzz, resulting, ultimately, in the transposition of lulz with activism. Once again, Anonymous had risen to the media's occasion—except this time, it was toward a political, and explicitly progressive, end.

Occupy Wall Street was the final nail in this coffin. Although the Occupy movement was first introduced by anti-consumerist magazine *Adbusters*,[28] the media focused on Anonymous's involvement, prominently featuring images of and interviews with protestors wearing Guy Fawkes masks.[29] Anonymous was credited with turning a "fledgling movement" into a "meme,"[30] and was lauded for transforming the Occupy protests into a "distinctive new movement,"[31] with little acknowledgment paid to the other groups and individuals propelling the movement forward, both off- and online.

Participating anons took full advantage of this platform and in interviews, Tweets, and YouTube videos, emphasized the connection between Anonymous and OWS protests, in some cases taking more credit than was probably warranted.[32] The ubiquitous Guy Fawkes mask, once a symbol of failure (the mask was first worn by "Epic Fail Guy") and then a symbol of lulz, had undergone yet another transformation—it was now a rallying cry for social justice. Furthermore, it was something anyone could pick up, put on, and use to challenge existing systems of inequity, a point emphasized in a video posted to BuzzFeed's front page in October 2011. As the accompanying blurb explains: "You might be surprised by what's behind the mask. People, young and old, male and female, perhaps not unlike you. Keeping with the tradition that there is no 'official' branch of Anonymous, this video serves to illustrate that anyone and everyone is capable of uniting under a common identity, or the guarded protection thereof."[33] In short, Anonymous was being framed as a global democratizing force, a point reiterated and further amplified by anons themselves, many of whom had only recently entered the activist fray.

Within the ranks of little-a Anonymous, resistance to the political gains made by Big-A Anonymous was widespread. In his article chronicling the first days of the OWS protests, reporter Saki Knafo interviewed a group of self-described lulzfags who had gathered outside the Church of Scientology New York branch, located just off Times Square. Rather than expressing support for the OWS arm of Anonymous, they decried the protestors as "annoying, deluded hippies" and "challenged their claim to the mantle of Anonymous."[34] This sentiment was common on /b/, precipitating a great deal of subcultural self-reflection. Many anons even discussed adopting a new mascot, as the Guy Fawkes mask had been appropriated by "new anon." As one anon explained:

Anonymous isn't supposed to represent anything. We did stuff for lulz, for lulz only. Not because we care what happens in the world, we found shit and made it amusing to us. Old anon would be in occupy wallstreet and trolling protestors to the max, not joining them. We used to represent nothing and were feared because of that, no one knew when we would act and what we would do. Even we didn't. Look at yourselves, we are discussing about our logo and how others recognize us? We are not supposed to have this kind of shit. We are supposed to be the unknown. We do not have ideals, we do not fight for anything, we do not care about anything.[35]

By late 2011, the connection between little-a and Big-A Anonymous had become so tenuous that a simple bifurcation of focus was no longer adequate. This was not, in other words, two main factions housed within a larger group; this was two distinct groups, called by the same name. Furthermore, as Hactivist Anon grew, Lulz Anon receded, suggesting that the cultural landscape has room for only one Anonymous at a time. Unlike Lulz Anon, which proved highly resistant to ideological incorporation (the process by which transgressive subcultural elements are integrated into mainstream culture, typically through commodification), Hactivist Anon has been particularly susceptible to such interventions, and has been embraced by everyone from Polish politicians[36] to Canadian fashion designers.[37]

Even Glenn Beck threw his Guy Fawkes mask into the ring. As part of a 2012 viral media campaign supporting his Mercury One Christian charity, Beck launched an Anonymous for Good campaign, which added a cartoon heart to Anonymous's iconic "everyman" logo.[38] In 2007, such an action would have resulted in swift and merciless retribution—recall Anonymous's pushback against Beck's colleague Bill O'Reilly. Glenn Beck's video, on the other hand, was met with no such indignation. Someone claiming to be Anon posted a response video on YouTube, but it was viewed by less than half of those who had watched Beck's original video. Anons on /b/ were slightly more vocal, though many of these conversations centered on what they described as the disappointing state of new anon. Otherwise, very little was said and even less was done. The Internet Hate Machine, this was not.

Subcultural Decline, Population Growth

In short, the sudden mainstream popularity of memes, coupled with increasingly positive media coverage surrounding hactivism, attracted a crush of new recruits to the troll space. New recruits meant new cultural values, and new cultural values meant new behaviors, and new behaviors resulted in a fundamental subcultural shift.

But not a population decrease. In fact, trolling subculture is in many ways *more* visible now than it was in 2008, a point borne out by 4chan's traffic stats. Despite Big-A Anonymous's perceived lulz deficit, traffic on 4chan doubled between 2010 and 2012, up to over 22 million hits per month,[39] and by its ten-year anniversary in October 2013, enjoyed 22.5 million monthly visitors.[40]

Nor has there been a shortage of high-profile coordinated trolling attacks. For example, in the wake of 2012's Hurricane Sandy, the GNAA (previously mentioned in chapter 7) spearheaded the "Sandy Loot Crew," a fictional group of Twitter users that claimed to have looted homes in the wake of the storm. The self-described "loot crew"—all of whom used images of African Americans as their profile pictures—posted images of the stolen items to the Twitter hashtag #SandyLootCrew, prompting a number of media outlets, including Alex Jones's Infowars, to post explicitly racist condemnations of the looters' "shameless" actions.[41]

And true to form, denizens of /b/ remain committed to lulz, as evidenced by their early 2014 feminism-themed ops, including Operation Bikini Bridge, a mock "thinspiration" trend fetishizing supine women with jutting hip bones (whose bikini line forms a bridge over their lower abdomen), as well as their push to popularize uncontrolled menstruation, described by participating trolls as "freebleeding."[42] 4chan's /b/ board also played a significant role in 2014's celebrity nude photo scandal,[43] in which a dozen high-profile celebrities' personal compromising photos were accessed via Apple's iCloud service and posted to /b/, where they quickly spread to other platforms and were further amplified by frenzied media coverage.

Unlike the troll space in previous years, however, particularly in the pre-mainstreaming period of 2006–2010, contemporary trolling no longer emanates from a single hotspot, and no longer necessarily falls under the same highly distinctive subcultural mantle. In 2014, one is as likely to encounter trollish behavior on Tumblr or reddit or Twitter as on 4chan, some of which flags itself as such via subtle memetic references and some of which does not. Some self-identifying trolls don't even bother trolling anonymously. The subcultural well may not be as deep, in other words, but the water now covers a much wider area.

The following chapter elaborates on this shift, and considers the political and legal implications of the increasing diffusiveness of the definition of trolling. Afterward, I offer perhaps not a conclusion—the story is, after all, still unfolding—but a framework with which to understand this changing online landscape.

9 Where Do We Go from Here? The Importance of Spinning Endlessly

Building upon the previous chapter, which focused on changes within the troll space and the cultural factors that precipitated those changes, this chapter addresses the increasingly fuzzy popular definition of trolling, which in mainstream media circles has been attributed to such a wide variety of behaviors that it has been rendered almost meaningless. After considering the legal implications of this definitional shift, the chapter provides a framework with which to understand online trolling behaviors, regardless of whether or not these behaviors meet the subcultural threshold. The chapter then forwards a practical response to the so-called troll problem, the summary of which could be understood thus: at bottom, the troll problem isn't a troll problem at all. It's a culture problem, immediately complicating any solution that mistakes the symptom for the disease.

The Future of Trolling and How to Stop It

Following the changes chronicled in chapter 8, trolling subculture has undergone—and in fact is still in the process of undergoing—a third major shift. Many of the trolls I've worked with have expressed profound frustration with this development, and deep antipathy for its constituent crop of trolls. As my long-standing research collaborator Paulie Socash explained in an email message: "These days trolling is dying because: the real trolls from way back when are done, and now it's just an all-encompassing term for being an ass on the internet and has shit to do with anonymity or guile or art or anything. It will actually provide a cop-out, I think, for real dirtbags who claim they were 'just trolling.' When that defense fails, trolling becomes synonymous with criminal activity."[1]

As evidenced by the dismay expressed by trolls on /b/ who are anxious about the future of Anonymous, Paulie is not alone in his concerns. Even if he is correct, however, even if subcultural trolling really is "dying," the frequency with which aggressive online behaviors are *described* as trolling has only increased. According to the myriad reports on the issue, trolling is everywhere, and includes everything from harassing celebrities on Twitter[2] to harassing people you know in real life[3] to feminist political activism[4] to child exploitation[5] to being a "total fucking dick" political pundit.[6]

The vast majority of this coverage is deeply critical and portrays trolling as an antagonistic, hateful, ever-present online danger. Coverage that isn't critical typically asserts that something is trolling without providing any further explanation of the term, or more curiously, disqualifies the most problematic iterations on the grounds that "real" trolling isn't cruel, a point made in 2012 by Australian journalist Claire Porter.[7] The more stories that are written, the more unwieldy the term; and the more unwieldy the term, the more difficult it is to know exactly what a person means when they talk about trolling.

As I explain in an article for *The Daily Dot*, I do not accept the basic premise that there is only one way to troll, and do not share many trolls' dismay over what they see as a bastardization of "their" word. Given the history of the term, which for over a decade was used to describe all stripes of online antagonism and deception, this most recent framing is actually closer to its original meaning. I am, however, wary of the legal and political implications of couching all acts of online aggression under a single umbrella category.[8]

This is no small point, as the question of definitions is far from merely semantic; what people call things often dictates what people are willing (or feel compelled) to do about them. Post enough stories condemning a poorly defined behavioral category that manages to subsume every asshole on the Internet, and eventually you'll start seeing legislation with the same kinds of equivocations—for example, anti-trolling legislation proposed by the Arizona legislature (which was ultimately defeated due to its insistence on "annoyance" as a legal threshold),[9] and which is currently being considered in the United Kingdom[10] and Australia.[11] These attempts at lockdown are unsurprising; nothing justifies legal intervention faster or more effectively than vaguely threatening abstract nouns, particularly when there exists no basic definitional criteria on which to base one's conclusions.

This is precisely why a basic definitional criterion is needed, even if its primary use is to demarcate the subcultural variety of trolling from the effects-based variety. Hastily conceived interventions designed to thwart trolling—especially when the term "trolling" is bandied about as a haphazard buzzword, don't help anyone, least of all the targets of antagonistic online behaviors. The question is, which solutions are the best solutions? How far should we be willing to go to protect users from trolling and other forms of online abuse?

Jonathan Zittrain considers similar questions in his prescient *The Future of the Internet and How to Stop It*. As Zittrain explains, while lockdown—the tethering of devices to proprietary software, essentially the process of erecting walled gardens for digital content—may seem appealing, the impulse is in fact counter-productive. Walled gardens may be less susceptible to bad code or security breaches, but they also preclude innovation, pigeon-hole users into corporate-approved behaviors, and all but invite panoptic surveillance. These pastures may indeed be safer, but they are by no means greener.[12]

One could make a similar argument about trolling. After all, the same Internet that provides the space and freedom for people to make jokes about Over 9000 Penises and post incendiary comments on dead strangers' Facebook pages also provides the space and freedom for people to organize, communicate securely, bypass oppressive censorship measures, and safely expose government corruption. Trolling may be an unpleasant side effect of such openness, but closing that which is open and naming that which is nameless risks creating far more problems than it would solve, particularly for those users who rely on online anonymity for reasons of political or personal safety. Attempt to smoke out the trolls, in other words, and you simultaneously smoke out the activists.

On the other hand, and as Zittrain warns, if the Internet is *too* open, if there are *no* behavioral checks, and consequently if the average user feels threatened on a regular basis, users will be much more willing to accept harsh preemptive and/or punitive measures.[13] In the context of trolling, these measures might include required proof of identification for website registration, (further) surveillance of online activities, or even the abolishment of online anonymity.

No matter how well intentioned, these sorts of broad, reactionary interventions are unlikely to have the intended effect. First, draconian measures designed to preempt antagonistic anonymous trolling and/or hacking behaviors would likely be subverted by the most experienced hands; in fact, they might spur novice trolls and hackers to better learn the existing system in order to better break the existing system. Average Internet users might be stymied, but not the people whose behaviors cause the most problems, and who happen to be some of the most sophisticated tinkerers on the Internet.

More importantly, there is no guarantee that an anonymity-free Internet would be a kinder, gentler Internet. History has proven again and again that people are perfectly capable of being atrocious to each other under their real names, a point University of Queensland psychology professor Alex Haslam argues in an interview with Vice Media's *Motherboard*. Citing his 2012 study with fellow professor Stephen Reicher exploring the nature of conformity within oppressive systems,[14] as well as a 1998 study conducted by social psychologists Tom Postmes and Russell Spears challenging the presumed correlation between anonymity and abuse (Postmes and Spears found little to no evidence supporting this assumption),[15] Haslam argues that anonymity is far less important than existing group dynamics. "If the norm of the group is to be destructive, well actually then anonymity can enhance that," Haslam explains. "But if the norm of the group is to be constructive, then anonymity can enhance that."[16]

The problem isn't anonymity; in other words, it's the norms under which particular groups are operating. Banning anonymous expression would therefore have little impact on groups already steeped in violence and abuse, and would risk stifling much more than online aggression—a high price to pay, especially when one considers the overwhelming political and social benefits of a free and open Internet.

Again, this is not to argue that nothing should be done to combat more extreme forms of online aggression. The trick, and one that Zittrain strongly advocates, is to find a way to preempt the need for widespread institutional lockdown.[17] The first and most important step would be to make every possible effort to understand exactly what one is dealing with before one attempts to respond. Politicians and members of the media, for example, would be well advised to acknowledge the full spectrum of trolling behaviors, which as this book has chronicled, can run the gamut from the harmless to the devastating. This point is particularly important in the drafting and publicizing of specific "anti-trolling" legislation. After all, what good is an anti-trolling law if no one can agree on what and who counts?

In addition to taking the time to define one's terms, it is critical for those responding to trolling behaviors—whether law enforcement or website administrators—to consider the impact of a given behavior before determining the appropriate course of action. From my perspective, the best criteria for helping guide these responses are the persistence and relative searchability of data. Simply put, do the offending behaviors affix themselves to a target's name? Are they Google search–indexed? Do they threaten a person's private or professional reputation? A "yes" to these questions should prompt one set of options, while a "no" should prompt another.

Make no mistake, even the most ephemeral antagonistic behaviors can be devastating to the target, and can linger in a person's mind long after the computer is powered down. This is especially true if the target is a member of a marginalized or otherwise underrepresented population, whose previous experience(s) of abuse or prejudice may trigger strong negative emotions when confronted with nasty online commentary. That said, the best practices for dealing with ephemeral, one-off interactions are not necessarily the best practices for dealing with persistent (i.e., searchable) harassment. Legal scholar Danielle Citron describes the latter category as cyber harassment or cyber stalking, and uses the "cyber-" prefix to highlight the unique ways in which digital technologies amplify and exacerbate abuse.[18] In these sorts of cases, where abusive behaviors are archived, searchable, and therefore inescapable for the victim, Citron advocates targeted legal interventions, some of which are already on the books and some of which would require significant legal reform. Such interventions are necessary, Citron argues, to "secure the necessary preconditions for victims' free expression,"[19] an outcome often minimized or outright overlooked in most debates about free speech online.

I agree wholeheartedly with Citron's approach, particularly when the behaviors in question render an individual incapable of leading a normal offline life. However, in cases where a person's reputation is not threatened, and where data disappears or at least doesn't "stick" to its target, site- and community-specific interventions are often the best avenues for remediation. These interventions can include amended Terms of Use agreements, efficient comment moderation protocols, and of course liberal use of the banhammer (the act of banning specific posters from a given thread or from a site entirely based on username and/or IP address). Rather than minimizing certain forms of online abuse or falling back on paternalistic declarations about power buttons (the implication being that if someone is offended by antagonistic online behaviors, it's the target's fault for turning on the computer), the establishment of a basic categorical distinction between ephemeral and persistent abuse would allow lawmakers and site administrators to respond thoughtfully and efficaciously to all forms of aggressive online behaviors. This, ultimately, should be the goal—to maximize effectiveness and minimize lockdown.

Building the Anti-Troll Army, One Fox News Pundit at a Time

Of course, individual trolls are not the only variable in the troll question. As I have emphasized throughout this study, trolling behaviors are directly reflective of the culture out of which they emerge. The jokes trolls make, the people trolls target, the means by which they achieve these ends— all are linked to the cultural conditions out of which the behaviors arise. Condemning these symptoms without addressing their ideological roots is unlikely to yield meaningful and truly transformative answers, no more so than putting a bandage over a broken arm is likely to set the fractured bone.

Consequently, if lawmakers and pundits really are serious about combating the most explicitly racist, misogynist, and homophobic iterations of trolling, they should first take active, combative steps against the most explicitly racist, misogynist, and homophobic discourses in mainstream media and political circles—discourses that only beget further trolling opportunities. After all, for every Todd Aiken, the Missouri congressman who insisted that the female body has ways of "shutting down" pregnancy caused by "legitimate rape,"[20] there will be a thousand trolls making rape jokes. For every segment of racist propaganda that Fox News frames as "legitimate" news, there will be a thousand trolls hurling racist epithets. For every bigoted slur uttered by a pray-away-the-gay hate monger, there will be a thousand trolls regurgitating homophobic and transphobic slurs. Furthermore, for every shrill, sensationalist article that condemns trolling behaviors while replicating trolling tactics, there will be a thousand trolls more than happy to rise to the media's occasion. In short, so long as mainstream institutions are steered by people who behave like trolls, there will always be an audience of trolls primed to maximize mainstream ugliness.

The ubiquity of trollish discourse isn't the only contributing factor to the troll problem. Another reason trolls continue to troll is that media outlets continue to ensure that the time and energy required to troll is well worth the effort. Not only do these outlets give trolls precisely what they want—specifically, a national platform—they validate the impulse to troll. The incentive to troll harder is particularly apparent, and particularly disruptive, in the wake of national tragedies. Take, for example, the all-out media onslaught following the mass shooting in Aurora, Colorado, particularly panic surrounding "Holmies," a group of self-professed supporters of shooter James Holmes. Though the Holmies were an extremely small group of Tumblr trolls, numbering between six and ten members directly following the shootings, its relatively meager output was framed by the media as if membership were in the tens of thousands. Spurred on by this attention, the Holmies began keeping a running tally of all the articles devoted to the Holmie "phenomenon," which, thanks to the media's intervention, had indeed become one.[21]

In this particular case (and this case is far from isolated), trolls had every reason to continue trolling, because as sensationalist media have proven again and again, these behaviors *work*, and not just for the trolls. The behaviors also work for mainstream media companies, since stories about trolling translate into page views, and page views translate into advertising revenue, and advertising revenue is the lifeblood of any successful media organization.

This is not to deny trolls agency. They choose to engage in trolling behaviors; they choose to hold up their end of the bargain. That said, until the conversation is directed toward those who engage in behaviors similar or identical to those of trolls, until sensationalist, exploitative media practices are no longer rewarded with page views and ad revenue—in short, until the mainstream is willing to step in front of the funhouse mirror and consider the contours of its own distorted reflection—the most aggressive forms of trolling will always have an outlet, and an audience. And so long as it does, these behaviors will implicate far more people than the trolls themselves. They will also, and just as damningly, implicate those who pick and choose when to affect outrage and when to shrug noncommittally. Or worse, when to sit back and chuckle cynically.

About That Bathwater

Lost in discussions about the form and function of trolling behaviors, the various definitional quandaries the term unearths, and the ways in which trolling behaviors are enabled by mainstream practices is the fact that trolling is, or at least can be, an extremely effective rhetorical strategy. First, unlike more traditional argumentative forms, particularly those that hew to the strictures of formal logic (or are merely delivered in a pedantic monotone), trolling has a way of snapping its audience to attention, either by activating emotional investment or by forwarding a claim so outrageous that one cannot help but engage in a dialogue.

Consider the effort to save Troy, Michigan's public library. Due to numerous budget cuts, the library in Troy was facing likely closure. The only thing that would save the library was a slight tax increase, which the local anti-taxation Tea Party vowed to oppose. Initially, the Tea Party successfully quashed support for the measure. But late in the campaign, Arc Worldwide, an advertising agency within the Leo Burnett Group, stepped in. Arc posed as a group called Safeguarding American Families (SAFE) and launched a multimedia campaign advocating the tax measure's defeat and declaring the group's intentions to hold a book burning party.[22] Citizens of Troy were outraged, and the public discourse quickly shifted from antitax to proliteracy. The measure passed, and the library was saved.

SAFE's proposed book burning party was, in other words, *trollbait*, and highly successful trollbait at that. Previous attempts to discuss the library's future and the importance of literacy generally fell on mostly disinterested ears, as did discussions of the necessary 0.07 percent tax increase. These were conversations about numbers and abstract hypotheticals, nothing to get all that worked up about. It wasn't until the library was threatened with a literal trial by fire that citizens became emotionally invested in the story, investment that in turn spurred action.

Second, while certain forms of trolling amount to little more than name-calling, more complex forms draw out a target's unspoken assumptions, allowing the troll to ascertain exactly what sort of argument one is dealing with, and furthermore, how best to respond. Harnessed for purely mischievous ends, these sorts of behaviors are often generative of little more than the troll's amusement. Directed thoughtfully, however, arguments imbued with trolling rhetoric have the potential to open avenues of discourse that wouldn't have been possible otherwise, either because the conversation never would have arisen or because the participants wouldn't have felt compelled to respond even if it had. In the case of SAFE's proposed book burning party, citizens were essentially trolled into answering the question "What's so important about books?," thus solidifying their support for the 0.07 percent tax increase.

Finally, and perhaps most importantly, trolling rhetoric is an extremely effective countertrolling strategy. This strategy—of actively trolling trolls—runs directly counter to the common imperative "don't feed the trolls," a statement predicated on the logic that trolls can only troll if their targets allow themselves to be trolled. Given that the fun of trolling inheres in the *game* of trolling—a game only the troll can win, and whose rules only the troll can modify—this is sound advice. If the target doesn't react, then neither can the troll. But even this decision buys into the trolls' game. The troll still sets the terms of their target's engagement; the troll still controls the timeline and the outcome.

The dynamic shifts considerably if the target counters with a second game, one that collapses the boundary between target and troll. In this new game, the troll *can* lose and, by taking umbrage at the possibility, falls victim to his or her own rigid rules. After all, it's emotion—particularly frustration or distress—that trips the troll's wire. In most cases, the troll's shame over having lost, or merely the possibility that he or she *could* lose, will often send the troll searching for more exploitable pastures.

I frequently utilized this strategy in my own dealings with random anonymous trolls, particularly on my quasi-academic blog. One particularly colorful example occurred in the wake of 2012's Aurora, Colorado movie theater shootings (described earlier in this chapter). As soon as the news broke, trolls on 4chan/b/ and reddit's r/4chan subreddit attempted to connect the shootings to 9gag, which by then had replaced Ebaumsworld as the preferred trolling scapegoat. After media outlets began reporting the trolls' fabrications as fact, I decided to post a short article debunking the claim that James Holmes had been a regular 9gag user and that he had posted about the shootings on-site.[23] Adrian Chen, who initially reiterated the 9gag connection, ended up linking to my article on Gawker, sending a wave of trolls onto my blog. For the next week, I received precisely the sorts of messages one might expect (figure 9.1).

I ignored most of these trolls, but chose to respond to a few that spoke directly to the accuracy of my article (and to those whose "Internet tough guy" routine warranted the text equivalent of an eye roll). One troll in particular reached out "out of concern for multiple Internet communities." As he explained:

While I respect your endeavour to study and document the common "troll" mentality, a lot of what you've posted is coming across as nothing more than a smear tactic against a number of communities.

You're articulate, which makes it easy for a lot of the things you say to come across as fact; so if you'd put a little more time into research for these articles, I wouldn't have a problem. This comment isn't meant to offend, and I apologise if I do so. I'm just voicing my concerns in a constructive manner, instead of dox'ing and ruining your life like I'm sure the victims of your articles are planning on.

It's disappointing really, because I truly enjoyed some of the content you've written. If I weren't concerned about the effect of some of your less accurate articles, I'd definitely be recommending this site to friends and family. If I sound like I'm full of shit, it's because I'm only young and as such don't have an abundance of formal education.

Regards,

Stephen[24]

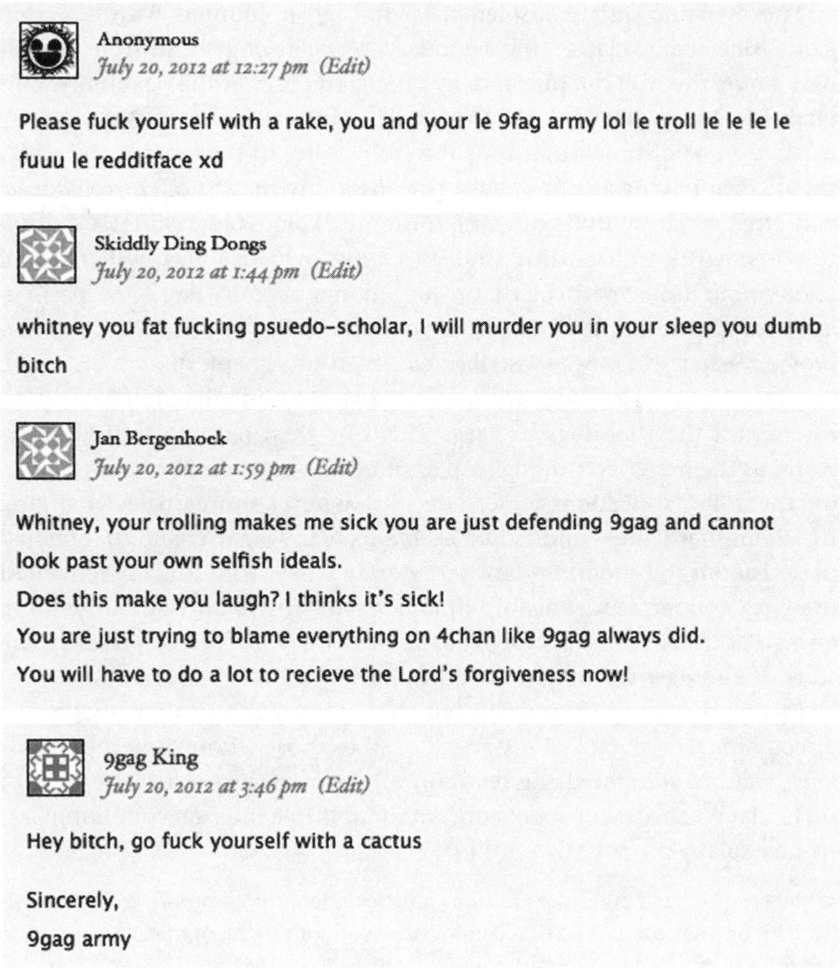

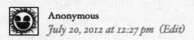
Anonymous
July 20, 2012 at 12:27 pm (Edit)

Please fuck yourself with a rake, you and your le 9fag army lol le troll le le le le
fuuu le redditface xd

Skiddly Ding Dongs
July 20, 2012 at 1:44 pm (Edit)

whitney you fat fucking psuedo-scholar, I will murder you in your sleep you dumb
bitch

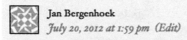
Jan Bergenhoek
July 20, 2012 at 1:59 pm (Edit)

Whitney, your trolling makes me sick you are just defending 9gag and cannot
look past your own selfish ideals.
Does this make you laugh? I thinks it's sick!
You are just trying to blame everything on 4chan like 9gag always did.
You will have to do a lot to recieve the Lord's forgiveness now!

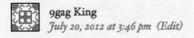
9gag King
July 20, 2012 at 3:46 pm (Edit)

Hey bitch, go fuck yourself with a cactus

Sincerely,

9gag army

Figure 9.1
Screenshot of comments posted to the author's July 20, 2012, blog post.

Rather than ignoring or deleting Stephen's comment (although I highly doubt that Stephen is the poster's real name), I decided to troll Stephen back, not just to send him a message but to declare to all the other trolls— particularly those posting sexually violent comments in response to my initial post—that I was aware of their game but had my own hand to play, thanks. So, pulling from what I knew about the community and what I could extrapolate from his statement, I wrote a sarcastic, condescending response thanking Stephen for his time and lauding him for his emotional investment in my work. I then asked him to please point out specific instances in my research where I had gotten my facts wrong, and pro- ceeded to preempt two potential points of criticism. I concluded by telling Stephen that I looked forward to his insights, and really appreciated his time and interest.[25]

Needless to say, Stephen did not respond. And why would he? By calling attention to the energy he'd invested in trolling me (or trying to troll me), I was essentially calling him a bad, inexperienced troll. Had he attempted to defend his trolling honor, he would have proven me right, and I would have won. He chose not to give me that satisfaction, thereby losing his own game. I am not ashamed to say that I laughed.

Trolling for Good?

However effective trolling rhetoric might be, particularly when dealing with unwanted trolling attention, the act of trolling is heavy with ideologi- cal baggage. No matter what purpose the act is meant to serve, it is and will always be predicated on some degree of antagonism. Ryan Milner argues that there is an important distinction between antagonism that facilitates robust dialogue—as was the outcome of SAFE's proposed book burning party—and antagonism that silences, marginalizes, and deni- grates.[26] In more straightforward cases like SAFE's book burning party, this distinction can be quite useful and provides an ethical metric for assessing specific instances of trolling. The distinction between "good" and "bad" antagonism becomes much more difficult to parse, however, when the act in question might facilitate robust dialogue for some and silence, marginal- ize, and denigrate others, a point of complication Milner readily con- cedes.[27] There is always the risk that when one antagonizes, even if one does so "for a good cause" (literacy, various counter-trolling strategies), one might also marginalize—the political and ethical implications of which hinge on who's doing the antagonizing and who's on the receiving end of those antagonisms.

Just as significantly, though perhaps more problematically, trolling is and will always be fundamentally asymmetrical: the troll, regardless of his or her motives, is roping a chosen target into a game of which the target may not even be aware, and subsequently to which he or she cannot consent. Compounding the basic asymmetry of trolling is the fact that the vast majority of trolls are gendered male, are raced as white, and are beneficiaries of a certain degree of economic privilege, and that the vast majority of their targets are members of underrepresented or otherwise marginalized populations.

But what happens when trolling rhetoric is harnessed for explicitly feminist purposes? Is there, or could there be, such a thing as a feminist troll? In an article posted to *Fembot*, an online feminist research collective, digital media and gender studies scholar Amanda Phillips considers the potential lessons of trolls and other online harassers (referred to collectively as "fucknecks") and insists that there is indeed a place for trolling rhetoric within feminist discourse. Wherever a person might go, she argues, whether online or even to an academic conference, there will be trolls. "Let's call it what it is," she argues, "and learn more effective strategies of provocation and deflection—to troll better, and to smash better those who troll us."[28] Given how culturally pervasive trolling has become, Phillips' point is well taken. If feminists don't find a way to harness existing trollish energy, it will be used against them.

I am inclined to take the argument one step further. In addition to serving an effective defensive function, something one deploys preemptively or in order to out-troll one's critics, feminist trolling can also be used for strategic intelligence gathering. By encouraging a suspected bigot and/or chauvinist to keep talking, interjecting only to goad the target into forwarding a stronger claim than he or she intended to disclose, feminist trolls are able to draw out the target's true loyalties—knowledge that can then be used to challenge or otherwise discredit an offending argument or person. That it also has the ability to befuddle and subsequently enrage a chauvinist—particularly when the chauvinist has taken pains to downplay his regressive political leanings—is an added bonus, at least for this feminist.

In 2012, the United States State Department sought to harness precisely this energy, for precisely these ends. Rather than trolling chauvinists, however, the State Department began trolling online extremists through a program called Viral Peace. According its founder, Shahed Amanullah, then senior technology advisor for the State Department, Viral Peace sought to use "logic, humor, satire, [and] religious arguments, not just to confront [extremists], but to undermine and demoralize them"—in other words, to troll hyper-masculinized wannabe terrorists into silence, thereby neutralizing potential threats before they have the chance to metastasize as offline violence. As Amanullah explained to *Wired*'s Spencer Ackerman, "[Online extremism] appeals to macho, it appeals to people's rebellious nature, it appeals to people who feel downtrodden." Consequently, it is very difficult to generate comparable anti-jihadist energy. "But it's easier," Ackerman wrote, paraphrasing Amanullah, "if the average would-be jihadi has his mystique challenged through the trial by fire that is online ridicule."[29]

As of 2014, Amanullah no longer works for the State Department, and Viral Peace is no longer a government-run program. It is, however, still operational, and in April 2014, Harvard University's Berkman Center for Internet & Society announced that it would be incorporating and building upon the Viral Peace project in order to combat youth-oriented hate speech and extremism online.[30] But the State Department trolls on; department officials currently run a verified Twitter account called "Think Again Turn Away," a program spearheaded by the interagency Center for Strategic Counterterrorism Communications (CSCC). Like its predecessor Viral Peace, Think Again Turn Away is designed to challenge would-be terrorists; unlike Viral Peace, this latest State Department venture advertises that it is a State Department program, even including the United States Department of State acronym in the program's Twitter handle (@Think_Again_DOS).[31]

Of course, the jury is still out on both Viral Peace and Think Again Turn Away. Not only are the projects navigating hitherto uncharted territory, success is an incredibly difficult criterion to define, let alone measure. It simply isn't possible to quantify the number of times someone who otherwise would have committed a violent act did not, a point former State Department senior counterterrorism advisor and CSCC cofounder Will McCants readily admits.[32] Still, the fact that the government (and as of 2014 Harvard's Berkman Center) is willing to train, fund, and oversee a professional class of Internet trolls speaks to the rhetorical power of coordinated provocation.

In China, the roles are reversed; instead of training trolls, the Chinese government is the target of trolling. But that's not the only point of distinction. Unlike Western trolling, which trades in spectacle, the Chinese variety is designed to travel under a series of governmental radars. Consequently, online instigators in China can't simply declare their trollish intentions. And so they must improvise, either by hiding messages in images (while the government is able to effectively censor specific key-words, it has more difficulty monitoring uploaded images),[33] by coding otherwise innocuous language with subversive meaning,[34] and/or by using what is called the "Human Flesh Search Engine,"[35] a loose online collective reminiscent of Anonymous, in order to subvert unjust social and political practices, stir up controversy, and cause mischief.[36]

The following example, which was recounted by social media artist An Xiao Mina during her presentation on the "Global Lulzes" panel at ROFLcon III, illustrates the subversive power of Chinese netizens. In 2011, a high-speed rail train crashed in Wenzhou, southern China. Initially, the govern-ment attempted to cover up the cause of the crash. Sina Weibo's users (Weibo is a Chinese microblogging platform similar in function and layout to Twitter) didn't buy this explanation, and posted countless image macros and subversive comics, with which the government censors couldn't keep pace. Not long after the crash, and as a direct result of these memetic interventions, the Chinese government was forced to reverse its position. In this way, Weibo users essentially trolled the Chinese government into publicly acknowledging both the crash and its cause.[37] While the actions of Chinese netizens may not be directly analogous to Western trolling, the basic impetus—to disrupt a given target's equilibrium or behavior in the name of some desired end—persists, suggesting that trolling rhetoric can be, and in fact has already proven to be, both culturally flexible and politi-cally efficacious.

So for the sake of argument—and this is an argument that I am inclined to agree with—let's say that certain forms of trolling can be justified, and that the antagonism(s) generated by these acts have a net positive social impact. Is the righteousness of a particular act compromised if it replicates precisely the cultural logics it seeks to dismantle? In an article analyzing the public voice of women (or lack thereof), classicist Mary Beard indirectly contextualizes this question in relation to feminist trolling. Beard opens her inquiry by turning to the beginning of Western literature, or very close to the beginning, specifically the ancient Greek epic the *Odyssey*. She describes an incident in which Telemachus, Odysseus and Penelope's son, scolds his mother for speaking freely in her own home. According to Telemachus, speech is the purview of men, and as such, he—and not his mother—should have the final and in fact the only say over what goes on in their household.[38]

Beard then compares this moment to our present pop cultural moment, in which women's voices online are silenced just as frequently, and for the same implicit reasons cited by Telemachus. If we want to understand why women are subjected to disproportionate abuse and derision online, Beard argues, we need to take the long view, one that sidesteps the overly simplistic assertion that specific hateful utterances are sexist. Aggressive speech directed at women is sexist, but it's symptomatic of something much deeper and much older than the contemporary attitudes of contemporary men toward contemporary women.

While Beard readily acknowledges that the Western tradition has been influenced and shaped by myriad cultural forces over the centuries, she stresses the enduring significance of the classical era, in the process contextualizing how conversations about classical tropes are immediately relevant to conversations about the contemporary digital media landscape—a very similar argument to the underlying thesis of this book, though with a much wider historical scope.

That, however, isn't the only overlap between Beard's argument and this study. Echoing chapter 7's critique of the adversary method, Beard discusses the impulse, common among women in positions of authority, to deliberately harness aspects of male rhetoric in order to be taken more seriously by subordinates, peers, and superiors. Although this approach might effectively convey authority and power, it doesn't get to the real issue: namely, the implication that speech, "serious" speech anyway, is naturally and necessarily gendered male. As such, the impulse to act like a man in order to be heard risks reinscribing precisely those structures that perpetuate gender inequality. A better approach, Beard argues, is to think critically and self-reflexively about our rhetorical operations. "We need," she argues, "to go back to some first principles about the nature of spoken authority, about what constitutes it, and how we have learned to hear authority where we do. And rather than push women into voice training classes to get a nice, deep, husky and entirely artificial tone, we should be thinking more about the faultlines and fractures that underlie dominant male discourse."[39]

Applied to trolling rhetoric, which is predicated on highly gendered notions of victory and domination, and which is used to silence, punish, and correct "soft" or otherwise feminized speech, Beard's conclusion is highly illuminating. It may be possible to deploy trolling rhetoric against trolls. It may be effective. It may be vindicating, even amusing. But what does it say when the solution to the problem contains a trace of the problem? What does it say when those invested in an anti-oppression framework engage in behaviors that are fundamentally asymmetrical, that actively seek to dominate and publicly humiliate one's opponent, and that, most problematically, preclude consent?

Just as Audre Lorde warned against using patriarchal rhetoric, patriarchal structures of organization, and patriarchal privileging of solidarity over difference to dismantle patriarchy,[40] I too am reluctant to wholeheartedly claim for the feminist cause a rhetorical mode so thoroughly steeped in male domination. On the other hand, if the goal is to dismantle patriarchal structures, and if feminist trolling helps accomplish those ends, then are the means, however problematic, retroactively justified? I look forward to further research that tackles these questions, including the question of how best to theorize the relationship between trolling and global activism. For now, I remain simultaneously intrigued by and wary of the political potential of trolling—a fitting end to a project and behavioral practice steeped in ambivalence.

Final Thoughts

As I explained in the introduction, this book is less about trolls and more about a culture in which trolls thrive. It is therefore fitting that my final takeaway point addresses trolls only indirectly, and instead focuses on the false security that comes from pitting a presumably innocent "us" against some seemingly antithetical "them." In this case, we—average Internet users—are reasonable, civil, and fair, while they—the ruthless trolls—are aggressive, misanthropic, and cruel.

Lewis Hyde's study of mythological trickster challenges such binary modes of thinking and argues that the line between us and them, good guy and bad guy, is rarely so straightforward.[41] "We may well hope our actions carry no moral ambiguity," Hyde writes. "But pretending that is the case when it isn't does not lead to greater clarity about right and wrong; it more likely leads to unconscious cruelty masked as inflated righteousness."[42] Furthermore, the assumption that we (whomever this universalizing "we" subsumes) couldn't possibly be wrong often obscures the ways in which normalized tropes encourage or even run parallel to precisely the individuals and behaviors condemned as aberrant.[43]

That, ultimately, is my argument here. Trolls may be destructive and callous; they may represent privilege gone berserk; they may be a significant reason why we can't have nice things online. But the uncomfortable fact is that trolls replicate behaviors and attitudes that in other contexts are actively celebrated ("This is how the West was won!") or simply taken as a given ("Boys will be boys"). Trolls certainly amplify the ugly side of mainstream behavior, but they aren't pulling their materials, chosen targets, or impulses from the ether. They are born of and fueled by the mainstream world—its behavioral mores, its corporate institutions, its political structures and leaders—however much the mainstream might rankle at the suggestion.

If this study has accomplished anything, then, it is to call attention to the overlap between us and them, and to encourage readers to spin endlessly their sense of what has happened—a line of questioning that is as likely to direct focus inward as it is to cast blame outward, and that provides a framework for thinking carefully and critically not just about the what of trolling, and not just the how, but the *why*. This why might not be a solution unto itself, but it is, at the very least, a start. And that is something.

Notes

Introduction

1. Ryan M. Milner, "Hacking the Social: Internet Memes, Identity Antagonism, and the Logic of Lulz," *The Fibreculture Journal* 22 (2013): paragraph 8, accessed March 23, 2014, http://twentytwo.fibreculturejournal.org/fcj-156-hacking-the -social-internet-memes-identity-antagonism-and-the-logic-of-lulz.

2. Suzanne Daley, "In Zambia, the Abandoned Generation," *New York Times*, September 18, 1998, accessed March 5, 2010, http://www.nytimes.com/1998/09/18/ world/in-zambia-the-abandoned-generation.html.

3. Ishbel Matheson, "Children High on Sewage," *BBC News*, July 30, 1999, accessed November 13, 2010, http://news.bbc.co.uk/2/hi/africa/406067.stm.

4. "Jenkem," *Encyclopedia Dramatica*, September 19, 2012, accessed September 19, 2012, https://encyclopediadramatica.es/Jenkem.

5. Ibid.

6. "'Drug' Made from Human Waste Making a Stink on Web, in Law Enforcement," *FoxNews*, November 7, 2007, accessed May 20, 2011, http://www.foxnews.com/ story/2007/11/06/drug-made-from-human-waste-causing-stink-on-web-in-law -enforcement.

7. "Fox News Reports on Jenkem," *YouTube*, November 7, 2007, accessed October 1, 2011, http://www.youtube.com/watch?v=2UsNbsjpuLc&feature=player_embedded.

8. "SAY NO TO JENKEM," *YouTube*, November 6, 2007, accessed October 1, 2011, http://www.youtube.com/watch?v=5-SB7kKwn1A&feature=player_embedded.

9. "'Drug' Making a Stink on Web."

10. "Police Training on How to Spot Nasty Drug," *MSNBC*, November 12, 2007, accessed March 5, 2013, http://web.archive.org/web/20071112023107/http://www .msnbc.msn.com/id/21684383.

11. Kelli Cheatham, "Police Warn about New Drug Made From Raw Sewage," *WSBT South Bend*, November 7, 2007, accessed March 5, 2013, http://web.archive.org/web/20071109120038/http://www.wsbt.com/news/11077771.html.

12. Mary Douglas, *Purity and Danger: An Analysis of Concepts of Pollution and Taboo* (London: Routledge and Kegan Paul, 1966), 1–50.

13. Janice Moulton, "A Paradigm of Philosophy: The Adversary Method," in *Discovering Reality, Second Edition: Feminist Perspectives on Epistemology, Metaphysics, Methodology, and Philosophy of Science*, ed. Sandra Harding and Merrill B. Hintikka (Dordrecht, The Netherlands: Kluwer, 1983), 149–164.

14. Lewis Hyde, *Trickster Makes This World: How Disruptive Imagination Creates Culture* (Edinburgh: Canongate, 1998).

15. Ibid., 2–14, 71, 283.

16. Ibid., 285–288.

17. Ibid., 287.

18. Ibid., 288.

19. Gabriella Coleman, "Hacker and Troller as Trickster," *Gabriellacoleman.org*, February 7, 2010, accessed June 10, 2010, http://gabriellacoleman.org/blog/?p=1902.

1   Defining Terms

1. "Troll," *Oxford English Dictionary*, accessed September 7, 2011, http://www.oxforddictionaries.com/us/definition/american_english/troll.

2. Michelle Tepper, "Usenet Communities and the Cultural Politics of Information," in *Internet Culture*, ed. David Porter (New York: Routledge, 1997), 39–55.

3. Judith Donath, "Identity and Deception in the Virtual World," in *Communities in Cyberspace*, ed. Mark A. Smith and Peter Kollock (New York: Routledge, 1999), 29–60.

4. Lincoln Dahlberg, "Computer Mediated Communication and the Public Sphere," *Journal of Computer Mediated Communication* 7, no. 1 (2001): 0, doi:10.1111/j.1083-6101.2001.tb00137.x.

5. Claire Hardacker, "Trolling in Asynchronous Computer-Mediated Communication: From User Discussions to Academic Definitions," *Journal of Politeness Research* 6, no. 2 (2010): 237, doi:10.1515/JPLR.2010.011.

6. Ibid., 225–235.

7. Kelly Bergstrom, "Don't Feed the Troll: Shutting Down Debate about Community Expectations on Reddit.com," *First Monday* 16, no. 8, accessed September 2, 2011, http://firstmonday.org/ojs/index.php/fm/article/view/3498/3029.

8. *Catfish*, directed by Henry Joost and Ariel Schulman (Universal City, CA: Universal Pictures, 2010).

9. "Senate Bill 1411," *California State Legislature*, 2010, accessed April 12, 2011, http://www.leginfo.ca.gov/pub/09-10/bill/sen/sb_1401-1450/sb_1411_bill_20100927 _chaptered.html.

10. "Troll," *Encyclopedia Dramatica*, December 12, 2004, accessed December 12, 2009 (website since deleted), http://encyclopediadramatica.com/Troll.

11. "FAQ," *4chan*, accessed October 23, 2009, http://www.4chan.org/faq.

12. Josh Quittner, "The War between alt.tasteless and rec.pets.cats," *Wired*, 1993, accessed June 10, 2013, http://www.wired.com/wired/archive/2.05/alt.tasteless_pr .html.

13. Anon1, Facebook messages exchanged with author, June–August 2011.

14. Andy Bennett and Keith Kahn-Harris, *After Subculture: Critical Studies in Contemporary Youth Culture* (London: Palgrave Macmillan Limited, 2004).

15. Richard Dawkins, *The Selfish Gene* (New York: Oxford University Press, 1976).

16. Jean Burgess, "'All Your Chocolate Rain Are Belong to Us?' Viral Video, YouTube, and the Dynamics of Participatory Culture," *Video Vortex Reader: Responses to YouTube* (Amsterdam: Institute of Network Cultures, 2008), 101–109; Ryan Milner, "The World Made Meme: Discourse and Identity in Participatory Media" (PhD diss., University of Kansas, 2012), accessed February 21, 2014, http://kuscholarworks. ku.edu/dspace/handle/1808/10256; Limor Shifman, *Memes in Digital Culture* (Cambridge, MA: MIT Press, 2013).

17. Henry Jenkins, Sam Ford, and Joshua Green, *Spreadable Media: Creating Value and Meaning in a Networked Culture* (New York: NYU Press, 2013).

18. Shifman, *Memes in Digital Culture*, 6; italics in the original.

19. Ryan M. Milner, "Media Lingua Franca: Fixity, Novelty, and Vernacular Creativity in Internet Memes," *Selected Papers of Internet Researchers* 3 (2013), accessed May 1, 2014, http://spir.aoir.org/index.php/spir/article/view/806.

20. "Ben Huh—Bio," *Bravotv.com*, 2014, accessed June 5, 2014. http://www.bravotv .com/people/ben-huh/bio.

21. Miki-em, "Rick Astley Does Live Rickroll at Macy's Thanksgiving Day Parade," *Laughing Squid*, November 27, 2008, accessed June 5, 2014, http://laughingsquid .com/rick-astley-does-live-rickroll-at-macys-thanksgiving-day-parade.

22. Tom Connor Mar, "The Internet Anthropologist's Field Guide to 'Rage Faces,'" *Ars Technica*, March 11, 2012, accessed June 5, 2014, http://arstechnica .com/tech-policy/2012/03/the-internet-anthropologists-field-guide-to-rage-faces/2.

23. moot on 4chan, quoted in Lee Knutilla, "User Unknown: 4chan, Anonymity and Contingency," *First Monday* 16, no. 10 (2011), accessed October 5, 2011, http://firstmonday.org/htbin/cgiwrap/bin/ojs/index.php/fm/article/viewArticle/3665/3055.

2 The Only Reason to Do Anything

1. "Lulz," *Encyclopedia Dramatica*, January 15, 2012, accessed January 15, 2012, http://encyclopediadramatica.ch/lulz.

2. Matthias Schwartz, "Malwebolence: The Trolls among Us," *New York Times*, August 8, 2008, accessed August 10, 2008, http://www.nytimes.com/2008/08/03/magazine/03trolls-t.html.

3. John Suler, "The Online Disinhibition Effect," *CyberPsychology & Behavior* 7, no. 3 (2004): 321.

4. Karl Marx, "The Fetishism of the Commodity and Its Secret," in *Capital* (New York: Penguin, 1867), 163–167.

5. "Jessi Slaughter," *Know Your Meme*, July 10, 2010, accessed June 20, 2011, http://knowyourmeme.com/memes/events/jessi-slaughter.

6. "ORIGINAL Jessi Slaughter before Emotional Breakdown (Bad Mouthed Girl)," *YouTube*, July 18, 2010, accessed March 20, 2012, http://www.youtube.com/watch?v=Yy4gGs8_90w&feature=player_embedded.

7. "Jessi Slaughter," *Know Your Meme*.

8. Mike Hubler and Diana Bell, "Computer-Mediated Humor and Ethos: Exploring Threads of Constitutive Humor in Online Communities," *Computers and Composition* 20, no. 3 (2003): 277–282.

9. James English, *Comic Transactions* (Ithaca: Cornell University Press, 1994), 16–19.

10. Milner, "Hacking the Social."

11. *Battletoads*, created by Tim and Chris Stamper (Twycross, Leicestershire, UK: Rare, 1991).

12. "Is This Battletoads," *Encyclopedia Dramatica*, February 26, 2010, accessed March 5, 2010 (website since deleted), http://encyclopediadramatica.com/Is_This_Battletoads.

13. Gabriella Coleman, "Our Weirdness Is Free," *Triple Canopy*, January 15, 2012, accessed January 16, 2012, http://canopycanopycanopy.com/issues/15/contents/our_weirdness_is_free.

14. Gregory Bateson, "A Theory of Play and Fantasy," in *Steps to an Ecology of Mind* (Chicago: University of Chicago Press, 1972), 177–193.

15. Anon2, Facebook messages exchanged with author, June–August, 2011.

16. Anon3, Facebook messages exchanged with author, June 2011–July 2011.

17. Erving Goffman, "Front," in *The Presentation of Self in Everyday Life* (New York: Doubleday, 1959), 22–30.

18. Henri Bergson, "On Laughter," in *Comedy*, ed. Wylie Sypher (Baltimore: Johns Hopkins University Press, 1956), 61–192.

19. Peter Partyvan, Facebook and Skype messages exchanged with author, 2011–2012.

20. Wilson Mouzone, Facebook and Skype messages exchanged with author, 2011–2012.

21. Anon2, Facebook messages exchanged with author.

3   Toward a Method/ology

1. Gershon Legman, *No Laughing Matter: Rational of the Dirty Joke* (New York: Bell, 1971).

2. Ibid., 21.

3. Dick Hebdige, *Subculture: The Meaning of Style* (New York: Routledge, 1972).

4. Mizuko Ito, "Virtually Embodied: The Reality of Fantasy in a Multi-User Dungeon," in *Internet Culture*, ed. David Porter (New York: Routledge, 1997), 87–111.

5. Lisa Nakamura, *Cybertypes: Race, Ethnicity, and Identity on the Internet* (New York: Routledge, 2002) and *Digitizing Race: Visual Cultures of the Internet* (Minneapolis: University of Minnesota Press, 2007).

6. danah boyd, "Why Youth Use Social Network Sites: The Role of Networked Publics in Teenage Social Life," in *Youth, Identity and Digital Media*, ed. David Buckingham (Cambridge, MA: MIT Press, 2009), 1–26.

7. Lisa Nakamura, Beth Kolko, and Gilbert Rodman, *Race in Cyberspace* (New York: Routledge, 2000).

8. Tom Boellstorff, *Coming of Age in Second Life* (Princeton: Princeton University Press, 2009).

9. danah boyd, "Taken Out of Context: American Teen Sociality in Networked Publics," *danah.org*, Fall 2008, accessed September 19, 2009, http://www.danah.org/papers/TakenOutOfContext.html.

10. Gabriella Coleman, "Phreakers, Hackers, and Trolls and the Politics of Transgression and Spectacle," in *The Social Media Reader*, ed. Michael Mandiberg (New York: NYU Press, 2010), 99–120.

11. Gabriella Coleman, *Coding Freedom: The Ethics and Aesthetics of Hacking* (Princeton: Princeton University Press, 2013).

12. Gabriella Coleman, *Hacker, Hoaxer, Whistleblower, Spy: The Story of Anonymous* (London: Verso Press, 2014).

13. Gabriella Coleman, "The Ethnographers Cunning: The Return of the Arm Chair and Keyboard Anthropologist" (paper presented at the annual meeting of the American Anthropological Association, Montreal, Canada, November 16, 2011).

14. Erin E. Buckels, Paul D. Trapnell, and Delroy L. Paulhus, "Trolls Just Want to Have Fun," *Personality and Individual Differences*, online before print February 8, 2014, accessed February 8, 2014, http://www.sciencedirect.com/science/article/pii/S0191886914000324.

15. Chris Mooney, "Internet Trolls Really Are Horrible People," *Slate*, February 14, 2014, accessed February 14, 2014, http://www.slate.com/articles/health_and _science/climate_desk/2014/02/internet_troll_personality_study_machiavellianism _narcissism_psychopathy.html.

16. Jenkins, Ford, and Green, *Spreadable Media*.

17. "Miracles," *YouTube*, April 6, 2010, accessed April 6, 2010, https://www.youtube .com/watch?v=_-agl0pOQfs.

18. Whitney Phillips, "'In Defense of Memes': My Essay from Spreadable Media," *Billions and Billions*, December 3, 2012, accessed December 3, 2012, http://billions -and-billions.com/2012/12/03/in-defense-of-memes-my-essay-from-spreadable -media.

19. Wilson Mouzone, Facebook and Skype messages exchanged with author.

4   The House That Fox Built

An early draft of this chapter was published online in the academic journal *Television and New Media* before it appeared in print on August 30, 2012. For the print version, see *Television and New Media* 14, no. 6 (November 2013): 494–509.

1. Taryn Sauthoff, "4chan: The Rude, Raunchy Underbelly of the Internet," *Fox News.com*, April 8, 2009, accessed April 8, 2009, http://www.foxnews.com/ story/2009/04/08/4chan-rude-raunchy-underbelly-internet.

2. Ibid.

3. "Outfoxed: Fox News Technique 'Some People Say,'" *YouTube*, May 9, 2007, accessed June 10, 2011, http://www.youtube.com/watch?v=NYA9ufivbDw.

4. Sauthoff, "4chan: The Rude, Raunchy Underbelly of the Internet."

5. Hebdige, *Subculture: The Meaning of Style*.

6. "FAQ," *4chan*.

7. Schwartz, "Malwebolence: The Trolls among Us."

8. Richard Dyer, *White* (New York: Routledge, 1997).

9. Ibid., 1–9.

10. Milner, "Hacking the Social," paragraph 45.

11. Ibid., paragraph 69.

12. Jamin Brophey-Warren, "Modest Web Site Is Behind a Bevy of Memes," *Wall Street Journal*, July 9, 2008, accessed June 10, 2009, http://online.wsj.com/news/articles/SB121564928060441097?mg=reno64-wsj&url=http%3A%2F%2Fonline.wsj.com%2Farticle%2FSB121564928060441097.html.

13. Lev Grossman, "The Master of Memes," *Time*, July 9, 2008, accessed July 20, 2009, http://content.time.com/time/magazine/article/0,9171,1821656,00.html.

14. Schwartz, "Malwebolence: The Trolls among Us."

15. Monica Hesse, "A Virtual Unknown: Meet 'moot,' the Secretive Internet Celeb Who Still Lives with Mom," *Washington Post*, February 17, 2009, accessed February 26, 2010, http://www.washingtonpost.com/wp-dyn/content/article/2009/02/16/AR2009021601565.html.

16. Nick Bilton, "One on One: Christopher Poole, Founder of 4chan," *New York Times*, March 19, 2010, accessed March 30, 2010, http://www.nytimes.com/glogin?URI=http://bits.blogs.nytimes.com/2010/03/19/one-on-one-christopher-poole-founder-of-4chan/&OQ=_phpQ3DtrueQ26_typeQ3DblogsQ26_rQ3D0&OP=719c062cQ2FqedQ2Fqv2Q2Fq888qRddQ25UQ7DesoudQ60d.

17. "Mainstreaming the Web," *ROFLcon*, May 24, 2010, accessed June 20, 2010, http://roflcon.org/2010/05/24/mainstreaming-the-web-complete-video.

18. "FAQ," *4chan*.

19. Finn Brunton, "Creating and Violating Anonymity in Online Communities: The Case of 4chan, Anon, and Dusty the Cat" (paper presented at the Privacy Research Group, New York University, New York, NY, February 24, 2010).

20. *We Are Legion*, directed by Brian Knappenberger (Venice, CA: Luminant Media, 2012).

21. Parmy Olson, "The March of the Trolls and Hactivists," *Forbes*, September 5, 2011, accessed March 5, 2012, http://www.forbes.com/sites/parmyolson/2011/09/05/march-of-the-trolls-and-hacktivists.

22. Erik Schonfeld, "Time Magazine Throws Up Its Hands as it Gets Pwnd by 4chan," *TechCrunch*, April 27, 2009, accessed June 5 2009, http://techcrunch.com/2009/04/27/time-magazine-throws-up-its-hands-as-it-gets-pwned-by-4chan.

23. Stanley Cohen, "Deviance and Moral Panics," in *Folk Devils and Moral Panics* (New York: Routledge, 1972), 11, 15–19.

24. "Archiving Internet Subculture," *The Web Ecology Project*, April 15, 2011, accessed May 5, 2014, http://www.webecologyproject.org/2011/04/archiving-internet-subculture-encyclopedia-dramatica.

25. The Web Ecology group's Encyclopedia Dramatica intervention was, ultimately, a lucky accident. In February 2011, Web Ecology members Seth Woodworth and Alex Leavitt were working on a network visualization project. In order to analyze existing topic clusters on Encyclopedia Dramatica, Woodworth downloaded the site's raw wiki markup (the unformatted code) as text files. After Encyclopedia Dramatica was deleted without warning—sending Internet researchers, myself included, into a panic—the Web Ecology group decided to post a zip archive of the scraped .txt files onto the Web Ecology blog. Using this data, a small army of Encyclopedia Dramatica users and admins were able to reconstruct the site, although all the pre–April 2011 edits were lost and all images had to be replaced by hand. Since 2011, the restored Encyclopedia Dramatica wiki has changed domains numerous times (from encyclopediadramatica.ch to encyclopediadramatica.se to encyclopediadramatica.es) and as of June 2014 is in the process of transferring its data to French servers.

26. "Anonymous," *Urban Dictionary*, November 3, 2006, accessed December 15, 2011, http://www.urbandictionary.com/define.php?term=Anonymous&page=6#.

27. "Anonymous on FOX 11 News," *YouTube*, July 27, 2007, accessed December 10, 2011, http://www.youtube.com/watch?v=DNO6G4ApJQY&feature=player_embedded.

28. Ibid.

29. DancingJesus94, 2010, comment on "Anonymous on FOX 11 News."

30. Douglas Thomas, *Hacker Culture* (Minneapolis: University of Minnesota Press, 2002), 37.

31. Nick Denton, "The Cruise Indoctrination Video Scientology Tried to Suppress," *Gawker*, January 15, 2008, accessed December 10, 2011, http://gawker.com/5002269/the-cruise-indoctrination-video-scientology-tried-to-suppress.

32. "Anonymous Proposes a Plan," *4chan Archive*, January 15, 2008, accessed December 3, 2011 (website since deleted), http://4chanarchive.org/brchive/dspl _thread.php5?thread_id=51051816.

33. Gabriella Coleman, "Old & New Net Wars over Free Speech, Freedom & Secrecy: Or How to Understand the Hacker & Lulz Battle against the Church of Scientology," *Vimeo*, December 10, 2010, accessed December 12, 2010, http://vimeo.com/ user3514769/videos.

34. Ibid.

35. "Message to Scientology," *YouTube*, January 21, 2008, accessed April 12, 2008, https://www.youtube.com/watch?v=JCbKv9yiLiQ.

36. *V for Vendetta*, directed by James McTeigue (Hollywood, CA: Warner Brothers, 2005).

37. "Anonymous," *Wikipedia*, February 12, 2008, accessed April 16, 2012, http:// en.wikipedia.org/w/index.php?title=Anonymous_(group)&dir=prev&action=history.

38. Helen Popkin, "Bill O'Reilly's Website Hacked," *MSNBC*, September 26, 2008, accessed October 1, 2008, http://www.nbcnews.com/id/26870105/ns/technology _and_science-tech_and_gadgets/t/bill-oreillys-web-site-hacked.

39. "Bill O'Reilly–Sarah Palin Email," *YouTube*, September 18, 2008, accessed December 3, 2011 (video since deleted), http://www.youtube.com/watch?v=hCSaF 4KC3eE&feature=player_embedded; "O'Reilly's Calling FBI on Palin Hackers & Lib Blog Posters," *YouTube*, September 18, 2008, accessed October 3, 2008, http://www .youtube.com/watch?v=zq1NK6P8870.

40. Dancho Danchev, "Bill O'Reilly's Website Hacked, Attackers Release Personal Details of Users," *ZDnet.com*, September 24, 2008, accessed October 1, 2009, http:// www.zdnet.com/security/?p=1958.

41. "Bill O'Reilly: A Far-Left Website Known as '4chan' Is Providing Child Pornography to Internet Pedophiles," *Reddit* (via *tinypic*), August 27, 2009, accessed September 2, 2009, http://www.reddit.com/r/pics/comments/9eslq/bill_oreilly_a _farleft_website _known_as_4chan_is.

42. "Operation Bill Can Haz Cheezburgers," *4chan*, November 7, 2009, accessed November 7, 2009 (thread since deleted), http://www.4chan.org.

43. "So Cash," *Encyclopedia Dramatica*, February, 19, 2008, accessed October 2, 2009 (website since deleted), http://encyclopediadramatica.com/So_cash.

44. Ibid.

45. Pierre Lévy, *Collective Intelligence*, trans. Robert Bononno (Cambridge: Perseus Books, 1997), 13.

46. "Pedobear," *Know Your Meme*, November 2011, accessed December 10, 2011, http://knowyourmeme.com/memes/pedobear.

47. "9000!!!!," *YouTube*, June 24, 2008, accessed July 13, 2009, http://www.youtube.com/watch?v=SiMHTK15Pik.

48. "Oprah Over 9000 Penises!," *Youtube*, October 3, 2008, accessed October 4, 2008 (video since deleted). http://www.youtube.com/watch?v=slDAPms8Tvs&feature=player_embedded.

49. "Oprah Over 9000 Penises f/ PEDOBEAR Remix," *YouTube*, October 10, 2008, accessed October 10, 2008 (video since deleted), http://www.youtube.com/watch?v=1A5Ysh5rl4g.

50. "Tom Cruise's Greatest Hits," *Oprah.com*, May 29, 2008, accessed May 5, 2014, http://www.oprah.com/oprahshow/Tom-Cruises-Greatest-Hits.

51. "Oprah Winfrey," *Encyclopedia Dramatica*, September 11, 2011, accessed September 11, 2011, http://encyclopediadramatica.ch/Oprah.

52. Guy Debord and Gil Wolman, "A User's Guide to *Détournement*," *Situationist International Anthology*, trans. and ed. Ken Knabb (Berkeley, CA: Bureau of Public Secrets, 1956), 14–21.

53. Anselm Jappe, *Guy Debord* (Berkeley: University of California Press, 1999), 59.

54. Douglas Kellner, "Media Culture and the Triumph of the Spectacle," in *Media Spectacle* (Routledge: New York, 2003), 1–33.

55. "Oprah Winfrey," *Encyclopedia Dramatica*.

56. "Gnomes," *South Park*, season 2, episode 17, written by Pam Brady, Trey Parker, and Matt Stone, first broadcast on Comedy Central, December 16, 1998.

5   LOLing at Tragedy

An early draft of this chapter, titled "LOLing at Tragedy: Facebook Trolls, Memorial Pages and Resistance to Grief Online," was published in the Internet studies journal *First Monday* 16, no. 12 (December 2011).

1. Elliot Oring, "Jokes and the Discourses on Disaster," *The Journal of American Folklore* 100, no. 397 (1987): 276–286.

2. Recall the previous discussion of "shit was SO cash"; hence "Paulie Socash." Similarly, my profile was a nod to the longstanding trolling joke that everyone on the Internet is actually named David.

3. Max Kelley, "Memories of Friends Departed Endure on Facebook," *Facebook*, October 26, 2010, accessed March 20, 2010, http://www.facebook.com/notes/facebook/memories-of-friends-departed-endure-on-facebook/163091042130.

4. Alexandria Topping, "Facebook to Launch Memorial Profiles of Deceased Users," *The Guardian*, May 2, 2010, accessed May 3, 2010, http://www.theguardian.com/ technology/2009/oct/27/facebook-user-memorials.

5. Kelley, "Memories of Friends Departed."

6. Lisa Miller, "R.I.P. on Facebook," *Newsweek*, March 1, 2010, accessed May 3, 2010, http://www.newsweek.com/2010/02/16/r-i-p-on-facebook.html.

7. Edicio Martinez, "Killer Whale Kills Trainer Footage: SeaWorld and Dawn Brancheau's Family Wants Video Suppressed," *CBS News*, March 9, 2010, accessed March 10, 2010, http://www.cbsnews.com/news/killer-whale-kills-trainer-footage -seaworld-dawn-brancheaus-family-wants-video-suppressed.

8. "Epic Beard Man," *Encyclopedia Dramatica*, February 27, 2010, accessed February 27, 2010 (website since deleted), http://encyclopediadramatica.com/Epic_Beard _Man.

9. Ibid.

10. Saul Relative, "Search for Chelsea King Shows Community Effort to Find Missing Poway Girl," *Yahoo Voices*, February 28, 2010, accessed March 1, 2012, http:// voices.yahoo.com/search-chelsea-king-shows-community-effort-to-5560523.html; Dean Schabner, "Chelsea King Searchers Move 'Heaven and Earth' to Find Girl," *ABC News*, February 27, 2010, accessed February 27, 2010, http://abcnews.go.com/ US/chelsea-king-missing-thursday/story?id=9966194.

11. "Chelsea's Light," *Facebook*, accessed March 10, 2010, https://www.facebook .com/chelseaslight.

12. "Help Find Chelsea King," *Facebook*, accessed March 15, 2010 (page since deleted), https://www.facebook.com.

13. Russell Goldman, "Cops Believe Chelsea King Was Raped and Murdered," *ABC News*, May 24, 2010, accessed May 24, 2010, http://abcnews.go.com/GMA/TheLaw/ chelsea-king-disappearance-suspect-linkedcases/story?id=9975272.

14. "I Bet This Pickle Can Get More Fans than Chelsea King," *Facebook*, 2010, accessed March 15, 2010 (page since deleted), https://www.facebook.com.

15. Created in early 2010, the Nickleback/Pickle page was based on the similarly titled "I Bet This Onion Ring Can Get More Fans than Justin Beiber." Like Justin Bieber/Onion Ring, Nickleback/Pickle was a runaway hit and amassed nearly 1.5 million fans, successfully surpassing the fan count on Nickleback's official Facebook page. Later variations on this meme included "Can This Poodle Wearing A Tinfoil Hat Get More Fans than Glenn Beck" and "I Bet This Shoe Can Get More Fans than Edward Cullin."

16. "Facebook Users Mock Death of Chelsea King," *10News*, May 2, 2010, accessed May 2, 2010 (page since deleted), http://www.10news.com/video/22759317/index.html.

17. Ibid.

18. Laura Roberts, "Kristian Digby, the BBC Presenter, May Have Died in Sex Game Gone Wrong," *The Telegraph*, March 2, 2010, accessed March 3, 2010, http://www.telegraph.co.uk/culture/tvandradio/7351843/Kristian-Digby-the-BBC-presenter-may-have-died-in-sex-game-gone-wrong.html.

19. Michael Lund, "What's Next for Facebook after Its Nightmare Week?" *The Punch*, May 7, 2010, accessed May 8, 2010, http://www.thepunch.com.au/articles/what-next-for-facebook-after-its-nightmare-week.

20. Tony Keim, "Facebook Troll Bradley Paul Hampson Jailed for Posting Child Porn on Tribute Sites of Dead Children," *The Courier Mail*, March 25, 2011, accessed May 1, 2013, http://www.couriermail.com.au/news/queensland/facebook-troll-bradley-paul-hampson-jailed-for-posting-child-porn-on-tribute-pages-for-dead-children/story-e6freoof-1226028117673.

21. "I Think Internet Trolls Are Losers," *Facebook*, accessed May 1, 2010 (page since deleted), https://www.facebook.com.

22. "Stop the Bullying," *Facebook*, accessed June 1, 2010 (page since deleted), https://www.facebook.com.

23. "Army against Low Life Trolls," *Facebook*, accessed April 1, 2010 (page since deleted), https://www.facebook.com.

24. "These Cruel Facebook 'Trolls' Need to Be Locked Up for Attacking RIP Groups!," *Facebook*, 2010, accessed April 1, 2010 (page since deleted), https://www.facebook.com.

25. "The Mike Lonston Experience," *Facebook*, 2010, accessed June 15, 2010 (page since deleted), https://www.facebook.com.

26. Lund, "What's Next for Facebook?"

27. Andrew Hough, "Facebook Vows New Security Measures to Combat Alarming 'Trolling' Abuse," *The Telegraph*, September 1, 2010, accessed September 2, 2010, http://www.telegraph.co.uk/technology%20/facebook/7939721/Facebook-vows-new-security-measures-to-combat-alarming-trolling-abuse-trend.html.

28. Miguel Helft, "Facebook Wrestles with Free Speech and Civility," *New York Times*, December 12, 2012, accessed December 12, 2010, http://www.nytimes.com/2010/12/13/technology/13facebook.html.

29. Frank, Facebook and Skype messages exchanged with the author, 2011–2012.

30. Phillips, "LOLing at Tragedy."

31. Soveri Ruthless, Skype messages exchanged with author, 2011.

32. Paulie Socash, Facebook and Skype messages exchanged with author, 2010–2012.

33. Peter Partyvan, Facebook and Skype messages exchanged with author, 2011–2012.

34. Wilson Mouzone, Facebook and Skype messages exchanged with author, 2011–2012.

35. "Memorial Page Tourism," *Encyclopedia Dramatica*, June 6, 2010, accessed June 9, 2010 (website since deleted), http://encyclopediadramatica.com/Memorial_Page _Tourism.

36. Paulie Socash, Facebook and Skype messages exchanged with author.

37. Ibid.

38. Alex Freedman, "We Can Pretty Much Say That We're Looking for the Worst," *Wnct.com*, August 19, 2011, accessed July 27, 2012, http://www2.wnct.com/ news/2010/aug /19/22/has-anyone-heard-jalesa-reynolds-scotland-neck-ar-340940.

39. Soveri Ruthless, Skype messages exchanged with author.

40. Oring, "Jokes and the Discourses on Disaster," 280.

41. Ibid., 280–283.

42. Ibid., 282.

43. "ABC 10 News Reaction," messages collected by the author on Facebook and Skype, May 2010.

44. John Hudson, "Gay Teen Suicide Sparks Debate over Cyber Bullying," *The Atlantic Wire*, October 1, 2010, accessed October 3, 2010, http://www.thewire.com/ national/2010/10/gay-teen-suicide-sparks-debate-over-cyber-bullying/22829.

45. "Online 'Trolls' Terrorize the Grieving," *The Today Show*, March 31, 2010, accessed March 31, 2010, http://www.today.com/video/today/36113365.

46. Beth Hale, "Tormented by Trolling: The Vile Web Craze Taunted Family of Bullied Girl after Her Death," *The Daily Mail*, February 26, 2011, accessed February 27, 2011, http://www.dailymail.co.uk/news/article-1360788/Natasha-MacBryde-suicide -Vile-web-craze-taunted-family-bullied-girl-death.html.

47. Tanith Carey, "'Help Me, Mummy. It's Hot Here in Hell': A Special Investigation into the Distress of Grieving Families Caused by the Sick Internet Craze of 'Troll-ing,'" *The Daily Mail*, September 24, 2011, accessed September 25, 2012, http://www .dailymail.co.uk/news/article-2041193/Internet-trolling-Investigation-distress -grieving-families-caused-trolls.html#ixzz1Yt6qEOwi.

48. David P. Phillips and Lundie L. Carstensen, "Clustering of Teenage Suicides after Television News Stories about Suicide," *New England Journal of Medicine* 315, no. 11 (1986): 685–689.

49. "Recommendations for Reporting on Suicide," *American Foundation for Suicide Prevention*, accessed January 5, 2010, https://www.afsp.org/news-events/for-the -media/reporting-on-suicide.

50. Hale, "Tormented by Trolling."

51. "Online 'Trolls' Terrorize the Grieving."

52. Christian Salazar, "Alexis Pilkington Facebook Horror: Cyber Bullies Harass Teen Even after Suicide," *Huffington Post*, May 25, 2010, accessed May 26, 2010, http:// www.huffingtonpost.com/2010/03/24/alexis-pilkington-faceboo_n_512482.html.

53. Pro Fessor, Facebook and Skype messages exchanged with author, 2011.

54. Paulie Socash, "It Finally Happened," email message to author, April 15, 2010.

6   Race and the No-Spin Zone

1. Stuart Hall, "The Whites of Their Eyes: Racist Ideologies and the Media," in *Silver Linings: Some Strategies for the Eighties*, ed. George Bridges and Rosalind Brunt (London: Lawrence and Wishart, 1981), 36–37.

2. Henry Jenkins, "If It Doesn't Spread, It's Dead," *Henryjenkins.org*, February 11, 2009, accessed July 12, 2010, http://henryjenkins.org/2009/02/if_it_doesnt_spread _its_dead_p.html.

3. Judith Butler, *Excitable Speech* (New York: Routledge, 1997).

4. Jane Hill, *The Everyday Language of White Racism* (Oxford: Wiley-Blackwell, 2008), 180.

5. Ibid.

6. Shelby Grad, "Sorting Out the Facts in the Obama-Joker 'Socialist' Posters around L.A," *Los Angeles Times*, August 3, 2009, accessed August 5, 2009, http://latimesblogs .latimes.com/lanow/2009/08/sorting-out-the-facts-in-obamajoker-socialist-posters -around-la.html.

7. Jonathan Jerald, "Mystery Obama/Joker Poster Appears in L.A," *Bedlam Magazine*, April 25, 2009, accessed August 8, 2009 (page since deleted), http://bedlammagazine .com/06news/mystery-obamajoker-poster-appears-la.

8. Patrick Courrielche, "The Artist Formally Known as Dissent," *Reason Magazine*, August 7, 2009, accessed August 10, 2009, http://reason.com/news/show/135293 .html.

9. *The Dark Knight*, directed by Christopher Nolan (Hollywood, CA: Warner Brothers, 2008).

10. "Batman," *Encyclopedia Dramatica*, August 17, 2009, accessed June 12, 2010 (site since deleted), http://encyclopediadramatica.com/Batman.

11. Ibid.

12. "Obama Joker," *Encyclopedia Dramatica*, August 29, 2009, accessed September 2, 2009 (site since deleted), http://encyclopediadramatica.com/Image:Obamajoker .png.

13. "A Tax Protest for the Productive People Who Drive Our Economy and Cannot Take Time Off Work to Protest," *Teabagparty*, accessed August 10, 2009 (post since deleted), http://www.teabagparty.org.

14. "10 Most Offensive Tea Party Signs," *Huffington Post*, April 16, 2009, accessed June 12, 2012, http://www.huffingtonpost.com/2009/04/16/10-most-offensive-tea -par_n_187554.html.

15. "Womb Raiders—Orly Taitz," *Colbert Nation*, July 28, 2009, accessed August 3, 2009, http://thecolbertreport.cc.com/the-colbert-report-videos/229691/july-28 -2009/womb-raiders---orly-taitz.

16. Bob Cesca, "Get Your Goddamn Government Hands Off My Medicare," *Huffington Post*, August 5, 2009, accessed August 6, 2009, http://www.huffingtonpost .com/bob-cesca/get-your-goddamn-governme_b_252326.html.

17. Paul Krugman, "The Town Hall Mob," *New York Times*, August 6, 2009, accessed August 8, 2009, http://www.nytimes.com/2009/08/07/opinion/07krugman.html.

18. Paul Krugman, "Tea Parties Forever," *New York Times*, April 12, 2009, Accessed May 1, 2014, http://www.nytimes.com/2009/04/13/opinion/13krugman.html.

19. Sarah Palin, "Statement on the Current Health Care Debate," *Facebook*, August 7, 2009, accessed August 10, 2010, https://www.facebook.com/note.php?note_id =113851103434.

20. Rachel Weiner, "Obama's NH Town Hall Brings Out Birthers, Deathers, and More," *Huffington Post*, August 13, 2009, accessed August 13 2009, http://www .huffingtonpost.com/2009/08/13/obamas-nh-town-hall-bring_n_258693.html.

21. Mike Stuckey, "Guns Near Obama Fuel 'Open-Carry' Debate," *MSNBC.com*, August 25, 2009, accessed August 26, 2009, http://www.nbcnews.com/id/32492783/ ns/us_news-life/t/guns-near-obama-fuel-open-carry-debate.

22. Tammy Bruce, "You Know B. Hussein Is in Trouble When . . . ," *Tammy.Bruce .com*, July 31, 2009, accessed August 2, 2009, http://tammybruce.com/2009/07/ you-know-b-hussein-is-in-trouble-when.html.

23. Pamela Geller, "The Worm Turns ☺," *Atlas Shrugs*, August 1, 2009, accessed August 5, 2009, http://atlasshrugs2000.typepad.com/atlas_shrugs/2009/08/the -worm-turns-.html.

24. Phillip Kennicott, "Obama as the Joker Betrays Racial Ugliness, Fears," *Washington Post*, August 6, 2009, accessed August 9, 2009, http://www.washingtonpost .com/wp-dyn/content/article/2009/08/05/AR2009080503876.html.

25. Stephen Mikulan, "New Anti-Obama 'Joker' Poster," *LA Weekly*, August 3, 2009, accessed August 5, 2009, http://www.laweekly.com/informer/2009/08/03/new-anti -obama-joker-poster.

26. Jerald, "Mystery Obama/Joker Poster Appears in L.A."

27. Mark Milian, "Shepard Fairey Has 'Doubts' about Intelligence of Obama Joker Artist," *Los Angeles Times*, August 10, 2009, accessed August 11, 2009, http:// latimesblogs.latimes.com/washington/2009/08/obama-joker-shepard-fairey.html.

28. David Ng, "Reading Into the Obama as Joker Poster . . . Or Not," *Los Angeles Times*, August 5, 2009, accessed August 6, 2009, http://latimesblogs.latimes.com/ culturemonster/2009/08/reading-into-the-obamaasjoker-poster-or-not.html.

29. Mark Milian, "Obama Joker Artist Unmasked: A Fellow Chicagoan," *Los Angeles Times*, August 17, 2009, accessed August 17, 2009, http://latimesblogs.latimes.com/ washington/2009/08/obama-joker-artist.html.

30. Ibid.

31. "Why So Serious," *Encyclopedia Dramatica*, August 17, 2009, accessed August 20, 2009 (site since deleted), http://encyclopediadramatica.com/Why_so_serious.

32. Comment posted to Jerald, "Mystery Obama/Joker Poster Appears in L.A," accessed August 8, 2009.

33. Matt Gertz and Eric Hananoki, "Corsi's Claim That Obama Posted 'False, Fake Birth Certificate' Flatly Rejected by Hawaii Health Department," *Media Matters*, August 15, 2008, accessed June 5, 2012, http://mediamatters.org/research/2008/08/15/ corsis-claim-that-obama-posted-false-fake-birth/144404.

34. Eric Hananoki, "Fox News Still Trafficking in Birth Certificate Theories," *Media Matters*, May 28, 2009, accessed June 8, 2012, http://mediamatters.org/ research/2009/05/28/fox-news-still-trafficking-in-birth-certificate/150597.

35. "Gibbs Finally Fields Birth Certificate Question," *Fox Nation*, May 27, 2009, accessed June 8, 2012 (page since deleted), http://nation.foxnews.com/ politics/2009/05/27/gibbs-finally-fields-birth-certificate-question.

36. Ellen, "Fox News Legitimizes Birthers," *News Hounds*, July 14, 2009, accessed June 20, 2012, http://www.newshounds.us/2009/07/14/fox_news_legitimizes_birthers.php.

37. Ibid.; "Fox News Again Posts Birther Story with Picture of Obama in Somali Clothes," *Media Matters*, July 20, 2009, accessed June 12, 2012, http://mediamatters .org/blog/2009/07/20/fox-nation-again-posts-birther-story-with-pictu/152203.

38. Tommy De Seno, "Obama's to Blame for Birther Movement," *Fox News*, July 29, 2009, accessed June 4, 2012, http://www.foxnews.com/opinion/2009/07/29/ tommy-seno-obama-birthers.

39. Hananoki, "Fox News Still Trafficking in Birth Certificate Theories."

40. Matthew Biedlingmaier, "Following McCain Rally Appearance, Bill Cunning-ham Uses Obama's Middle Name Seven Times on Hannity and Colmbs," *Media Matters*, February 27, 2008, accessed June 3, 2012, http://mediamatters.org/ research/2008/02/27/following-mccain-rally-appearance-bill-cunningh/142696.

41. "Obama Smeared as Former 'Madrassa' Student, Possible Covert Muslim Extrem-ist," *Think Progress*, January 19, 2007, accessed June 4, 2012, http://thinkprogress .org/media/2007/01/19/9711/fox-obama-madrassa.

42. "Fox News—Barack Obama—This Is HUGE!," *YouTube*, January 31, 2007, accessed June 20, 2012, http://www.youtube.com/watch?v=nw6LBbeXTww.

43. Judy, "Fox and Friends 'Corrects' Obama Madrassa Claim," *News Hounds*, January 22, 2007, accessed June 23, 2012, http://www.newshounds.us/2007/01/22/ fox_and_friends_corrects_obama_madrassa_claim.php.

44. "Terrorist Fist Jab," *YouTube*, June 7, 2008, accessed June 13, 2012, http://www .youtube.com/watch?v=G_vmQrTi3aM.

45. Deborah, "Laura Ingraham Tells O'Reilly What's Wrong with Michelle Obama and Joe Biden," *News Hounds*, August 26, 2008, accessed June 5, 2012, http://www .newshounds.us/2008/08/26/laura_ingraham_tells_oreilly_whats_wrong_with _michelle_obama_and_joe_biden.php.

46. "Fox Host Glenn Beck: Obama Is a 'Racist,'" *Huffington Post*, August 28, 2009, accessed June 12, 2012, http://www.huffingtonpost.com/2009/07/28/fox-host -glenn-beck-obama-n_246310.html.

47. David Neiwert, "Lou Dobbs and the Birthers: Mainstreaming Fringe Ideas for Ratings Eventually Will Catch Up with You," *Crooks and Liars*, July 27, 2009, accessed March 20, 2014, http://crooksandliars.com/david-neiwert/lou-dobbs-and -birthers-why-making-ca.

48. Brian Selter, "On Television and Radio, Talk of Obama's Citizenship," *New York Times*, July 24, 2009, accessed March 20, 2014, http://mediadecoder.blogs.nytimes .com/2009/07/24/on-television-and-radio-talk-of-obamas-citizenship/?hp.

49. Matea Gold, "CNN Chief Addresses Obama Birth Controversy," *Los Angeles Times*, July 25, 2009, accessed March 20, 2014, http://articles.latimes.com/2009/ jul/25/entertainment/et-cnnobama25.

50. Tim Mak, "MSNBC Drops Pat Buchanan," *Politico*, February 17, 2012, accessed March 20, 2014, http://www.politico.com/news/stories/0212/73014.html.

51. "We President Now (image macro)," *4chan/b/*, November 5, 2008, accessed November 5, 2008 (thread since deleted). http://boards.4chan.org/b.

52. "Ingraham Guest Host Bruce on the Obamas: 'We've Got Trash in the White House,'" *Media Matters*, March 23, 2009, accessed June 23, 2009, http://mediamatters .org/video/2009/03/23/ingraham-guest-host-bruce-on-the-obamas-weve-go/148502.

53. "Barack Obama's Small Town Guns and Religion Comments," *YouTube*, April 11, 2008, accessed June 15, 2009, http://www.youtube.com/watch?v=DTxXUufI3jA.

7   Dicks Everywhere

1. "'I Learned It by Watching You' Anti-Drug PSA," public service announcement produced in 1987 by Partnership for a Drug-Free Tomorrow, video posted to *YouTube*, October 1, 2006, accessed March 12, 2012, http://www.youtube.com/ watch?v=Y-Elr5K2Vuo.

2. Christie Davies, "Jokes That Follow Mass-Mediated Disasters in a Global Electronic Age," in *Of Corpse: Death and Humor in Folklore and Popular Culture*, ed. Peter Narvaez (Logan: Utah State University Press, 2003), 15–35.

3. Ibid., 16–17.

4. Ibid., 19.

5. Ibid., 23–26.

6. Ibid., 33–34.

7. Bill Ellis, "Making a Big Apple Crumble: The Role of Humor in Constructing A Global Response to Disaster," in *Of Corpse: Death and Humor in Folklore and Popular Culture*, ed. Peter Narvaez (Logan: Utah State University Press, 2003), 35–79.

8. Henry Jenkins, "What Happened before YouTube," in *YouTube: Online Video and Participatory Culture*, ed. Jean Burgess and Joshua Green (New York: Polity, 2009), 117, 121–123.

9. A Google Trends comparison of the terms "goatse" and "lolcat" from 2006 to 2014 reveals that searches for "goatse" outnumber those for "lolcat" at a ratio of 36:15. The graph also reveals that overall search volume for "goatse" has been consistently higher than search volume for "lolcat" since September 2009, http:// www.google.com/trends/explore#q=goatse%2C%20lolcat&cmpt=q.

10. Eli Pariser, "Beware Online Filter Bubbles," *TED.com*, May 2011, accessed June 5, 2011, http://www.ted.com/talks/eli_pariser_beware_online_filter_bubbles.

11. Mark Zuckerberg quoted in David Kirkpatrick, *The Facebook Effect: The Inside Story of the Company That Is Connecting the World* (New York: Simon and Schuster, 2010), 296.

12. Greg Leuch, "Shaved Bieber," *Gleuch.com*, May 2010, accessed December 10, 2011, http://gleu.ch/projects/shaved-bieber.

13. Greg Leuch, "Olwimpics Browser Blocker," *F.A.T. Lab*, July 28, 2012, accessed July 28, 2012, http://fffff.at/olwimpics.

14. Mike Allen, "Before Golf, Bush Decries Latest Deaths in Mideast," *Washington Post*, August 5, 2002, accessed June 5, 2010 (page since deleted), http://www.washingtonpost.com/ac2/wp-dyn/A43789-2002Aug4?language=printer; "Now Watch This Drive!," *YouTube*, January 7, 2007, accessed March 5, 2012, http://www.youtube.com/watch?v=Z3p9y_OEAdc.

15. "Moment of Zen: Bush Plays Golf," *The Daily Show*, August 5, 2002, accessed March 5, 2012, http://thedailyshow.cc.com/watch/mon-august-5-2002/moment-of-zen---bush-plays-golf.

16. *Fahrenheit 911*, directed by Michael Moore (Hollywood, CA: Lion's Gate, 2004).

17. "At O'Hare, President Says 'Get on Board,'" *Whitehouse.gov*, September 27, 2001, accessed March 4, 2012, http://georgewbush-whitehouse.archives.gov/news/releases/2001/09/20010927-1.html.

18. "Bush Iraq WMDs Joke Backfires," *BBC*, March 26, 2004, accessed March 5, 2012, http://news.bbc.co.uk/2/hi/3570845.stm.

19. "Memorandum on the Geneva Conventions," *Center for American Progress*, May 18, 2004, accessed March 17, 2014, http://americanprogress.org/issues/terrorism/news/2004/05/18/753/memorandum-on-the-geneva-conventions.

20. "Lulz," *Encyclopedia Dramatica*.

21. Jenkins, "What Happened before YouTube," 109–110.

22. Coleman, "Old & New Net Wars over Free Speech, Freedom & Secrecy."

23. "Joe Biden: Noun + Verb + 9/11 = Giuliani Vocabulary," *YouTube*, October 31, 2007, accessed October 31, 2012, http://www.youtube.com/watch?v=DteDRD6cbbM.

24. Janice Moulton, "A Paradigm of Philosophy: The Adversary Method," in *Discovering Reality, Second Edition: Feminist Perspectives on Epistemology, Metaphysics, Methodology, and Philosophy of Science*, ed. Sandra Harding and Merrill B. Hintikka (Dordrecht, The Netherlands: Kluwer, 1983), 149–164.

25. Pierre Bourdieu, *Masculine Domination* (Stanford: Stanford University Press, 2001), 56.

26. Moulton, "A Paradigm of Philosophy."

27. Ibid., 149–150.

28. Arthur Schopenhauer, *The Art of Controversy*, trans. T. Bailey Saunders (LaVergne, TN: Kessinger Books, 1896).

29. Ibid., 4.

30. Ibid., 12.

31. Ibid., 17.

32. Ibid., 32.

33. Ibid., 12–32.

34. "Socrates," *Encyclopedia Dramatica*, November 12, 2010, accessed December 1, 2010 (site since deleted), http://encyclopediadramatica.com/Socrates.

35. Ibid.

36. "Free Speech Trolls," *Huffington Post Live*, October 19, 2012, accessed October 19, 2012, http://live.huffingtonpost.com/r/segment/is-anonymity-good-for/5079868778c90a4bef000172.

37. Plato, "Meno," *Five Dialogues: Euthyphro, Apology, Crito, Meno, Phaedo*, 2nd ed., trans. G. M. A. Grube and John M. Cooper (Indianapolis: Hackett Publishing Company, 2002), 58–92.

38. Ibid., 69–70.

39. Paul W. Gooch, "Irony and Insight in Plato's *Meno*," *Laval Théologique et Philosophique* 43, no. 2 (1987): 189–204, accessed May 2, 2014, doi:10.7202/400301ar; Jacob Klein. *A Commentary on Plato's* Meno (Chicago: University of Chicago Press, 1989), 255.

40. Robert Nisbet, *History of the Idea of Progress* (New York: Basic Books, 1980).

41. Howard Rheingold, *The Virtual Community: Homesteading on the Virtual Frontier* (Cambridge, MA: MIT Press, 1993).

42. John Perry Barlow, "Declaration of the Independence of Cyberspace," *Electronic Frontier Foundation*, February 8, 1996, accessed July 6, 2012, https://projects.eff.org/~barlow/Declaration-Final.html.

43. Ibid.

44. Ibid.

45. "Habbo Hotel," *Encyclopedia Dramatica*, March 9, 2010, accessed February 28, 2010 (page since deleted), http://encyclopediadramatica.com/Habbo_Hotel.

46. Jason Scott, "Before the LOL: ROFLcon 2008," *Archive.org*, April 1, 2008, accessed June 1, 2010, https://archive.org/details/RespectablyFrench.ROFLCon.BeforetheLOL.

47. Steven Levy, *Hackers* (New York: Penguin, 1984).

48. Ibid., 39–49.

49. Ibid., 102.

50. Gabriella Coleman, *Coding Freedom: The Ethics and Aesthetics of Hacking* (Princeton: Princeton University Press, 2013).

51. "Jailbait" refers to sexualized images of minors; "creepshots" are images taken of women and uploaded to the Internet without their consent.

52. "Free Speech Trolls."

53. Schwartz, "Malwebolence: The Trolls among Us."

54. Greg Sandoval, "The End of Kindness: Weev and the Cult of the Angry Young Man, *The Verge*, September 12, 2013, accessed September 12, 2013, http://www
.theverge.com/2013/9/12/4693710/the-end-of-kindness-weev-and-the-cult-of-the
-angry-young-man.

55. Adrian Chen, "'The Best Fucking Thing That Could Possibly Happen': Hacker Convict Weev Bids Farewell to Freedom," *Gawker*, March 22, 2013, accessed March 22, 2013, http://gawker.com/5991737/the-best-fucking-thing-that-could-possibly
-happen-hacker-convict-weev-bids-farewell-to-freedom; Jon Ronson, "Security Alert: Notes from the Frontline of the War in Cyberspace," *The Guardian*, May 3, 2013, accessed May 4, 2014, http://www.theguardian.com/technology/2013/may/04/
security-alert-war-in-cyberspace.

8   The Lulz Are Dead, Long Live the Lulz

1. Nicholas Carlson, "Even with 8.2 Million Uniques, Only Worth $45,000," *Business Insider*, March 19, 2010, accessed March 20, 2010, http://www.businessinsider
.com/even-with-82-million-uniques-4chan-is-only-worth-45000-2010-3#ixzz1
BQK7qVfL.

2. "FAQ," *4chan*, 2009, accessed October 23, 2009, http://www.4chan.org/faq.

3. Ken Fisher, "4chan's moot Takes Pro-Anonymity to TED 2010," *Ars Techinca*, February 11, 2010, accessed February 20, 2010, http://arstechnica.com/staff/
2010/02/4chans-moot-takes-pro-anonymity-to-ted-2010.

4. "Operation Black Rage Thread," *4chan Archive*, November 18, 2010, accessed December 10, 2011 (website since deleted), http://4chanarchive.org/brchive/dspl
_thread.php5?thread_id= 288070260&x=Operation+Black+Rage.

5. "Re: Anonymous—Old Spice," *YouTube*, July 13, 2010, accessed April 19, 2012, http://www.youtube.com/watch?v=LWCVhGzrAT0.

6. The bulk of these posts were made on July 14, 2010. As I always would when a trolling story of note would break, I parked myself in front of the computer and archived everything I could. The folder I devoted to the Old Spice's Re: Anonymous ad is one of the strangest things on my computer—and after six years of this sort of research, that's really saying something.

7. Pamela Vaughan, "Memejacking: The Complete Guide for Creating Memes for Marketing," *Hubspot*, July 6, 2012, accessed October 24, 2012, http://blog.hubspot .com/blog/tabid/6307/bid/33363/Memejacking-The-Complete-Guide-to-Creating -Memes-for-Marketing.aspx#ixzz2A8kQ3e1M.

8. Chris Menning, "Meme Agent Ben Lashes Bites the Hand That Feeds," *Modern Primate,* May 7, 2012, accessed May 7, 2012, http://www.modernprimate.com/ meme-agent-ben-lashes-bites-the-hand-that-feeds-and-the-sun-is-still-terrible.

9. In his ROFLcon III keynote address, Jonathan Zittrain recounted the Operation Black Rage story, and during the Q&A segment one of the Know Your Meme interns forwarded himself as the person with whom Hot Topic had spoken in order to dispel the rage face racism rumor.

10. "Mainstreaming the Web," *ROFLcon*, May 24, 2010, accessed June 20, 2010 (website since deleted), http://roflcon.org/2010/05/24/mainstreaming-the-web -complete-video.

11. I attended ROFLcon II as a third-year PhD student. At that point I hadn't gone public with any of my research, and hardly anyone, save for a few friends and professors, even knew what my dissertation was about. Sitting in the audience of the "Mainstreaming the Web" panel, I had a very different relationship to my object of study than I did when I sat down to revise my dissertation manuscript for publication. In 2010, I was merely a bystander attempting to take as many notes as possible. By 2014, I had long since abandoned my role as bystander. Not only had I granted dozens of media interviews, many of which had debunked various misconceptions about the troll space, I'd published a handful of academic and popular press articles on the subject of trolling and meme culture, and had even been asked to speak at 2012's ROFLcon III on a panel titled "Adventures in Aca-meme-ia." I had, in other words, become every bit as complicit in helping demystify and disseminate meme culture as the ROFLcon II panelists—a position further solidified by the publication of this book.

12. Poole, "Mainstreaming the Web."

13. As organizers Tim Hwang and Christina Xu explained in the conference program, titled Choose Your Own ROFLcon, the series—and perhaps by implication

meme culture generally—had simply run its course; the time had come to "[put] this trilogy to bed and [ride] out into the sunset."

14. "Chris Poole Part 1/3—ROFLCON 2012—Solo Panel," *YouTube*, May 10, 2012, accessed May 20, 2012, http://www.youtube.com/watch?v=O5adlMZFVEA.

15. Anonymous, "Disgusts," *4chan/b/*, February 13, 2012, message board post (thread since deleted), http://www.4chan.org.

16. Anonymous, "Greater Good," *4chan/b/*, February 21, 2012, message board post (thread since deleted), http://www.4chan.org.

17. Anonymous, "Shitposting," *4chan/b/*, February 19, 2012, message board post (thread since deleted), http://www.4chan.org.

18. Anonymous, "Sheep," *4chan/b/*, February 20, 2012, message board post (thread since deleted), http://www.4chan.org.

19. Ibid.

20. Anonymous, "Greater Good," *4chan/b/*, February 21, 2012, message board post (thread since deleted), http://www.4chan.org.

21. Julian Dibbell, "The Assclown Offensive: How to Enrage the Church of Scientology," *Wired*, September 21, 2009, accessed June 2, 2009, http://archive.wired.com/culture/culturereviews/magazine/17-10/mf_chanology?currentPage=all.

22. Ibid.

23. Bianca Bosker, "Gene Simmons Threatens Hacker Group, Responds to 'Popcorn Farts,'" *Huffington Post*, October 18, 2010, accessed October 20, 2010, http://www.huffingtonpost.com/2010/10/18/gene-simmons-threatens-ha_n_766114.html.

24. "Anonymous Hactivists Say Wikileaks War to Continue," *BBC*, December 9, 2010, accessed December 9, 2010, http://www.bbc.co.uk/news/technology-11935539.

25. Yasmine Ryan, "Anonymous and the Arab Uprisings," *Al Jazeera*, May 19, 2011, accessed June 1, 2012, http://www.aljazeera.com/news/middleeast/2011/05/201151917634659824.html.

26. Gabriella Coleman, "Our Weirdness Is Free," *Triple Canopy*, January 15, 2012, accessed January 16, 2012, http://canopycanopycanopy.com/issues/15/contents/our_weirdness_is_free.

27. Saki Knafo, "LulzSec, Sony, and The Rise of a New Breed of Hacker," *Huffington Post*, June 7, 2011, accessed July 20, 2012, http://www.huffingtonpost.com/2011/06/07/lulzsec-sony-and-the-rise_n_872814.html.

28. Martin Kaste, "Exploring Occupy Wall Street's 'Adbuster' Origins," *NPR*, October 20, 2011, accessed October 25, 2012, http://www.npr.org/2011/10/20/141526467/exploring-occupy-wall-streets-adbuster-origins.

29. Robert Johnson, "Anonymous Occupation of Wall Street—Here Is What You Missed," *Business Insider*, September 17, 2011, accessed October 10, 2012, http://www.businessinsider.com/anonymous-occupy-wall-street-2011-9?op=1.

30. Saki Knafo, "Occupy Wall Street and Anonymous: Turning a Fledgling Movement into a Meme," *Huffington Post*, October 20, 2011, accessed December 20, 2011, http://www.huffingtonpost.com/2011/10/20/occupy-wall-street-anonymous-connection_n_1021665.html.

31. Ayesha Kazmi, "How Anonymous Emerged to Occupy Wall Street," *The Guardian*, September 26, 2011, accessed October 13, 2012, http://www.theguardian.com/commentisfree/cifamerica/2011/sep/27/occupy-wall-street-anonymous.

32. Sean Captain, "The Real Role of Anonymous in Occupy Wall Street," *Fast Company*, October 17, 2011, accessed November 5, 2011, http://www.fastcompany.com/node/1788397.

33. "Anonymous' Identity Revealed!," *BuzzFeed*, 2011, accessed May 1, 2012, http://www.buzzfeed.com/unwantedpermutations/anonymous-identity-revealed.

34. Knafo, "Occupy Wall Street and Anonymous."

35. Anonymous, "We Do Not Have Ideals," *4chan/b/*, November 6, 2011, message board post (thread since deleted), http://www.4chan.org.

36. Mike Masnick, "Polish Politicians Don Guy Fawkes/Anonymous Masks to Protest ACTA Signing," *TechDirt*, January 26, 2012, accessed January 27, 2012, https://www.techdirt.com/articles/20120126/12313917555/polish-politicians-don-guy-fawkesanonymous-masks-to-protest-acta-signing.shtml.

37. Derick Chetty, "Toronto Fashion Week: Adrian Wu's Message Baffles Audience," *Toronto Star*, March 13, 2012, accessed March 13, 2012, http://www.thestar.com/life/fashion_style/2012/03/13/toronto_fashion_week_adrian_wus_message_baffles_audience.html.

38. "Anonymous for Good," *YouTube*, January 24, 2012, accessed January 24, 2012, http://www.youtube.com/watch?v=yMl2lDLXUkY.

39. Adrian Chen, "4chan's Moment Is Over, Even Though It's More Popular than Ever," *Gawker*, July 12, 2012, accessed July 12, 2012, http://gawker.com/5925535/4chans-moment-is-over-even-though-its-more-popular-than-ever.

40. Fernando Alfonso III, "Now 10 Years Old, 4chan Is the Most Important Site You Never Visit," *The Daily Dot*, October 1, 2013, accessed February 1, 2014, http://www.dailydot.com/business/4chan-10-years-christopher-moot-poole.

41. Paul Joseph Watson, "Shameless Looters Display Stolen Goods on Twitter," *Alex Jones' Infowars*, October 31, 2012, accessed October 31, 2012, http://www.infowars.com/shameless-looters-display-stolen-goods-on-twitter.

42. Fernando Alfonso III, "4chan Is Trying to Make 'Free Bleeding' the Latest Twitter Trend," *The Daily Dot*, February 1, 2014, accessed February 10, 2014, http://www .dailydot.com/lol/free-bleeding-is-a-4chan-hoax.

43. Caroline Moss, "Nude Photos of Jennifer Lawrence, Kate Upton, Ariana Grande Leak in Massive Hack," *Business Insider*, August 31, 2014, accessed August 31, 2014, http://www.businessinsider.com/4chan-nude-photo-leak-2014-8.

9 Where Do We Go from Here?

1. Paulie Socash, "That's Not Trolling," email message to author, October 12, 2012.

2. Holly Byrnes, "Charlotte Dawson Won't Be Silenced by Twitter Trolls," *The Telegraph*, September 11, 2012, accessed October 31, 2012, http://www.dailytelegraph .com.au/charlotte-dawson-wont-be-silenced-by-twitter-trolls/story-e6freuy9 -1226472066006.

3. Leo Traynor, "The Day I Confronted My Troll," *The Guardian*, September 26, 2012, accessed September 29, 2012, http://www.theguardian.com/commentis free/2012/sep/26/day-confronted-troll.

4. Erin Ryan, "Trolling Polititians' Facebook Pages with Vaginal News is the Hot New Trend," *Jezebel*, March 20, 2012, accessed October 5, 2012, http://jezebel .com/5894635/trolling-politicians-facebook-pages-with-vaginal-news-is-hot-new -trend.

5. Adrian Chen, "Unmasking Violentacrez, the Biggest Troll on the Web," *Gawker*, October 12, 2012, accessed October 12, 2012, http://gawker.com/5950981/ unmasking-reddits-violentacrez-the-biggest-troll-on-the-web.

6. Erin Ryan, "Miserable Troll Ann Coulter Forced to Cancel Speaking Engagement Because Everyone Hates Her," *Jezebel*, October 26, 2012, accessed October 27, 2012, http://jezebel.com/5955193/miserable-troll-ann-coulter-forced-to-cancel-speaking -engagement-because-everyone-hates-her.

7. Claire Porter, "I'm Taking Back the 'T' word: Bullies Are Not Trolls," *The Punch*, October 17, 2012, accessed October 18, 2012 (website since deleted), http://www .thepunch.com.au/articles/im-taking-back-the-t-word.

8. Whitney Phillips, "A Brief History of Trolls," *The Daily Dot*, May 20, 2013, accessed May 20, 2013, http://www.dailydot.com/opinion/phillips-brief-history-of -trolls.

9. "House Bill 2549," *Arizona State Legislature*, April 2012, accessed April 15, 2012, http://www.azleg.gov//FormatDocument.asp?inDoc=/legtext/50leg/2r/bills/ hb2549s.htm&Session_ID=107.

10. Samuel Gibbs, "Cyber-Bullies Could Face Two Years in Jail under New Internet Troll Rules," *The Guardian*, March 26, 2014, accessed May 2, 2014, http://www .theguardian.com/technology/2014/mar/26/cyber-bullies-tougher-penalties -internet-troll.

11. Renee Viellaris, "Internet Trolls and Cyber-Bullies Face Jail under Amended Commonwealth Law," *The Courier-Mail*, November 30, 2013, accessed January 13, 2014, http://www.couriermail.com.au/news/queensland/internet-trolls-and -cyberbullies-face-jail-under-amended-commonwealth-law/story-fnihsrf2 -1226771735572?nk=86c846653f7c941e16d5959fec680673.

12. Jonathan Zittrain, *The Future of the Internet and How to Stop It* (New Haven, CT: Yale University Press, 2008).

13. Ibid., 149–152.

14. Alexander S. Haslam and Stephen Reicher, "Contesting the 'Nature' of Conformity: What Milgram and Zimbardo's Studies Really Show," *PLOS Biology* 10, no. 11 (2012): e1001426, accessed March 10, 2013, doi:10.1371/journal.pbio.1001426.

15. Tom Postmes and Russell Spears, "Deindividuation and Antinormative Behavior: A Meta-Analysis," *Psychological Bulletin* 123, no. 3 (1998): 238–259.

16. McLean Gordon, "You're as Evil as Your Social Network: What the Prison Experiment Got Wrong," *Motherboard*, December 11, 2012, accessed on December 12, 2012, http://motherboard.vice.com/blog/you-are-as-evil-as-your-social-network -alexander-haslam-on-what-the-prison-experiment-got-wrong.

17. Zittrain, *The Future of the Internet and How to Stop It*, 175–199.

18. Danielle Citron, *Hate 3.0* (Cambridge, MA: Harvard University Press, 2014), 3.

19. Ibid., 20.

20. Chris Gentilviso, "Todd Aiken on Abortion: 'Legitimate Rape' Victims Have 'Ways to Try to Shut That Whole Thing Down," *Huffington Post*, October 19, 2012, accessed October 20, 2012, http://www.huffingtonpost.com/2012/08/19/todd-akin -abortion-legitimate-rape_n_1807381.html?utm_hp_ref=todd-akin.

21. Whitney Phillips, "On Feeding the Holmies," *Billions and Billions*, July 31, 2012, accessed August 1, 2012, http://billions-and-billions.com/2012/07/31/on-feeding -the-holmies.

22. Cory Doctorow, "Award-Winning Book-Burning Hoax Saves Troy, MI Libraries," *BoingBoing*, June 16, 2012, accessed October 14, 2012, http://boingboing .net/2012/06/16/award-winning-book-burning-hoa.html.

23. Whitney Phillips, "Oh Boy," *Billions and Billions*, July 20, 2012, accessed July 20, 2012, http://billions-and-billions.com/2012/07/20/oh-boy.

24. Stephen, July 20, 2012, comment on Whitney Phillips, "About," *Billions and Billions*, accessed July 20, 2012, http://billions-and-billions.com/about.

25. Whitney Phillips, responses to troll comments on the author's "About" page, *Billions and Billions*, July 20, 2012, accessed July 20, 2012, http://billions-and-billions.com/about.

26. Ryan Milner, "Dialogue Is Important, Even When It's Impolite," *New York Times*, August 19, 2014, accessed August 19, 2014, http://www.nytimes.com/roomfordebate/2014/08/19/the-war-against-online-trolls/dialogue-is-important-even-when-its-impolite.

27. Ibid.

28. Amanda Phillips, "5 Things Academics Might Learn from How the Rowdy Social Justice Blogosphere Handles Fucknecks," *Fembot Collective*, April 10, 2012, accessed April 10, 2012, http://fembotcollective.org/blog/2012/04/10/im-not-offended-im-contemptuous-5-things-academics-might-learn-from-how-the-rowdy-social-justice-blogosphere-handles-fucknecks.

29. Spenser Ackerman, "Newest U.S. Counterterrorism Strategy: Trolling," *Wired*, July 18, 2012, accessed July 18, 2012, http://www.wired.com/2012/07/counterterrorism-trolls/all.

30. "Harvard's Berkman Center to Launch Global Research and Action Network Focused on Youth-Oriented Hate Speech Online," *Berkman Center for Internet and Society*, April 16, 2014, accessed April 18, 2014, http://cyber.law.harvard.edu/node/9108.

31. Asawin Suebsaeng, "The State Department Is Actively Trolling Terrorists on Twitter," *Mother Jones*, March 5, 2014, accessed March 5, 2014, http://www.motherjones.com/politics/2014/02/state-department-cscc-troll-terrorists-twitter-think-again-turn-away.

32. Ibid.

33. Adam Bluestein, "What Twitter Can Learn from Weibo: Field Notes from Global Tech Ethnographer Tricia Wang," *Fast Company*, July 11, 2012, accessed July 11, 2012, http://www.fastcompany.com/node/1842561.

34. Jiashan Wu, email message to author, July 27, 2012.

35. "Human Flesh Search Engine," *Know Your Meme*, January 1, 2012, accessed July 15, 2012, http://knowyourmeme.com/memes/subcultures/human-flesh-search-engine.

36. The website chinaSMACK, an archive of the Chinese Internet's most popular content, is an excellent resource for those interested in this sort of playful online engagement, as is the website ChinaHush.

37. "When Lulzes Go Global," *YouTube*, May 22, 2012, accessed June 1, 2012, http://www.youtube.com/watch?v=RDDi4Dj-EQI.

38. Mary Beard, "The Public Voice of Women," *London Review of Books*, February 14, 2014, accessed February 14, 2014, http://www.lrb.co.uk/v36/n06/mary-beard/the-public-voice-of-women.

39. Ibid.

40. Audre Lorde, "The Master's Tools Will Never Dismantle the Master's House," in *Feminism and Race*, ed. Kum-Kum Bhavnani (New York: Oxford University Press, 1984), 89–92.

41. Hyde, *Trickster Makes This World*.

42. Ibid., 10–11.

43. Ibid.

Bibliography

Primary Sources

"10 Most Offensive Tea Party Signs." *Huffington Post*, April 16, 2009. Accessed June 12, 2012. http://www.huffingtonpost.com/2009/04/16/10-most-offensive-tea -par_n_187554.html.

"9000!!!!" *YouTube*, June 24, 2008. Accessed July 13, 2009. http://www.youtube .com/watch?v=SiMHTK15Pik.

"ABC Reaction." Messages collected by the author on Facebook and Skype. May 2010.

Anon1. Facebook messages exchanged with author. June–August 2011.

Anon2. Facebook messages exchanged with author. June–August 2011.

Anon3. Facebook messages exchanged with author. June–July 2011.

Anonymous. "Changes." *4chan/b/*, February 21, 2012. Message board post (thread since deleted). http://www.4chan.org.

Anonymous. "Disgusts." *4chan/b/*, February 13, 2012. Message board post (thread since deleted). http://www.4chan.org.

Anonymous. "Greater Good." *4chan/b/*, February 21, 2012. Message board post (thread since deleted). http://www.4chan.org.

Anonymous. "Lamejokes." *4chan/b/*, February 20, 2012. Message board post (thread since deleted). http://www.4chan.org.

Anonymous. "Sheep." *4chan/b/*, February 20, 2012. Message board post (thread since deleted). http://www.4chan.org.

Anonymous. "Shitposting." *4chan/b/*, February 19, 2012. Message board post (thread since deleted). http://www.4chan.org.

Anonymous. "We Do Not Have Ideals." *4chan/b/*, November 6, 2011. Message board post (thread since deleted). http://www.4chan.org.

"Anonymous." *Wikipedia*, February 12, 2008. Accessed April 16, 2012. http://en.wikipedia.org/w/index.php?title=Anonymous_(group)&dir=prev&action=history.

"Anonymous." *Urban Dictionary*, November 3, 2006. Accessed December 15, 2011. http://www.urbandictionary.com/define.php?term=Anonymous&page=6#.

"Anonymous Calls Gamestop." *YouTube*, April 4, 2008. Accessed June 2, 2010. http://www.youtube.com/watch?v=cvEThh1RMlQ&feature=player_embedded.

"Anonymous Credo." *Urban Dictionary*, May 9, 2007. Accessed December 15, 2011. http://www.urbandictionary.com/define.php?term=Anonymous&defid=2409401.

"Anonymous' Identity Revealed!" *BuzzFeed*, 2011. Accessed May 1, 2012. http://www.buzzfeed.com/unwantedpermutations/anonymous-identity-revealed.

"Anonymous for Good." *YouTube*, January 24, 2012. Accessed January 24, 2012. http://www.youtube.com/watch?v=yMl2lDLXUkY.

"Anonymous Hactivists Say Wikileaks War to Continue." *BBC*, December 9, 2010. Accessed December 9, 2010. http://www.bbc.co.uk/news/technology-11935539.

"Anonymous on FOX 11 News." *YouTube*, July 27, 2007. Accessed December 10, 2011. http://www.youtube.com/watch?v=DNO6G4ApJQY&feature=player_embedded.

"Anonymous Proposes a Plan." *4chan Archive*, January 15, 2008. Accessed December 3, 2011 (website since deleted). http://4chanarchive.org/brchive/dspl_thread.php5?thread_id=51051816.

"Archiving Internet Subculture." *The Web Ecology Project*, April 15, 2011. Accessed May 5, 2014. http://www.webecologyproject.org/2011/04/archiving-internet-subculture-encyclopedia-dramatica.

"Army against Low Life Trolls." *Facebook*, 2010. Accessed April 1, 2010 (page since deleted). http://www.facebook.com.

"A Tax Protest for the Productive People Who Drive Our Economy and Cannot Take Time Off Work to Protest." *Teabagparty*, 2009. Accessed August 10, 2009 (post since deleted). http://www.teabagparty.org.

"At O'Hare, President Says 'Get on Board.'" *Whitehouse.gov*, September 27, 2001. Accessed March 4, 2012. http://georgewbushwhitehouse.archives.gov/news/releases/2001/09/20010927-1.html.

"Barack Obama's Small Town Guns and Religion Comments." *YouTube*, April 11, 2008. Accessed June 15, 2009. http://www.youtube.com/watch?v=DTxXUufI3jA.

Barlow, John Perry. "Declaration of the Independence of Cyberspace." *Electronic Frontier Foundation*, February 8, 1996. Accessed July 6, 2012. https://projects.eff .org/~barlow/Declaration-Final.html.

"Batman." *Encyclopedia Dramatica*, August 17, 2009. Accessed June 12, 2010 (website since deleted). http://encyclopediadramatica.com/Batman.

Battletoads. Created by Tim and Chris Stamper. 1991. Twycross, Leicestershire, United Kingdom: Rare.

"Ben Huh—Bio." *BravoTV.com*, 2014. Accessed June 5, 2014. http://www.bravotv .com/people/ben-huh/bio.

"Bill O'Reilly—Sarah Palin Email." *YouTube*, September 18, 2008. Accessed December 3, 2011 (video since deleted). http://www.youtube.com/watch?v=hCSaF4KC3eE&fe ature=player_embedded.

"Bill O'Reilly: A Far-Left website Known as '4chan' Is Providing Child Pornography to Internet Pedophiles." *Reddit* (via *tinypic*), August 27, 2009. Accessed September 2, 2009. http://www.reddit.com/r/pics/comments/9eslq/bill_oreilly_a_farleft_website _known_as_4chan_is.

Bilton, Nick. "One on One: Christopher Poole, Founder of 4chan." *New York Times*, March 19, 2010. Accessed March 30, 2010. http://www.nytimes.com/glogin ?URI=http://bits.blogs.nytimes.com/2010/03/19/one-on-one-christopher-poole -founder-of-4chan/&OQ=_phpQ3DtrueQ26_typeQ3DblogsQ26_rQ3D0&OP=719 c062cQ2FqedQ2Fqv2Q2Fq888qRddQ25UQ7DesoudQ60d.

Bosker, Bianca. "Gene Simmons Threatens Hacker Group, Responds to 'Popcorn Farts.'" *Huffington Post*, October 18, 2010. Accessed October 20, 2010. http://www .huffingtonpost.com/2010/10/18/gene-simmons-threatens-ha_n_766114.html.

Brophey-Warren, Jamin. "Modest Web Site Is Behind a Bevy of Memes." *The Wall Street Journal*, July 9, 2008. Accessed June 10, 2009. http://online.wsj.com/news/ articles/SB121564928060441097?mg=reno64-wsj&url=http%3A%2F%2Fonline.wsj .com%2Farticle%2FSB121564928060441097.html.

Bruce, Tammy. "You Know B. Hussein Is in Trouble When . . . ," *Tammy Bruce.com*, July 31, 2009. Accessed August 2, 2009. http://tammybruce.com/2009/07/you -know-b-hussein-is-in-trouble-when.html.

Byrnes, Holly. "Charlotte Dawson Won't Be Silenced by Twitter Trolls." *The Telegraph*, September 11, 2012. Accessed October 31, 2012. http://www.dailytelegraph .com.au/news/charlotte-dawson-wont-be-silenced-by-twitter-trolls/story-e6freuy9 -1226472066006.

Camber, Rebecca, and Simon Neville. "Sick Internet 'Troll' Who Posted Vile Messages and Videos Taunting the Death of Teenagers Is Jailed for 18 WEEKS." *The Daily*

Mail, September 14, 2011. Accessed September 14, 2011. http://www.dailymail
.co.uk/news/article-2036935/Natasha-MacBryde-death-Facebook-internet-troll-Sean
-Duffy-jailed.html.

"Can This Poodle Wearing a Tinfoil Hat Get More Fans than Glenn Beck." *Facebook*,
2010. Accessed March 13, 2010 (page since deleted). http://www.facebook.com.

Carey, Tanith. "'Help Me, Mummy. It's Hot Here in Hell': A Special Investigation
into the Distress of Grieving Families Caused by the Sick Internet Craze of 'Trolling.'" *The Daily Mail*, September 24, 2011. Accessed September 25, 2012. http://
www.dailymail.co.uk/news/article-2041193/Internet-trolling-Investigation-distress
-grieving-families-caused-trolls.html#ixzz1Yt6qEOwi.

Carlson, Nicholas. "Even with 8.2 Million Uniques, Only Worth $45,000." *Business
Insider*, March 19, 2010. Accessed March 20, 2010. http://www.businessinsider.com/
even-with-82-million-uniques-4chan-is-only-worth-45000-2010-3#ixzz1BQK7qVfL.

Catfish. Directed by Henry Joost and Ariel Schulman. 2010. Universal City, CA:
Universal Pictures.

Cesca, Bob. "Get Your Goddamn Government Hands Off My Medicare." *Huffington
Post*, August 5, 2009. Accessed August 6, 2009. http://www.huffingtonpost.com/
bob-cesca/get-your-goddamn-governme_b_252326.html.

Cheatham, Kelli. "Police Warn about New Drug Made From Raw Sewage." *WSBT
South Bend*, November 7, 2007. Accessed March 5, 2013. http://web.archive.org/
web/20071109120038/http://www.wsbt.com/news/11077771.html.

"Chelsea King." *Facebook*, 2010. Accessed April 10, 2010 (page since deleted). http://
www.facebook.com.

"Chelsea King Fans: Why Aren't You Helping to Find Jalesa Reynolds?" *Facebook*,
2010. Accessed June 1, 2010 (page since deleted). http://www.facebook.com.

"Chelsea's Light." *Facebook*, 2010. Accessed March 10, 2010. http://www.facebook
.com/chelseaslight.

Chen, Adrian. "Unmasking Violentacrez, the Biggest Troll on the Web." *Gawker*,
October 12, 2012. Accessed October 12, 2012. http://gawker.com/5950981/
unmasking-reddits-violentacrez-the-biggest-troll-on-the-web.

Chen, Adrian. "'The Best Fucking Thing That Could Possibly Happen': Hacker
Convict Weev Bids Farewell to Freedom." *Gawker*, March 22, 2013. Accessed March
22, 2013. http://gawker.com/5991737/the-best-fucking-thing-that-could-possibly
-happen-hacker-convict-weev-bids-farewell-to-freedom.

Chetty, Derick. "Toronto Fashion Week: Adrian Wu's Message Baffles Audience."
Toronto Star, March 13, 2012. Accessed March 13, 2012. http://www.thestar.com/

living/fashion/article/1145546--toronto-fashion-week-adrian-wu-s-message-baffles
-audience.

"Chris Poole Part 1/3—ROFLCON 2012—Solo Panel." *YouTube*, May 10, 2012.
Accessed May 20, 2012. http://www.youtube.com/watch?v=O5adlMZFVEA.

"Couple Wins $14 Million after Un-masking Anonymous Internet Trolls Who
Labeled them Sexual Deviants." *The Daily Mail*, April 24, 2012. Accessed April
24, 2012. http://www.dailymail.co.uk/news/article-2134613/Couple-wins-14million
-masking-anonymous-internet-trolls-labeled-sexual-deviants.html?ito=feeds
-newsxml.

Daley, Suzanne. "In Zambia, the Abandoned Generation." *New York Times*, September 18, 1998. Accessed March 5, 2010. http://www.nytimes.com/1998/09/18/world/
in-zambia-the-abandoned-generation.html.

Danchev, Dancho. "Bill O'Reilly's Website Hacked, Attackers Release Personal
Details of Users." *ZDnet.com*, September 24, 2008. Accessed October 1, 2009. http://
blogs.zdnet.com/security/?p=1958.

The Dark Knight. Directed by Christopher Nolan. 2008. Hollywood: Warner
Brothers.

Denton, Nick. "The Cruise Indoctrination Video Scientology Tried to Suppress."
Gawker, January 15, 2008. Accessed December 10, 2011. http://gawker.com/5002269/
the-cruise-indoctrination-video-scientology-tried-to-suppress.

De Seno, Tommy. "Obama's to Blame for Birther Movement." *Fox News*, July 29,
2009. Accessed June 4, 2012. http://www.foxnews.com/opinion/2009/07/29/
tommy-seno-obama-birthers.

Dickinson, Alex. "Facebook Moves to Protect Memorial Pages from Offensive 'Trolling.'" *News.com.au*, May 2, 2010. Accessed May 2, 2010. http://www.news.com.au/
technology/facebook-moves-to-protect-memorial-pages-from-offensive-trolling/
story-e6frfro0-1225847737623.

"'Drug' Made from Human Waste Making a Stink on Web, in Law Enforcement."
FoxNews, November 7, 2007. Accessed May 20, 2011. http://www.foxnews.com/
story/2007/11/06/drug-made-from-human-waste-causing-stink-on-web-in-law
-enforcement.

"Epic Beard Man." *Encyclopedia Dramatica*, February 27, 2010. Accessed February 27,
2010 (website since deleted). http://encyclopediadramatica.com/Epic_Beard_Man.

"Facebook Users Mock Death of Chelsea King." *10News*, May 2, 2010. Accessed May
2, 2010 (page since deleted). http://www.10news.com/video/22759317/index.html.

"FAQ." *4chan*, 2009. Accessed October 23, 2009. http://www.4chan.org/faq.

Fahrenheit 911. Directed by Michael Moore. 2004. Hollywood, CA: Lion's Gate.

"Fox Host Glenn Beck: Obama Is a 'Racist.'" *Huffington Post*, August 28, 2009. Accessed June 12, 2012. http://www.huffingtonpost.com/2009/07/28/fox-host -glenn-beck-obama_n_246310.html.

"Fox News—Barack Obama—This Is HUGE!" *YouTube*, January 31, 2007. Accessed June 20, 2012. http://www.youtube.com/watch?v=nw6LBbeXTww.

"Fox News Reports on Jenkem." *YouTube*, November 7, 2007. Accessed October 1, 2011. http://www.youtube.com/watch?v=2UsNbsjpuLc&feature=player_embedded.

Frank. Facebook and Skype messages exchanged with author. 2011–2012.

Freedman, Alex. "We Can Pretty Much Say That We're Looking for the Worst." *Wnct.com*, August 19, 2011. Accessed July 27, 2012. http://www2.wnct.com/ news/2010/aug /19/22/has-anyone-heard-jalesa-reynolds-scotland-neck-ar-340940.

"Free Speech Trolls." *Huffington Post Live*, October 19, 2012. Accessed October 19, 2012. http://live.huffingtonpost.com/r/segment/is-anonymity-good-for/5079868778 c90a4bef000172.

"The Game." *Encyclopedia Dramatica*, November 29, 2010. Accessed December 15, 2010 (website since deleted). http://encyclopediadramatica.com/index.php?title =The_Game&action=history.

Geller, Pamela. "The Worm Turns ☺." *Atlas Shrugs*, August 1, 2009. Accessed August 5, 2009. http://atlasshrugs2000.typepad.com/atlas_shrugs/2009/08/the-worm-turns -.html.

Gentilviso, Chris. "Todd Aiken on Abortion: 'Legitimate Rape' Victims Have 'Ways to Try to Shut That Whole Thing Down.'" *Huffington Post*, October 19, 2012. Accessed October 20, 2012. http://www.huffingtonpost.com/2012/08/19/todd-akin-abortion -legitimate-rape_n_1807381.html?utm_hp_ref=todd-akin.

Gibbs, Samuel. "Cyber-bullies Could Face Two Years in Jail Under New Internet Troll Rules." *The Guardian*, March 26, 2014. Accessed May 2, 2014. http://www.theguardian .com/technology/2014/mar/26/cyber-bullies-tougher-penalties-internet-troll.

"Gibbs Finally Fields Birth Certificate Question." *Fox Nation*, May 27, 2009. Accessed June 8, 2012 (page since deleted). http://nation.foxnews.com/politics/2009/05/27/ gibbs-finally-fields-birth-certificate-question.

Glor, Jeff. "Cyberbullying Continued after Teen's Death." *CBS News*, March 29, 2010. Accessed March 29, 2010. http://www.cbsnews.com/2100-500202_162-6343077 .html.

Gold, Matea. "CNN Chief Addresses Obama Birth Controversy." *Los Angeles Times*, July 25, 2009. Accessed March 20, 2014. http://articles.latimes.com/2009/jul/25/ entertainment/et-cnnobama25.

Goldman, Russell. "Cops Believe Chelsea King Was Raped and Murdered." *ABC News*, May 24, 2010. Accessed May 24, 2010. http://abcnews.go.com/GMA/TheLaw/chelsea-king-disappearance-suspect-linkedcases/story?id=9975272.

"Gnomes." *South Park*, season 2, episode 17. Written by Pam Brady, Trey Parker, and Matt Stone. December 16, 1998. Los Angeles, CA: Comedy Central.

"Habbo Hotel—Where Else?" *Sulake.com*, 2010. Accessed February 20, 2010. http://www.sulake.com/habbo.

"Habbo Hotel." *Encyclopedia Dramatica*, March 9, 2010. Accessed February 28, 2010 (website since deleted). http://encyclopediadramatica.com/Habbo_Hotel.

Hale, Beth. "Tormented by Trolling: The Vile Web Craze Taunted Family of Bullied Girl after Her Death." *The Daily Mail*, February 26, 2011. Accessed February 27, 2011. http://www.dailymail.co.uk/news/article-1360788/Natasha-MacBryde-suicide-Vile-web-craze-taunted-family-bullied-girl-death.html.

"Harvard's Berkman Center to Launch Global Research and Action Network Focused on Youth-Oriented Hate Speech Online." *Berkman Center for Internet and Society*, April 16, 2014. Accessed April 18, 2014. http://cyber.law.harvard.edu/node/9108.

"Help Find Chelsea King." *Facebook*, 2010. Accessed March 15, 2010 (page since deleted). http://www.facebook.com.

Holt, Kris. "Australia Considers Tougher Anti-Trolling Laws." *The Daily Dot*, September 17, 2012. Accessed October 20, 2012. http://www.dailydot.com/news/australia-anti-troll-laws.

Hough, Andrew. "Facebook Vows New Security Measures to Combat Alarming 'Trolling' Abuse." *The Telegraph*, September 1, 2010. Accessed September 2, 2010. http://www.telegraph.co.uk/technology /facebook/7939721/Facebook-vows-new-security-measures-to-combat-alarming-trolling-abuse-trend.htm.

"House Bill 2549." *Arizona State Legislature*, April 2012. Accessed April 15, 2012. http://www.azleg.gov//FormatDocument.asp?inDoc=/legtext/50leg/2r/bills/hb2549s.htm&Session_ID=107.

"Human Flesh Search Engine." *Know Your Meme*, January 1, 2012. Accessed July 15, 2012. http://knowyourmeme.com/memes/subcultures/human-flesh-search-engine.

Hwang, Tim, and Christina Xu. *Choose Your Own ROFLcon: ROFLcon III Program*. Boston: Lulu.com, 2012.

"I Bet This Onion Ring Can Get More Fans than Justin Bieber." *Facebook*, 2010. Accessed June 1, 2010 (page since deleted). http://www.facebook.com.

"I Bet This Pickle Can Get More Fans than Chelsea King." *Facebook*, 2010. Accessed March 15, 2010 (page since deleted). http://www.facebook.com.

"I Bet This Shoe Can Get More Fans than Edward Cullin." *Facebook*, 2010. Accessed May 1, 2010 (page since deleted). http://www.facebook.com.

"'I Learned It by Watching You' Anti-Drug PSA." Public service announcement produced in 1987 by Partnership for a Drug-Free Tomorrow. *YouTube*, October 1, 2006. Accessed March 12, 2012. http://www.youtube.com/watch?v=Y-Elr5K2Vuo.

"Is This Battletoads." *Encyclopedia Dramatica*, February 26, 2010. Accessed March 5, 2010 (website since deleted). http://encyclopediadramatica.com/Is_This _Battletoads.

"I Think Internet Trolls Are Losers." *Facebook*, 2010. Accessed May 1, 2010 (page since deleted). http://www.facebook.com.

"Jenkem." *Encyclopedia Dramatica*, September 19, 2012. Accessed September 19, 2012. https://encyclopediadramatica.es/Jenkem.

Jerald, Jonathan. "Mystery Obama/Joker Poster Appears in L.A." *Bedlam Magazine*, April 25, 2009. Accessed August 8, 2009. http://bedlammagazine.com/06news/ mystery-obamajoker-poster-appears-la.

"Jessi Slaughter." *Know Your Meme*, July 10, 2010. Accessed June 20, 2011. http:// knowyourmeme.com/memes/events/jessi-slaughter.

"Joe Biden: Noun + Verb + 9/11 = Giuliani Vocabulary." *YouTube*, October 31, 2007. Accessed October 31, 2012. http://www.youtube.com/watch?v=DteDRD6cbbM.

Keim, Tony. "Facebook Troll Bradley Paul Hampson Jailed for Posting Child Porn on Tribute Sites of Dead Children." *The Courier Mail*, March 25, 2011. Accessed May 1, 2013. http://www.couriermail.com.au/news/queensland/facebook-troll-bradley -paul-hampson-jailed-for-posting-child-porn-on-tribute-pages-for-dead-children/ story-e6freoof-1226028117673.

Leuch, Greg. "Shaved Bieber." *Gleuch.com*, May 2010. Accessed December 10, 2011, http://gleuch.com/projects/shaved-bieber.

Leuch, Greg. "Olwimpics Browser Blocker." *F.A.T. Lab*, July 28, 2012. Accessed July 28, 2012. http://fffff.at/olwimpics.

"Lulz." *Encyclopedia Dramatica*, January 15, 2012. Accessed January 15, 2012. http:// encyclopediadramatica.ch/lulz.

"Mainstreaming the Web." *ROFLcon*, May 24, 2010. Accessed June 20, 2010 (website since deleted). http://roflcon.org/2010/05/24/mainstreaming-the-web -complete-video.

Mak, Tim. "MSNBC Drops Pat Buchanan." *Politico*, February 17, 2012. Accessed March 20, 2014. http://www.politico.com/news/stories/0212/73014.html.

"Marble Cake Also the Game." *Buzzfeed*, 2009. Accessed June 5, 2010. http://www
.buzzfeed.com/reddit/also-the-work-of-4chan-pic.

Martinez, Edicio. "Killer Whale Kills Trainer Footage: SeaWorld and Dawn Brancheau's Family Wants Video Suppressed." *CBS News*, March 9, 2010. Accessed March
10, 2010. http://www.cbsnews.com/news/killer-whale-kills-trainer-footage-seaworld
-dawn-brancheaus-family-wants-video-suppressed.

Masnick, Mike. "Polish Politicians Don Guy Fawkes/Anonymous Masks to Protest
ACTA Signing." *TechDirt*, January 26, 2012. Accessed January 27, 2012. http://www
.techdirt.com/articles/20120126/12313917555/polish-politicians-don-guy
-fawkesanonymous-masks-to-protest-acta-signing.shtml.

Matheson, Ishbel. "Children High on Sewage." *BBC News*, July 30, 1999. Accessed
November 13, 2010. http://news.bbc.co.uk/2/hi/africa/406067.stm.

"Memorandum on the Geneva Conventions." *Center for American Progress*, May 18,
2004. Accessed March 17, 2014. http://www.americanprogress.org/issues/terrorism/
news/2004/05/18/753/memorandum-on-the-geneva-conventions.

"Memorial Page Tourism." *Encyclopedia Dramatica*, June 6, 2010. Accessed June 9,
2010 (website since deleted). http://encyclopediadramatica.com/Memorial_Page
_Tourism.

"Message to Scientology." *YouTube*, January 21, 2008. Accessed April 12, 2008.
http://www.youtube.com/watch?v=JCbKv9yiLiQ.

"Michael Fertik Talks to ABC News 20/20 about Online Ghouls." *YouTube*, June 27,
2011. Accessed April 24, 2012. http://www.youtube.com/watch?v=JivyHVNc7fI&
feature=player_ embedded.

Michaels, Sean. "Nickleback Lose Popularity Contest to a Pickle." *The Guardian*,
February 28, 2010. Accessed February 28, 2010. http://www.guardian.co.uk/
music/2010/feb/24/nickelback-popularity-contest-pickle.

"The Mike Lonston Experience." *Facebook*, 2010. Accessed June 15, 2010 (page since
deleted). http://www.facebook.com.

Mikulan, Stephen. "New Anti-Obama 'Joker' Poster." *LA Weekly*, August 3, 2009.
Accessed August 5, 2009. http://www.laweekly.com/informer/2009/08/03/new-anti
-obama-joker-poster.

Milian, Mark. "Obama Joker Artist Unmasked: A Fellow Chicagoan." *Los Angeles
Times*, August 17, 2009. Accessed August 17, 2009. http://latimesblogs.latimes.com
/washington /2009/08/obama-joker-artist.html.

"Miracles." *YouTube*, April 6, 2010. Accessed April 6, 2010. https://www.youtube
.com/watch?v=_-agl0pOQfs.

"Moment of Zen: Bush Plays Golf." *The Daily Show*, August 5, 2002. Accessed March 5, 2012. http://www.thedailyshow.com/watch/mon-august-5-2002/moment-of-zen ---bush-plays-golf.

Moss, Caroline. "Nude Photos of Jennifer Lawrence, Kate Upton, Ariana Grande Leak in Massive Hack." *Business Insider*, August 31, 2014. Accessed August 31, 2014. http://www.businessinsider.com/4chan-nude-photo-leak-2014-8.

"Now Watch This Drive!" *YouTube*, January 7, 2007. Accessed March 5, 2012. http://www.youtube.com/watch?v=Z3p9y_OEAdc.

"Obama Joker." *Encyclopedia Dramatica*, August 29, 2009. Accessed September 2, 2009 (website since deleted). http://encyclopediadramatica.com/Image:Obamajoker.png.

"Online 'Trolls' Terrorize the Grieving." *The Today Show*, March 31, 2010. Accessed March 31, 2010. http://www.today.com/video/today/36113365.

"Operation Bill Can Haz Cheezburgers." *4chan,* November 7, 2009. Accessed November 7, 2009 (thread since deleted). http://www.4chan.org.

"Operation Black Rage Thread." *4chan Archive*, November 18, 2010. Accessed December 10, 2011 (website since deleted). http://4chanarchive.org/brchive/dspl_thread.php5?thread_id= 288070260&x=Operation+Black+Rage.

"Oprah Over 9000 Penises!" *YouTube*, October 3, 2008. Accessed October 4, 2008 (video since deleted). http://www.youtube.com/watch?v=slDAPms8Tvs&feature=player_embedded.

"Oprah Over 9000 Penises f/ PEDOBEAR Remix." *YouTube*, October 10, 2008. Accessed October 10, 2008 (video since deleted). http://www.youtube.com/watch?v=1A5Ysh5rl4g.

"Oprah Winfrey." *Encyclopedia Dramatica*, September 11, 2011. Accessed September 11, 2011. http://encyclopediadramatica.ch/Oprah.

"O'Reilly's Calling FBI on Palin Hackers & Lib Blog Posters." *YouTube*, September 17, 2008. Accessed October 3, 2008 (video since deleted). http://www.youtube.com/watch?v=zq1NK6P8870.

"ORIGINAL Jessi Slaughter before Breakdown (Bad Mouthed Girl)." *YouTube*, July 18, 2010. Accessed March 20, 2012. http://www.youtube.com/watch?v=Yy4gGs8_90w&feature=player_embedded.

"Outfoxed: Fox News Technique 'Some People Say.'" *YouTube*, May 9, 2007. Accessed June 10, 2011. http://www.youtube.com/watch?v=NYA9ufivbDw.

Owens, Jason. "Friends, Family Celebrate Chelsea King at Poway Memorial." *SDNN*, March 20, 2010. Accessed March 21, 2011 (page since deleted). http://www.sdnn

.com/sandiego/2010-03-13/news/friends-family-celebrate-chelsea-kingat-poway
-memorial.

Palin, Sarah. "Statement on the Current Health Care Debate." *Facebook*, August 7, 2009. Accessed August 10, 2010. https://www.facebook.com/note.php?note
_id=113851103434.

Pariser, Eli. "Beware Online Filter Bubbles." *TED.com*, May 2011. Accessed June 5, 2011. http://www.ted.com/talks/eli_pariser_beware_online_filter_bubbles.html.

Paulie Socash. Facebook and Skype messages exchanged with author. 2010–2012.

Paulie Socash. "It Finally Happened." Email message to author. April 15, 2010.

Paulie Socash. "That's Not Trolling." Email message to author. October 12, 2012.

"Pedobear." *Know Your Meme*, November 2011. Accessed December 10, 2011. http://
knowyourmeme.com/memes/pedobear.

Peter Partyvan. Facebook and Skype messages exchanged with author. 2011–2012.

Phillips, Whitney. "The House That Fox Built: Anonymous, Spectacle, and Cycles of Amplification." *Television and New Media* 14, no. 6 (2013): 494–509. Accessed September 1, 2014. doi:10.1177/1527476412452799.

Phillips, Whitney. "LOLing at Tragedy: Facebook Trolls, Memorial Pages, and Resistance to Grief Online." *First Monday* 16, no. 12 (2011): 0. Accessed September 1, 2014. http://firstmonday.org/article/view/3168/3115.

Phillips, Whitney. "Oh Boy." *Billions and Billions*, July 20, 2012. Accessed July 20, 2012. http://billions-and-billions.com/2012/07/20/oh-boy.

Phillips, Whitney. "On Feeding the Holmies." *Billions and Billions*, July 31, 2012. Accessed August 1, 2012. http://billions-and-billions.com/2012/07/31/on-feeding
-the-holmies.

Phillips, Whitney. "Responses to Troll Comments on the Author's 'About' Page. *Billions and Billions*, July 20, 2012. Accessed July 20, 2012. http://billions-and
-billions.com/2012/07/20/about.

Plato. "Meno." In *Five Dialogues: Euthyphro, Apology, Crito, Meno, Phaedo*, 2nd ed., translated by G. M. A. Grube and John M. Cooper, 58–92. Indianapolis: Hackett Publishing Company, 2002.

"Police Training on How to Spot Nasty Drug." *MSNBC*, November 12, 2007. Accessed March 5, 2013. http://web.archive.org/web/20071112023107/http://www.msnbc
.msn.com/id/21684383.

Popkin, Helen. "Bill O'Reilly's Website Hacked." *MSNBC*, September 26, 2008. Accessed October 1, 2008. http://www.nbcnews.com/id/26870105/ns/technology
_and_science-tech_and_gadgets/t/bill-oreillys-web-site-hacked.

Pro Fessor. Facebook and Skype messages exchanged with author. 2011.

Quittner, Josh. "The War between alt.tasteless and rec.pets.cats." *Wired*, 1993. Accessed June 10, 2013. http://www.wired.com/wired/archive/2.05/alt.tasteless _pr.html.

"Re: Anonymous—Old Spice." *YouTube*, July 13, 2010. Accessed April 19, 2012. http://www.youtube.com/watch?v=LWCVhGzrAT0.

Relative, Saul. "Search for Chelsea King Shows Community Effort to Find Missing Poway Girl." *Yahoo Voices*, February 28, 2010. Accessed March 1, 2012. http://voices .yahoo.com/search-chelsea-king-shows-community-effort-to-5560523.html.

Roberts, Laura. "Kristian Digby, the BBC Presenter, May Have Died in Sex Game Gone Wrong." *The Telegraph*, March 2, 2010. Accessed March 3, 2010. http://www .telegraph.co.uk/culture/tvandradio/7351843/Kristian-Digby-the-BBC-presenter -may-have-died-in-sex-game-gone-wrong.html.

Sauthoff, Taryn. "4chan: The Rude, Raunchy Underbelly of the Internet." *Fox News. com*, April 8, 2009. Accessed April 8, 2009. http://www.foxnews.com/story/ 2009/04/08/4chan-rude-raunchy-underbelly-internet.

"SAY NO TO JENKEM." *YouTube*, November 6, 2007. Accessed October 1, 2011. http://www.youtube.com/watch?v=5-SB7kKwn1A&feature=player_embedded.

Schabner, Dean. "Chelsea King Searchers Move 'Heaven and Earth' to Find Girl." *ABC News*, February 27, 2010. Accessed February 27, 2010. http://abcnews.go.com/ US/chelsea-king-missing-thursday/story?id=9966194.

Schonfeld, Erik. "Time Magazine Throws Up Its Hands as It Gets Pwnd by 4chan." *TechCrunch*, April 27, 2009. Accessed June 5, 2009. http://techcrunch.com/2009/04/27/ time-magazine-throws-up-its-hands-as-it-gets-pwned-by-4chan.

Scott, Jason. "Before the LOL: ROFLcon 2008." *Archive.org*, April 1, 2008. Accessed June 1, 2010. https://archive.org/details/RespectablyFrench.ROFLCon. BeforetheLOL.

"Senate Bill 1411." *California State Legislature*, 2010. Accessed April 12, 2011. http:// www.leginfo.ca.gov/pub/09-10/bill/sen/sb_1401-1450/sb_1411_bill_20100927 _chaptered.html.

"Sheriff Gore Confirms Body in Chelsea King Case." *SDNN*, March 2, 2010. Accessed March 5, 2010. http://www.sdnn.com/sandiego/2010-03-02/local-county-news/ body-found-in-chelsea-king-case.

"So Cash." *Encyclopedia Dramatica*, February, 19, 2008. Accessed October 2, 2009 (website since deleted). http://encyclopediadramatica.com/So_cash.

"Socrates." *Encyclopedia Dramatica*, November 12, 2010. Accessed December 1, 2010 (website since deleted). http://encyclopediadramatica.com/Socrates.

Soveri Ruthless. Skype messages exchanged with author. 2011.

Stephen. Comment on author's "About" page. *Billions and Billions*, July 20, 2012. Accessed July 20, 2012. http://billions-and-billions.com/2012/07/20/about.

"Stop the Bullying." *Facebook*, 2010. Accessed June 1, 2010 (page since deleted). http://www.facebook.com.

"Terrorist Fist Jab." *YouTube*, June 7, 2008. Accessed June 13, 2012. http://www .youtube.com/watch?v=G_vmQrTi3aM.

"These Cruel Facebook 'Trolls' Need to Be Locked Up for Attacking RIP Groups!" *Facebook*, 2010. Accessed April 1, 2010 (page since deleted). http://www.facebook .com.

"Tom Cruise's Greatest Hits." *Oprah.com*, May 29, 2008. Accessed May 5, 2014. http://www.oprah.com/oprahshow/Tom-Cruises-Greatest-Hits.

"Troll." *Encyclopedia Dramatica*, December 12, 2004. Accessed December 12, 2009 (website since deleted). http://encyclopediadramatica.com/Troll.

"Trolls." *Encyclopedia Dramatica*, April 7, 2010. Accessed December 20, 2010 (website since deleted). http://encyclopediadramatica.com/Trolls.

"Trolls." *Encyclopedia Dramatica*, April 5, 2012. Accessed November 10, 2012. http:// encyclopediadramatica.se/Trolls.

V for Vendetta. Directed by James McTeigue. 2005. Hollywood, CA: Warner Brothers.

Watson, Paul Joseph. "Shameless Looters Display Stolen Goods on Twitter." *Alex Jones' Infowars*, October 31, 2012. Accessed October 31, 2012. http://www.infowars .com/shameless-looters-display-stolen-goods-on-twitter.

We Are Legion. Directed by Brian Knappenberger. 2012. Venice: Luminant Media.

Weiner, Rachel. "Obama's NH Town Hall Brings Out Birthers, Deathers, and More." *Huffington Post*, August 13, 2009. Accessed August 13, 2009. http://www .huffingtonpost.com/2009/08/13/obamas-nh-town-hall-bring_n_258693.html.

"We President Now (image macro)." *4chan/b/*, November 5, 2008. Image accessed November 5, 2008 (thread since deleted). http://boards.4chan.org/b.

"When Lulzes Go Global." *YouTube*, May 22, 2012. Accessed June 1, 2012. http:// www.youtube.com/watch?v=RDDi4Dj-EQI.

Wilson Mouzone. Facebook and Skype messages exchanged with author. 2011–2012.

"Womb Raiders—Orly Taitz." *Colbert Nation*, July 28, 2009. Accessed August 3, 2009. http://www.colbertnation.com/the-colbert-report-videos/229691/july-28-2009/ womb-raiders---orly-taitz.

"Why So Serious." *Encyclopedia Dramatica*, August 17, 2009. Accessed August 20, 2009 (website since deleted). http://encyclopediadramatica.com/Why_so_serious.

Wu, Jiashan Email message to author. July 27, 2012.

Secondary Sources

Ackerman, Spenser. "Newest U.S. Counterterrorism Strategy: Trolling." *Wired*, July 18, 2012. Accessed July 18, 2012. http://www.wired.com/2012/07/counterterrorism-trolls/all.

Alfonso, Fernando, III. "4chan Is Trying to Make 'Free Bleeding' the Latest Twitter Trend." *The Daily Dot*, February 1, 2014. Accessed February 10, 2014. http://www.dailydot.com/lol/free-bleeding-is-a-4chan-hoax.

Alfonso, Fernando, III. "Now 10 Years Old, 4chan Is the Most Important Site You Never Visit." *The Daily Dot*, October 1, 2013. Accessed February 1, 2014. http://www.dailydot.com/business/4chan-10-years-christopher-moot-poole.

Allen, Mike. "Before Golf, Bush Decries Latest Deaths in Mideast." *Washington Post*, August 5, 2002. Accessed June 5, 2010 (page since deleted). http://www.washingtonpost.com/ac2/wp-dyn/A43789-2002Aug4?language=printer.

Ball, James. "You Calling That a Troll? Are You Winding Me Up?" *The Guardian*, June 12, 2012. Accessed June 12, 2012. http://www.guardian.co.uk/commentisfree/2012/jun/12/troll-winding-me-up.

Bateson, Gregory. "A Theory of Play and Fantasy." In *Steps to an Ecology of Mind*, 177–193. Chicago: University of Chicago Press, 1972.

Beard, Mary. "The Public Voice of Women." *London Review of Books*, February 14, 2014. Accessed February 14, 2014. http://www.lrb.co.uk/2014/02/14/mary-beard/the-public-voice-of-women.

Bennett, Andy, and Kahn-Harris, Keith. *After Subculture: Critical Studies in Contemporary Youth Culture*. London: Palgrave Macmillan Limited, 2004.

Bergson, Henri. "On Laughter." In *Comedy*, edited by Wylie Sypher, 61–192. Baltimore: Johns Hopkins University Press, 1956.

Bergstrom, Kelly. "Don't Feed the Troll: Shutting Down Debate about Community Expectations on Reddit.com." *First Monday* 16, no. 8 (2011). Accessed September 2, 2011. http://firstmonday.org/ojs/index.php/fm/article/view/3498/3029.

Bernstein, Michael, Monroy-Hernández, Andrés, Harry, Drew, André, Paul, Panovich, Katrina, and Greg Vargas. "4chan and /b/: An Analysis of Anonymity and Ephemerality in a Large Online Community." *Association for the Advancement of*

Artificial Intelligence. Accessed August 20, 2011. http://projects.csail.mit.edu/chanthropology/4chan.pdf.

Biedlingmaier, Matthew. "Following McCain Rally Appearance, Bill Cunningham Uses Obama's Middle Name Seven Times on Hannity and Colmbs." *Media Matters*, February 27, 2008. Accessed June 3, 2012. http://mediamatters.org/research/2008/02/27/following-mccain-rally-appearance-bill-cunningh/142696.

Bluestein, Adam. "What Twitter Can Learn from Weibo: Field Notes from Global Tech Ethnographer Tricia Wang." *Fast Company*, July 11, 2012. Accessed July 11, 2012. http://www.fastcompany.com/node/1842561.

Boellstorff, Tom. *Coming of Age in Second Life*. Princeton: Princeton University Press, 2009.

Bourdieu, Pierre. *Masculine Domination*. Stanford: Stanford University Press, 2001.

Bowcott, Owen. "Bill Targeting Internet 'Trolls' Gets Weary Welcome from Websites." *The Guardian*, June 12, 2012. Accessed October 5, 2012. http://www.guardian.co.uk/technology/2012/jun/12/bill-internet-trolls-wary-welcome.

boyd, danah. "Taken Out of Context: American Teen Sociality in Networked Publics." *danah.org*, Fall 2008. Accessed September 19, 2009. http://www.danah.org/papers/TakenOutOfContext.html.

boyd, danah. "Why Youth Use Social Network Sites: The Role of Networked Publics in Teenage Social Life." In *Youth, Identity and Digital Media*, edited by David Buckingham, 1–26. Cambridge, MA: MIT Press, 2009.

Brunton, Finn. "Creating and Violating Anonymity in Online Communities: The Case of 4chan, Anon, and Dusty the Cat." Paper presented at the Privacy Research Group, New York University, New York, NY, February 24, 2010.

Buckels, Erin E., Paul D. Trapnell, and Deroy L. Paulhus. "Trolls Just Want to Have Fun." *Personality and Individual Differences*, online before print February 8, 2014. Accessed February 8, 2014. http://www.sciencedirect.com/science/article/pii/S0191886914000324.

Burgess, Jean. "'All Your Chocolate Rain Are Belong to Us?' Viral Video, YouTube and the Dynamics of Participatory Culture." In *Video Vortex Reader: Responses to YouTube*, edited by Geert Lovink and Sabine Niederer, 101–109. Amsterdam: Institute of Network Cultures, 2008.

"Bush Iraq WMDs Joke Backfires." *BBC*, March 26, 2004. Accessed March 5, 2012. http://news.bbc.co.uk/2/hi/3570845.stm.

Butler, Judith. *Excitable Speech*. New York: Routledge, 1997.

Captain, Sean. "The Real Role of Anonymous in Occupy Wall Street." *Fast Company*, October 17, 2011. Accessed November 5, 2011. http://www.fastcompany.com/node/1788397.

Chen, Adrian. "4chan's Moment Is Over, Even Though It's More Popular than Ever." *Gawker*, July 12, 2012. Accessed July 12, 2012. http://gawker.com/5925535/4chans-moment-is-over-even-though-its-more-popular-than-ever.

Citron, Danielle. *Hate 3.0*. Cambridge: Harvard University Press, 2014.

Cohen, Stanley. "Deviance and Moral Panics." In *Folk Devils and Moral Panics*, 1–20. New York: Routledge, 1972.

Coleman, Gabriella. *Coding Freedom: The Ethics and Aesthetics of Hacking*. Princeton: Princeton University Press, 2013.

Coleman, Gabriella. "The Ethnographers Cunning: The Return of the Arm Chair and Keyboard Anthropologist." Paper presented at the annual meeting of the American Anthropological Association, Montreal, Canada, November 16, 2011.

Coleman, Gabriella. *Hacker, Hoaxer, Whistleblower, Spy: The Story of Anonymous*. London: Verso Press, 2014.

Coleman, Gabriella. "Hacker and Troller as Trickster." *Gabriellacoleman.org*, February 7, 2010. Accessed June 10, 2010. http://gabriellacoleman.org/blog/?p=1902.

Coleman, Gabriella. "Old & New Net Wars over Free Speech, Freedom & Secrecy: Or How to Understand the Hacker & Lulz Battle against the Church of Scientology." *Vimeo*, December 10, 2010. Accessed December 12, 2010. http://vimeo.com/user3514769/videos.

Coleman, Gabriella. "Our Weirdness Is Free." *Triple Canopy*, January 15, 2012. Accessed January 16, 2012. http://canopycanopycanopy.com/issues/15/contents/our_weirdness_is_free.

Coleman, Gabriella. "Phreakers, Hackers, and Trolls and the Politics of Transgression and Spectacle." In *The Social Media Reader*, edited by Michael Mandiberg, 99–120. New York: NYU Press, 2010.

Connor Mar, Tom. "The Internet Anthropologist's Field Guide to 'Rage Faces.'" *Ars Technica*, March 11, 2012. Accessed June 5, 2014. http://arstechnica.com/tech-policy/2012/03/the-internet-anthropologists-field-guide-to-rage-faces/2.

Courrielche, Patrick. "The Artist Formally Known as Dissent." *Reason Magazine*, August 7, 2009. Accessed August 10, 2009. http://www.reason.com/news/show/135293.html.

Dahlberg, Lincoln. "Computer Mediated Communication and the Public Sphere." *Journal of Computer Mediated Communication* 7, no. 1 (2001): 0. Accessed September 18, 2012. doi:10.1111/j.1083-6101.2001.tb00137.x.

Davies, Christie. "Jokes That Follow Mass-Mediated Disasters in a Global Electronic Age." In *Of Corpse: Death and Humor in Folklore and Popular Culture*, edited by Peter Narvaez, 15–35. Logan: Utah State University Press, 2003.

Dawkins, Richard. *The Selfish Gene.* New York: Oxford University Press, 1976.

Deborah. "Laura Ingraham Tells O'Reilly What's Wrong with Michelle Obama and Joe Biden." *News Hounds*, August 26, 2008. Accessed June 5, 2012. http://www .newshounds.us/2008/08/26/laura_ingraham_tells_oreilly_whats_wrong_with _michelle_obama_and_joe_biden.php.

Debord, Guy, and Gil Wolman. "A User's Guide to *Détournement.*" In *Situationist International Anthology*, translated and edited by Ken Knabb, 14–21. Berkeley, CA: Bureau of Public Secrets, 1956.

Dibbell, Julian. "The Assclown Offensive: How to Enrage the Church of Scientology." *Wired*, September 21, 2009. Accessed June 2, 2009. http://www.wired.com/ culture/culturereviews/magazine/17-10/mf_chanology/?currentPage=all.

Dibbell, Julian. "Mutilated Furries, Flying Phalluses: Put the Blame on Griefers, the Sociopaths of the Virtual World." *Wired*, January 18, 2008. Accessed March 23, 2008. http://www.wired.com/gaming/virtualworlds/magazine/16-02/mf_goons.

Dibbell, Julian. "S*." In *My Tiny Life: Crime and Passion in a Virtual World*, 235–267. New York: Henry Holt, 1998.

Doctorow, Cory. "Award-Winning Book-Burning Hoax Saves Troy, MI Libraries." *BoingBoing*, June 16, 2012. Accessed October 14, 2012. http://boingboing.net/ 2012/06/16/award-winning-book-burning-hoa.html.

Donath, Judith. "Identity and Deception in the Virtual World." In *Communities in Cyberspace*, edited by Mark A. Smith and Peter Kollock, 29–60. New York: Routledge, 1999.

Douglas, Mary. *Purity and Danger: An Analysis of Concepts of Pollution and Taboo.* London: Routledge and Kegan Paul, 1966.

Dyer, Richard. *White.* New York: Routledge, 1997.

Ellen. "Fox News Legitimizes Birthers." *News Hounds*, July 14, 2009. Accessed June 20, 2012. http://www.newshounds.us/2009/07/14/fox_news_legitimizes_birthers .php.

Ellis, Bill. "Making a Big Apple Crumble: The Role of Humor in Constructing A Global Response to Disaster." In *Of Corpse: Death and Humor in Folklore and Popular Culture*, edited by Peter Narvaez, 35–79. Logan: Utah State University Press, 2003.

English, James. *Comic Transactions.* Ithaca: Cornell University Press, 1994.

Fisher, Ken. "4chan's moot Takes Pro-Anonymity to TED 2010." *Ars Techinca*, February 11, 2010. Accessed February 20, 2010. http://arstechnica.com/staff/palatine /2010/02/4chans-moot-takes-pro-anonymity-to-ted-2010.ars.

Fitzpatrick, David, and Drew Griffin. "Man Behind 'Jailbait' Post Exposed, Loses Job." *Anderson Cooper 360*, October 19, 2012. Accessed October 19, 2012. http:// www.cnn.com/2012/10/18/us/internet-troll-apology/index.html.

"Fox News Again Posts Birther Story with Picture of Obama in Somali Clothes." *Media Matters*, July 20, 2009. Accessed June 12, 2012. http://mediamatters.org/ blog/2009/07/20/fox-nation-again-posts-birther-story-with-pictu/152203.

"Fox News Still Obsessing Over Obama's Birth Certificate." *Media Matters*, July 14, 2009. Accessed June 3, 2012. http://mediamatters.org/blog/2009/07/14/updated -fox-nation-still-obsessing-over-obamas/152001.

Gertz, Matt, and Eric Hananoki. "Corsi's Claim That Obama Posted 'False, Fake Birth Certificate' Flatly Rejected by Hawaii Health Department." *Media Matters*, August 15, 2008. Accessed June 5, 2012. http://mediamatters.org/research/2008/08/15/ corsis-claim-that-obama-posted-false-fake-birth/144404.

Goffman, Erving. "Front." In *The Presentation of Self in Everyday Life*, 22–30. New York: Doubleday, 1959.

Gooch, Paul W. "Irony and Insight in Plato's *Meno*." *Laval Théologique et Philosophique* 43, no. 2 (1987): 189–204. Accessed May 2, 2014. doi:10.7202/400301ar.

Gordon, McLean. "You're as Evil as Your Social Network: What the Prison Experiment Got Wrong." *Motherboard*, December 11, 2012. Accessed December 12, 2012. http://motherboard.vice.com/blog/you-are-as-evil-as-your-social-network-alexander -haslam-on-what-the-prison-experiment-got-wrong.

Grad, Shelby. "Sorting Out the Facts in the Obama-Joker 'Socialist' Posters around L.A." *Los Angeles Times*, August 3, 2009. Accessed August 5, 2009. http:// latimesblogs.latimes.com/lanow/2009/08/sorting-out-the-facts-in-obamajoker -socialist-posters-around-la.html.

Grossman, Lev. "The Master of Memes." *Time*, July 9, 2008. Accessed July 20, 2009. http://content.time.com/time/magazine/article/0,9171,1821656,00.html.

Grossman, Lev. "Now in Paper Version: The 4chan guy." *Time: Techland*, July 10, 2008. Accessed July 14, 2009. http://techland.time.com/2008/07/10/now_in _papervision_the_4chan_g.

Hall, Stuart. "The Whites of Their Eyes: Racist Ideologies and the Media." In *Silver Linings: Some Strategies for the Eighties*, edited by George Bridges and Rosalind Brunt, 28–52. London: Lawrence and Wishart, 1981.

Hananoki, Eric. "Fox News Still Trafficking in Birth Certificate Theories." *Media Matters*, May 28, 2009. Accessed June 8, 2012. http://mediamatters.org/research/2009/05/28/fox-news-still-trafficking-in-birth-certificate/150597.

"Hannity Advances Obama Birth Certificate Conspiracies." *Media Matters*, July 16, 2009. Accessed July 20, 2012. http://mediamatters.org/video/2009/07/16/hannity-advances-obama-birth-certificate-conspi/152096.

Hardacker, Claire. "Trolling in Asynchronous Computer-Mediated Communication: From User Discussions to Academic Definitions." *Journal of Politeness Research* 6, no. 2 (2010): 225–235. Accessed March 12, 2013. doi:10.1515/JPLR.2010.011.

Haslam, Alexander S., and Stephen Reicher. "Contesting the 'Nature' of Conformity: What Milgram and Zimbardo's Studies Really Show." *PLOS Biology* 10, no. 11 (2012): 0. Accessed March 10, 2013. doi:10.1371/journal.pbio.1001426.

Hebdige, Dick. *Subculture: The Meaning of Style*. New York: Routledge, 1972.

Helft, Miguel. "Facebook Wrestles with Free Speech and Civility." *New York Times*, December 12, 2012. Accessed December 12, 2010. http://www.nytimes.com/2010/12/13/technology/13facebook.html.

Hesse, Monica. "A Virtual Unknown: Meet 'moot,' the Secretive Internet Celeb Who Still Lives with Mom." *Washington Post*, February 17, 2009. Accessed February 26, 2010. http://www.washingtonpost.com/wp-dyn/content/article/2009/02/16/AR2009021601565.html.

Hill, Jane. *The Everyday Language of White Racism*. Oxford: Wiley-Blackwell, 2008.

Hubler, Mike and Diana Bell. "Computer-Mediated Humor and Ethos: Exploring Threads of Constitutive Humor in Online Communities." *Computers and Composition* 20, no. 3 (2003): 277–294.

Hudson, John. "Gay Teen Suicide Sparks Debate over Cyber Bullying." *The Atlantic Wire*, October 1, 2010. Accessed October 3, 2010. http://www.theatlanticwire.com/national/2010/10/gay-teen-suicide-sparks-debate-over-cyber-bullying/22829.

Hyde, Lewis. *Trickster Makes This World: How Disruptive Imagination Creates Culture*. Edinburgh: Canongate, 1998.

"Ingraham Guest Host Bruce on the Obamas: 'We've Got Trash in the White House.'" *Media Matters*, March 23, 2009. Accessed June 23, 2009. http://mediamatters.org/video/2009/03/23/ingraham-guest-host-bruce-on-the-obamas-weve-go/148502.

Ito, Mizuko. "Virtually Embodied: The Reality of Fantasy in a Multi-User Dungeon." In *Internet Culture*, edited by David Porter, 87–111. New York: Routledge, 1997.

Jappe, Anselm. *Guy Debord*. Berkeley: University of California Press, 1999.

Jenkins, Henry. "If It Doesn't Spread, It's Dead." *Henryjenkins.org*, February 11, 2009. Accessed July 12, 2010. http://www.henryjenkins.org/2009/02/if_it_doesnt_spread _its_dead_p.html.

Jenkins, Henry. "What Happened before YouTube." In *YouTube: Online Video and Participatory Culture*, edited by Jean Burgess and Joshua Green, 109–126. New York: Polity, 2009.

Jenkins, Henry, Ford, Sam, and Green, Joshua. *Spreadable Media: Creating Value and Meaning in a Networked Culture*. New York: NYU Press, 2013.

Johnson, Robert. "Anonymous Occupation of Wall Street—Here Is What You Missed." *Business Insider*, September 17, 2011. Accessed October 10, 2012. http:// www.businessinsider.com/anonymous-occupy-wall-street-2011-9?op=1.

Judy. "Fox and Friends 'Corrects' Obama Madrassa Claim." *News Hounds*, January 22, 2007. Accessed June 23, 2012. http://www.newshounds.us/2007/01/22/fox_and _friends_corrects_obama_madrassa_claim.php.

Kaste, Martin. "Exploring Occupy Wall Street's 'Adbuster' Origins." *NPR*, October 20, 2011. Accessed October 25, 2012. http://www.npr.org/2011/10/20/141526467/ exploring-occupy-wall-streets-adbuster-origins.

Kazmi, Ayesha. "How Anonymous Emerged to Occupy Wall Street." *The Guardian*, September 26, 2011. Accessed October 13, 2012. http://www.guardian.co.uk/ commentisfree/cifamerica/2011/sep/27/occupy-wall-street-anonymous.

Kelley, Max. "Memories of Friends Departed Endure on Facebook." *Facebook*, October 26, 2010. Accessed March 20, 2010. http://www.facebook.com/notes/facebook/ memories-of-friends-departed-endure-on-facebook/163091042130.

Kellner, Douglas. "Media Culture and the Triumph of the Spectacle." In *Media Spectacle*, 1–33. Routledge: New York, 2003.

Kennicott, Phillips. "Obama as the Joker Betrays Racial Ugliness, Fears." *Washington Post*, August 6, 2009. Accessed August 9, 2009. http://www.washingtonpost.com/ wp-dyn/content/article/2009/08/05/AR2009080503876.html.

Kirkpatrick, David. *The Facebook Effect: The Inside Story of the Company That Is Connecting the World*. New York: Simon and Schuster, 2010.

Klein, Jacob. *A Commentary on Plato's Meno*. Chicago: University of Chicago Press, 1989.

Knafo, Saki. "LulzSec, Sony, and The Rise of a New Breed of Hacker." *Huffington Post*, June 7, 2011. Accessed July 20, 2012. http://www.huffingtonpost.com/2011/06/07/ lulzsec-sony-and-the-rise_n_872814.html.

Knafo, Saki. "Occupy Wall Street and Anonymous: Turning a Fledgling Movement into a Meme." *Huffington Post*, October 20, 2011. Accessed December 20, 2011.

http://www.huffingtonpost.com/2011/10/20/occupy-wall-street-anonymous
-connection_n_1021665.html.

Knutilla, Lee. "User Unknown: 4chan, Anonymity and Contingency." *First Monday* 16, no. 10 (2011). Accessed October 5, 2011. http://firstmonday.org/htbin/cgiwrap/ bin/ojs/index.php/fm/article/viewArticle/3665/3055.

Krugman, Paul. "Tea Parties Forever." *New York Times*, April 12, 2009. Accessed May 1, 2014. http://www.nytimes.com/2009/04/13/opinion/13krugman.html.

Krugman, Paul. "The Town Hall Mob." *New York Times*, August 6, 2009. Accessed August 8, 2009. http://www.nytimes.com/2009/08/07/opinion/07krugman.html.

Legman, Gershon. *No Laughing Matter: Rational of the Dirty Joke*. New York: Bell, 1971.

Lévy, Pierre. *Collective Intelligence*. Translated by Robert Bononno. Cambridge: Perseus Books, 1997.

Levy, Steven. *Hackers*. New York: Penguin, 1984.

Lorde, Audre. "The Master's Tools Will Never Dismantle the Master's House." In *Feminism and Race*, edited by Kum-Kum Bhavnani, 89–92. New York: Oxford University Press, 1984.

Lund, Michael. "What's Next for Facebook after Its Nightmare Week?" *The Punch*, May 7, 2010. Accessed May 8, 2010. http://www.thepunch.com.au/articles/ what-next-for-facebook-after-its-nightmare-week.

Marx, Karl. "The Fetishism of the Commodity and Its Secret." In *Capital*, 163–177. New York: Penguin, 1867.

Menning, Chris. "Meme Agent Ben Lashes Bites the Hand That Feeds." *Modern Primate*, May 7, 2012. Accessed May 7, 2012. http://www.modernprimate.com/ meme-agent-ben-lashes-bites-the-hand-that-feeds-and-the-sun-is-still-terrible.

Miki-em. "Rick Astley Does Live Rickroll at Macy's Thanksgiving Day Parade." *Laughing Squid*, November 27, 2008. Accessed June 5, 2014. http://laughingsquid.com/ rick-astley-does-live-rickroll-at-macys-thanksgiving-day-parade.

Milian, Mark. "Shepard Fairey Has 'Doubts' about Intelligence of Obama Joker Artist." *Los Angeles Times*, August 10, 2009. Accessed August 11, 2009. http:// latimesblogs.latimes.com/washington/2009/08/obama-joker-shepard-fairey.html.

Miller, Lisa. "R.I.P. on Facebook." *Newsweek*, March 1, 2010. Accessed May 3, 2010. http://www.newsweek.com/2010/02/16/r-i-p-on-facebook.html.

Milner, Ryan M. "Dialogue Is Important, Even When It's Impolite." *The New York Times*, August 19, 2014. Accessed August 19, 2014. http://www.nytimes.com/

roomfordebate/2014/08/19/the-war-against-online-trolls/dialogue-is-important
-even-when-its-impolite.

Milner, Ryan M. "Hacking the Social: Internet Memes, Identity Antagonism, and
the Logic of Lulz." *The Fibreculture Journal* 22 (2013). Accessed March 23, 2014.
http://twentytwo.fibreculturejournal.org/fcj-156-hacking-the-social-internet
-memes-identity-antagonism-and-the-logic-of-lulz.

Milner, Ryan M. "Media Lingua Franca: Fixity, Novelty, and Vernacular Creativity
in Internet Memes." *Selected Papers of Internet Researchers* 3 (2013). Accessed May 1,
2014. http://spir.aoir.org/index.php/spir/article/view/806.

Milner, Ryan M. "The World Made Meme: Discourse and Identity in Participatory
Media." PhD diss., University of Kansas, 2012. Accessed February 21, 2014. http://
kuscholarworks.ku.edu/dspace/handle/1808/10256.

Mooney, Chris. "Internet Trolls Really Are Horrible People." *Slate*, February 14, 2014.
Accessed February 14, 2014. http://www.slate.com/articles/health_and_science/
climate_desk/2014/02/internet_troll_personality_study_machiavellianism_narcissism
_psychopathy.html.

Moulton, Janice. "A Paradigm of Philosophy: The Adversary Method." In *Discovering
Reality: Feminist Perspectives on Epistemology, Metaphysics, Methodology, and Philosophy
of Science*, edited by Sandra Harding and Merrill B. Hintikka, 149–164. Dordrecht,
The Netherlands: Kluwer, 1983.

Moyer, Christine. "Cyberbullying a High-Tech Health Risk for Young Patients."
American Medical News, November 15, 2010. Accessed December 10, 2010. http://
www.ama-assn.org/amednews/2010/11/15/prl21115.htm.

Nakamura, Lisa. *Cybertypes: Race, Ethnicity, and Identity on the Internet*. New York:
Routledge, 2002.

Nakamura, Lisa. *Digitizing Race: Visual Cultures of the Internet*. Minneapolis: University of Minnesota Press, 2007.

Nakamura, Lisa, Beth Kolko, and Gilbert Rodman. *Race in Cyberspace*. New York:
Routledge, 2000.

Neiwert, David. "Lou Dobbs and the Birthers: Mainstreaming Fringe Ideas for
Ratings Eventually Will Catch Up with You." *Crooks and Liars*, July 27, 2009.
Accessed March 20, 2014. http://crooksandliars.com/david-neiwert/lou-dobbs-and
-birthers-why-making-ca.

Ng, David. "Reading Into the Obama as Joker Poster . . . Or Not." *Los Angeles
Times*, August 5, 2009. Accessed August 6, 2009. http://latimesblogs.latimes.com/
culturemonster/2009/08/reading-into-the-obamaasjoker-poster-or-not.html.

Nisbet, Robert. *History of the Idea of Progress*. New York: Basic Books, 1980.

"Obama Smeared as Former 'Madrassa' Student, Possible Covert Muslim Extremist." *Think Progress*, January 19, 2007. Accessed June 4, 2012. http://thinkprogress.org/media /2007/01/19/9711/fox-obama-madrassa.

Olson, Parmy. "The March of the Trolls and Hactivists." *Forbes*, September 5, 2011. Accessed March 5, 2012. http://www.forbes.com/sites/parmyolson/2011/09/05/march-of-the-trolls-and-hacktivists.

Oring, Elliot. "Jokes and the Discourses on Disaster." *Journal of American Folklore* 100, no. 397 (1987): 276–286.

Phillips, Amanda. "5 Things Academics Might Learn from How the Rowdy Social Justice Blogosphere Handles Fucknecks." *Fembot Collective*, April 10, 2012. Accessed April 10, 2012. http://fembotcollective.org/blog/2012/04/10/im-not-offended-im -contemptuous-5-things-academics-might-learn-from-how-the-rowdy-social-justice -blogosphere-handles-fucknecks.

Phillips, David P., and Lundie L. Carstensen. "Clustering of Teenage Suicides after Television News Stories about Suicide." *New England Journal of Medicine* 315, no. 11 (1986): 685–689.

Phillips, Whitney. "A Brief History of Trolls." *The Daily Dot*, May 20, 2013. Accessed May 20, 2013. http://www.dailydot.com/opinion/phillips-brief-history-of-trolls.

Phillips, Whitney. "'In Defense of Memes': My Essay from Spreadable Media." *Billions and Billions*, December 3, 2012. Accessed December 3, 2012. http://billions-and -billions.com/2012/12/03/in-defense-of-memes-my-essay-from-spreadable-media.

Porter, Claire. "I'm Taking Back the 'T' Word: Bullies Are Not Trolls." *The Punch*, October 17, 2012. Accessed October 18, 2012 (website since deleted). http://www .thepunch.com.au/articles/im-taking-back-the-t-word.

Postmes, Tom, and Russell Spears. "Deindividuation and Antinormative Behavior: A Meta-Analysis." *Psychological Bulletin* 123, no. 3 (1998): 238–259.

"Recommendations for Reporting on Suicide." *American Foundation for Suicide Prevention*, 2010. Accessed January 5, 2010. https://www.afsp.org/news-events/for-the-media/reporting-on-suicide.

Rheingold, Howard. *The Virtual Community: Homesteading on the Virtual Frontier*. Cambridge, MA: MIT Press, 1993.

Ronson, Jon. "Security Alert: Notes from the Frontline of the War in Cyberspace." *The Guardian*, May 3, 2013. Accessed May 4, 2014. http://www.theguardian.com/technology/2013/may/04/security-alert-war-in-cyberspace.

Ryan, Erin. "Miserable Troll Ann Coulter Forced to Cancel Speaking Engagement Because Everyone Hates Her." *Jezebel*, October 26, 2012. Accessed October 27, 2012. http://jezebel.com/5955193/miserable-troll-ann-coulter-forced-to-cancel-speaking -engagement-because-everyone-hates-her.

Ryan, Erin. "Trolling Polititians' Facebook Pages with Vaginal News Is the Hot New Trend." *Jezebel*, March 20, 2012. Accessed October 5, 2012. http://jezebel .com/5894635/trolling-politicians-facebook-pages-with-vaginal-news-is-hot -new-trend.

Ryan, Yasmine. "Anonymous and the Arab Uprisings." *Al Jazeera*, May 19, 2011. Accessed June 1, 2012. http://www.aljazeera.com/news/middleeast/2011/05/ 201151917634659824.html.

Salazar, Christian. "Alexis Pilkington Facebook Horror: Cyber Bullies Harass Teen Even after Suicide." *Huffington Post*, May 25, 2010. Accessed May 26, 2010. http:// www.huffingtonpost.com/2010/03/24/alexis-pilkington-faceboo_n_512482.html.

Sandoval, Greg. "The End of Kindness: Weev and the Cult of the Angry Young Man." *The Verge*, September 12, 2013. Accessed September 12, 2013. http://www.theverge .com/2013/9/12/4693710/the-end-of-kindness-weev-and-the-cult-of-the-angry -young-man.

Schopenhauer, Arthur. *The Art of Controversy*. Translated by T. Bailey Saunders. LaVergne, TN: Kessinger Books, 1896.

Schwartz, Matthias. "Malwebolence: The Trolls among Us." *New York Times*, August 8, 2008. Accessed August 10, 2008. http://www.nytimes.com/2008/08/03/ magazine/03trolls-t.html.

Selter, Brian. "On Television and Radio, Talk of Obama's Citizenship." *New York Times*, July 24, 2009. Accessed March 20, 2014. http://mediadecoder.blogs.nytimes. com/2009/07/24/on-television-and-radio-talk-of-obamas-citizenship/?hp.

Shanahan, Leo. "Facebook Responds: Shock at Obscenities, No Policy Changes Planned." *The Punch*, February 26, 2010. Accessed February 27, 2010. http://www .thepunch.com.au/articles/facebook-responds-shock-at-obscenities-apology -planned.

Shifman, Limor. *Memes in Digital Culture*. Cambridge, MA: MIT Press, 2013.

Stivale, Charles. "Spam: Heteroglossia and Harassment in Cyberspace." In *Internet Culture*, edited by David Porter, 133–145. New York: Routledge, 1997.

Stuckey, Mike. "Guns Near Obama Fuel 'Open-Carry' Debate." *MSNBC.com*, August 25, 2009. Accessed August 26, 2009. http://www.nbcnews.com/id/32492783/ns/ us_news-life/t/guns-near-obama-fuel-open-carry-debate.

Suebsaeng, Asawin. "The State Department Is Actively Trolling Terrorists on Twitter." *Mother Jones*, March 5, 2014. Accessed March 5, 2014. http://www.motherjones.com/ politics/2014/02/state-department-cscc-troll-terrorists-twitter-think-again -turn-away.

Suler, John. "The Online Disinhibition Effect." *CyberPsychology & Behavior* 7, no. 3 (2004): 321–326.

Tepper, Michelle. "Usenet Communities and the Cultural Politics of Information." In *Internet Culture*, edited by David Porter, 39–55. New York: Routledge, 1997.

Thomas, Douglas. *Hacker Culture*. Minneapolis: University of Minnesota Press, 2002.

Topping, Alexandria. "Facebook to Launch Memorial Profiles of Deceased Users." *The Guardian*, May 2, 2010. Accessed May 3, 2010. http://www.guardian.co.uk/technology/2009/oct/27/facebook-user-memorials.

Traynor, Leo. "The Day I Confronted My Troll." *The Guardian*, September 26, 2012. Accessed September 29, 2012. http://www.guardian.co.uk/commentisfree/2012/sep/26/day-confronted-troll.

"Troll." *Oxford English Dictionary*. Accessed September 7, 2011. http://www.oxforddictionaries.com/us/definition/american_english/troll.

Turkle, Sherry. "Virtuality and Its Discontents." In *Life on Screen: Identity in the Age of the Internet*, 233–254. New York: Touchstone, 1996.

Vaughan, Pamela. "Memejacking: The Complete Guide for Creating Memes for Marketing." *Hubspot*, July 6, 2012. Accessed October 24, 2012. http://blog.hubspot.com/blog/tabid/6307/bid/33363/Memejacking-The-Complete-Guide-to-Creating-Memes-for-Marketing.aspx#ixzz2A8kQ3e1M.

Viellaris, Renee. "Internet Trolls and Cyber-Bullies Face Jail under Amended Commonwealth Law." *The Courier-Mail*, November 30, 2013. Accessed January 13, 2014. http://www.couriermail.com.au/news/queensland/internet-trolls-and-cyberbullies-face-jail-under-amended-commonwealth-law/story-fnihsrf2-1226771735572?nk=86c846653f7c941e16d5959fec680673.

Yaniv, Oren. "Long Island Teen's Suicide Linked to Cruel Cyberbullies, Formspring.me Site: Police." *New York Daily News*, March 25, 2010. Accessed March 26, 2010. http://www.nydailynews.com/news/crime/long-island-teen-suicide-linked-cruel-cyberbullies-formspring-site-police-article-1.173441.

Zittrain, Jonathan. *The Future of the Internet and How to Stop It*. New Haven, CT: Yale University Press, 2008.

Index